Queer Theory

READERS IN CULTURAL CRITICISM
General Editor: *Catherine Belsey*

Posthumanism	*Neil Badmington*
Theorizing Ireland	*Claire Connolly*
Postmodern Debates	*Simon Malpas*
Queer Theory	*Iain Morland and*
	Annabelle Willox
Reading the Past	*Tamsin Spargo*
Performance Studies	*Erin Striff*
Reading Images	*Julia Thomas*
Gender	*Anna Tripp*

Readers in Cultural Criticism
Series Standing Order
ISBN 0–333–78660–2 hardcover
ISBN 0–333–75236–8 paperback
(outside North America only)

You can receive future titles in this series as they are published by placing a standing order. Please contact your bookseller or, in case of difficulty, write to us at the address below with your name and address, the title of the series and the ISBN quoted above.

Customer Services Department, Macmillan Distribution Ltd
Houndmills, Basingstoke, Hampshire RG21 6XS, England

Queer Theory

Edited by Iain Morland and Annabelle Willox

Published 2005 by
PALGRAVE MACMILLAN
Houndmills, Basingstoke, Hampshire RG21 6XS and
175 Fifth Avenue, New York, N.Y. 10010
Companies and representatives throughout the world

PALGRAVE MACMILLAN is the global academic imprint of the Palgrave
Macmillan division of St. Martin's Press, LLC and of Palgrave Macmillan Ltd.
Macmillan® is a registered trademark in the United States, United Kingdom
and other countries. Palgrave is a registered trademark in the European
Union and other countries.

ISBN 1–4039–1693–4 hardback
ISBN 1–4039–1694–2 paperback

This book is printed on paper suitable for recycling and made from fully
managed and sustained forest sources.

A catalogue record for this book is available from the British Library.

Library of Congress Cataloging-in-Publication Data

Queer theory / edited by Iain Morland and Annabelle Willox.
         p. cm. – (Readers in cultural criticism)
     Includes bibliographical references and index.
     ISBN 1–4039–1693–4 (cloth) – ISBN 1–4039–1694–2 (pbk.)
       1. Homosexuality–Philosophy. 2. Lesbianism–Philosophy. 3. Gender
   identity–Philosophy. I. Morland, Iain, 1978– II. Willox, Annabelle, 1975– III. Series.

HQ76.25.Q3843 2004
306.76′6–dc22
                                                                    2004042101

10   9   8   7   6   5   4   3   2   1
14   13   12   11   10   09   08   07   06   05

Printed and bound in China

Contents

List of Figures

General Editor's Preface

Culture is the element we inhabit as subjects.

Culture embraces the whole range of practices, customs and representations of a society. In their rituals, stories and images, societies identify what they perceive as good and evil, proper, sexually acceptable, racially other. Culture is the location of values, and the study of cultures shows how values vary from one society to another, or from one historical moment to the next.

But culture does not exist in the abstract. On the contrary, it is in the broadest sense of the term textual, inscribed in the paintings, operas, sculptures, furnishings, fashions, bus tickets and shopping lists which are the currency of both aesthetic and everyday exchange. Societies invest these artefacts with meanings, until in many cases the meanings are so 'obvious' that they pass for nature. Cultural criticism denaturalizes and defamiliarizes these meanings, isolating them for inspection and analysis.

The subject is what speaks, or, more precisely, what signifies, and subjects learn in culture to reproduce or to challenge the meanings and values inscribed in the signifying practices of the society that shapes them.

If culture is pervasive and constitutive for us, if it resides in the documents, objects and practices that surround us, if it circulates as the meanings and values we learn and reproduce as good citizens, how in these circumstances can we practise cultural *criticism*, where criticism implies a certain distance between the critic and the culture? The answer is that cultures are not homogeneous; they are not even necessarily coherent. There are always other perspectives, so that cultures offer alternative positions for the subjects they also recruit. Moreover, we have a degree of power over the messages we reproduce. A minor modification changes the script, and may alter the meaning; the introduction of a negative constructs a resistance.

The present moment in our own culture is one of intense debate. Sexual alignments, family values, racial politics, the implications of economic differences are all hotly contested. And positions are taken up not only in explicit discussions at political meetings, on television and in the pub. They are often reaffirmed or challenged implicitly in films and advertisements, horoscopes and lonely-hearts columns. Cultural criticism analyses all these forms in order to assess their hold on our consciousness.

There is no interpretative practice without theory, and the more sophisticated the theory, the more precise and perceptive the reading it makes possible. Cultural theory is as well defined now as it has ever been, and as strongly contested as our social values. There could not, in consequence, be a more exciting time to engage in the theory and practice of cultural criticism.

Catherine Belsey
Cardiff University

Acknowledgements

The editors wish to thank Catherine Belsey, Loren Cameron, Diane Elam, Jared Gee, Dan Pitcher, Jay Prosser, Nikki Sullivan, and Sonya Barker, Felicity Noble, Anna Sandeman and Kate Wallis at Palgrave Macmillan.

We also wish to thank the contributors – in particular those who genially let us edit their excellent work.

Annabelle also thanks her friends for watching from a safe distance, and Di Carr for curry, *Kes* and Manchester United.

The editors and publishers wish to thank the following for permission to use copyright material:

Suzanna Danuta Walters, for 'From Here to Queer: Radical Feminism, Postmodernism, and the Lesbian Menace (Or, Why Can't a Woman Be More Like a Fag?)', in *Signs: Journal of Women in Culture and Society*, 21:4 (1996), pp. 830–69; reproduced by permission of University of Chicago Press.

Patrick Califia, for 'Gay Men, Lesbians, and Sex: Doing It Together', in *Public Sex: The Culture of Radical Sex* (1994), pp. 183–9; reproduced by permission of Cleis Press.

Larry Kramer, for '1,112 and Counting', in *We are Everywhere: A Historical Sourcebook of Gay and Lesbian Politics*, ed. Mark Blasius and Shane Phelan (1997), pp. 578–86, reproduced by permission of Routledge, Inc.

Carol Queen, for 'The Leather Daddy and the Femme', © 1998, 2003 by Carol Queen, pp. 9–29; reprinted with permission of Down There Press, San Francisco. These selections constitute the first two chapters of a longer erotic novel.

Marjorie Garber, for the extract from *Vice Versa: Bisexuality and the Eroticism of Everyday Life* (1997), pp. 268–83; reproduced by permission of Taylor & Francis and the Beth Vesel Literary Agency.

Peter Hegarty and Cheryl Chase, for the extract from 'Intersex Activism, Feminism and Psychology: Opening a Dialogue on Theory, Research and Clinical Practice', in *Feminism and Psychology*, 10:1 (2000), pp. 117–32; reprinted by permission of Sage Publications Ltd.

Eve Kosofsky Sedgwick, for the extract from *Epistemology of the Closet*, © 1990 Regents of the University of California, pp. 22–48; reproduced by permission of California University Press.

Donald E. Hall, for 'A Brief, Slanted History of "Homosexual" Activity', in *Queer Theories* (2003), pp. 21–47; reprinted by permission of Palgrave Macmillan.

Stephen Whittle, for 'Gender Fucking or Fucking Gender?', in *Blending Genders: Social Aspects of Cross-Dressing and Sex-Changing*, ed. Richard Ekins and Dave King (1996), pp. 196–214; reproduced by permission of Routledge, Ltd.

Judith Butler, for the extract from *Excitable Speech: A Politics of the Performative*, © Routledge, Inc. 1997, pp. 103–26; reproduced by permission of Routledge, Inc.

William J. Spurlin, for 'I'd Rather be the Princess than the Queen! Mourning Diana as a Gay Icon', from *Mourning Diana: Nation, Culture and the Performance of Grief*, ed. Adrian Kear and Deborah Lynn Steinberg (1999), pp. 155–68; reproduced by permission of Routledge, Ltd.

Mark Norris Lance and Alessandra Tanesini, for 'Identity Judgements, Queer Politics', in *Radical Philosophy*, 100 (March/April 2000), pp. 42–51; reproduced by permission of Radical Philosophy.

Every effort has been made to trace the copyright holders but if any have been inadvertently overlooked the publishers will be pleased to make the necessary arrangement at the first opportunity.

1

Introduction

Iain Morland and Annabelle Willox

I

What makes a theory queer? What does it mean to describe oneself as queer? Is 'queer' an adjective, a noun or a verb? Is 'queer' something that you *do* or something that you *are*? Perhaps you become queer by doing certain things – for instance, by being seen to be reading this book. Maybe you are hiding its cover behind *Cosmopolitan* or *Men's Health*. Alternatively, if you *are* queer, are the things that you do queer enough? Are you in the closet, or are you out and proud; are you on the scene, or furtively surfing the internet for same-sex pornography? There is little contemporary distinction between a practising heterosexual and a heterosexual in theory, but the corresponding difference is critical for queers. What does this tell us about the contested character of 'queer' as simultaneously an exultant identity claim and a derogatory label, a topic of intense academic debate and a politically correct fuss? In the late 1990s, two seemingly unrelated events brought the term 'queer' into common parlance, but also into dispute. One was the prime time presentation of the British mini-series *Queer as Folk*, later screened and remade internationally.[1] The second was a nail bomb.

On 23 February 1999, *Queer as Folk* hit UK television screens, and sparked both the public's imagination and its condemnation. With the catchphrase 'being gay has never looked so cool', the show idealized gay male life in Manchester, England. Queerness became fashionable. *Queer as Folk*'s beautiful, healthy and wealthy main characters portrayed queer as a trendy, sexy way to be. The urban gay scene was set up by the show as bright, loud, busy and fun – everything the straight world was not. Gay character Vince, horrified upon his visit to the one straight pub in the series, observed that 'There are people talking in sentences with no punchline and they don't even care. Can you believe it, they've got toilets in which no one's ever had sex.'[2] According to *Queer as Folk*, the drab, mundane world of straights could do no better than to have a makeover by the wonderful world of queers. The predictable moral backlash to the series served only to reinforce the idea of queer as a brash and unapologetic lifestyle – the *fin-de-siècle* consumerist incarnation of Patrick Califia's call for freedom of sexual expression and identity in 'Gay Men, Lesbians, and Sex: Doing It Together', his 1983 essay chosen for this volume.[3] The question provoked by *Queer as Folk*, then, is the extent to which 'queer' has become a euphemism for gay, white, male affluence. This is the question of queer identity, and so of the identity of queer.

Queer as a political strategy arose in the 1980s as a hybrid of the issues raised by the gay and lesbian civil rights movements, the 'sex wars' over pornography and censorship amongst feminists, and the early 1980s AIDS epidemic. Suzanna Danuta Walters' article 'From Here to Queer: Radical Feminism, Postmodernism, and the Lesbian Menace' explains and interrogates these contexts, while Donald E. Hall's 'A Brief, Slanted History of "Homosexual" Activity' critically charts the longer genealogy of queer. Subcultural disenfranchisement from the sometimes conservative itineraries of same-sex and feminist movements produced splinter groups that eventually rallied behind the shared threat of AIDS. Activism, no longer organized around common lifestyles and experiences, became centred on the terrifying capriciousness of illness, described movingly in Larry Kramer's 1983 rallying call, '1,112 and Counting'.

Identity politics, so important historically to activists such as the suffragettes, seemed redundant. With the realization that AIDS did not target social or biological groups – that its spread was dependent instead on the acts in which people engaged – came an awareness that identities were no indicator of vulnerability, and no shield from risk. So queer activism's necessity and urgency lay in its challenge to the notion that identities could classify people, keep people safe, and keep them alive. It was a strategy, not an identity. Put differently, the message of queer activism was that politics could be queer, but folk could not.

But Stuart (Brian in the US version), one of *Queer as Folk*'s principal characters, is. He is individualist, consumerist, and apparently queer. Stuart is fashionable, wearing only expensive designer labels; he is portrayed as compellingly sexy, and has a voracious appetite for anonymous sex; he works in public relations, and flaunts his high disposable income through a company jeep and the incessant use of his cellular phone. The other main characters work in high-earning sectors such as management and law: they can afford luxury goods and gym bodies. The only unfit gay person in the UK series, Phil, dies after two episodes from a drug overdose, while the oldest person in the US remake, Ted, is comatosed for the same reason. It seems that in the world of *Queer as Folk*, in contrast to the world of queer activism and AIDS, youth and beauty can protect you. This politicization of aesthetics is sharply different from the queerly playful, inclusive imagination of Del LaGrace Volcano and Indra Windh in the new composition 'GenderFusion'. Toned, tanned queers like Stuart will apparently go on to inherit the capitalist earth.

II

On Friday, 30 April 1999, at 6:37 pm, a nail bomb exploded in the Admiral Duncan pub in Soho, London. This was the third London bombing in the same month, after attacks in Brixton on 17 April and Brick Lane on 24 April. Both earlier bombs met with condemnation, concern and calls for the government to tackle the unmistakable threat of racism. Different about the final bombing was the reaction to a specifically homophobic hate crime. Prime Minister Tony Blair responded: 'When the gay community is attacked and innocent people are murdered, all the good people of Britain, whatever their race, their lifestyle, their class unite in revulsion and determination to bring the evil people to justice.'[4] Blair's statement, together with the Prince of Wales's visit to the Soho survivors, made clear the official view that the gay community was a respectable minority. This endorsement would seem to mark the success of queer activism.

Yet the minority status of 'queer' is coterminous with its invisibility. Blair's rhetoric conspicuously made no reference to sexuality, implying that the 'gay community' were defined principally by their chosen, alternative 'lifestyle'. Notice that he separates even as he links the scandal of an 'attack' on homosexuals and the 'murder' of innocents: it is not transparent that the *killing of homosexuals* should itself incite revulsion. A similar erasure of sexuality in media coverage of Diana, Princess of Wales's visits to gay AIDS patients is observed by William J. Spurlin in his paper 'I'd Rather Be the Princess than the Queen! Mourning Diana as a Gay Icon'. Blair's comment, like the portrayal of a jubilantly gay way of life by *Queer as Folk*, is double-edged. The appeal to innocence elides the homophobia that motivated the bombing. The call for justice is couched in terms of *everything but* sexuality: what made the bombing shocking was that people were murdered while they were out innocently enjoying (that is, consuming) their lifestyle. We are to be appalled by the abstract 'evil' of the perpetrators. The media correspondingly focused on a heterosexual woman who was killed in the blast, downplaying the sexuality of her two murdered friends.[5]

It is at this point that rhetoric and practice, the spheres of queer theory and political action, collide. If queer theory is not about identities but about actions and ways of living, then in an important sense queer politics *is* about shared lifestyles. But simultaneously, we recall, 'queer' began as a strategy that linked disparate groups with exceedingly different lives and sexual practices. The title *Queer as Folk* is derived from a Northern English colloquialism, 'there's nowt so queer as folk', meaning 'people are strange'. Queerness calls at once for a celebration of a diversity of identities, but also for a cultural diversity that surpasses the notion of identity. So is queer still queer, and is it important for 'queerness' to refer always to the same communities, acts, and beliefs?

III

Paradoxically, the intermittent but inimitable violence of theory shows that the referential slipperiness of 'queer' may be politically vital. While transgender became the academic exemplar of queer theory, troubling deliciously not only gender but also the corollary issues of sexuality, patriarchy and sexual difference, transsexuality posed a problem, as Stephen Whittle recounts in his article 'Gender Fucking or Fucking Gender?'. Castigated by such eminent gender theorists as Germaine Greer, transsexual people have seemed to reconstitute the gender binary by bringing the dichotomously sexed body sharply and stubbornly back into focus as the necessary vehicle of desire.[6] Moreover, by appearing to demonstrate that your identity is defined by your ability to change your identity, transsexuality might be seen as the *reductio ad absurdum* of queer theory.[7] Therefore the difficulty faced by queer as a sexually inclusive and socially progressive movement is to account for those instances where it unseats its own authority by the use of examples that take on an ethical life of their own. Such a mission raises awkward academic questions: Would a truly queer university course be wholly taught and attended by queers? Or should the opposite be the case, and who is fit to decide?

Certainly the primary challenge posed by queer theory, as Eve Kosofsky Sedgwick shows in her essay 'Axiomatic', is to hegemonic understandings of the relations between identity, sex, gender and sexuality. Whereas Western culture has attempted to ossify these relations in the name of patriarchy, and feminism has tended to want to reconfigure them while preserving their conventional descriptive force, queer theory politicizes sex, gender and sexuality in a way that severs the notion of identity from any stable reference points. In this way, queerness resists the regimes, critiqued by Marjorie Garber in 'The Return to Biology', of measuring, categorizing, and knowing the truth of sexual orientation.

Now there are at least three distinctly queer alternatives to traditional conceptions of identity: on the one hand, there is a *performative* or speech act approach, which is explained by Judith Butler's paper 'Contagious Word: Paranoia and "Homosexuality" in the Military'. On another hand, identities can be understood *normatively* as community commitments, according to Mark Norris Lance and Alessandra Tanesini in 'Identity Judgements, Queer Politics'. On the third hand (queer theory likes to disrupt conventional parameters of embodiment), a vision of identity as *performance* or phenomenological presentation is demonstrated by Carol Queen's story 'The Leather Daddy and the Femme'. Further kinds of queer subjectivity jostle invigoratingly within and between the texts collected in this volume – intersexed, transsexual, invert, anti-homophobe, HIV positive, bisexual, married, male lesbian, leather daddy, royal princess . . .

IV

Our point is that queer comes into being through the turbulent conjunction of theory and politics. This is why it matters whether *Queer as Folk* is properly representative – a seemingly hair-splitting demand which would rarely be made of heterosexual drama.[8] Consider likewise the scrutiny to which we subjected Prime Minister Blair's response to the Admiral Duncan bombing. And the same is true of transsexuality's challenge to academic gender studies. In these situations and many others, queer makes a political summons to accountability that blurs the difference between theory and activism. The current crisis over the medical management of intersex people is a further relevant example. In 'Intersex Activism, Feminism and Psychology', Cheryl Chase and Peter Hegarty talk about how the lack of follow-up and comparative medical research into patients with, and without, genital surgery means that paternalistic treatment protocols are at once flimsy and intractable. So the challenges to institutionalized homophobia and sexism by intersexed activists, like the projects of other queer movements, have been disparaged as politically correct conjecture – as mere *queer theory* – for the very reasons that their activism pickets and lobbies against. In this way, queer calls the distinction between politics and theory into question, while itself being incessantly queried by the same distinction.

The future of queer is unknown. We have purposively composed our Introduction before finding out what Mandy Merck has written in her specially commissioned Afterword to this volume. But queer's future is not a mystery simply because the future is by definition unknowable. On the contrary, queer theory's political commitment is specifically to the unknowability, the non-identifiability, of its own identity in the future.

2

From Here to Queer: Radical Feminism, Postmodernism, and the Lesbian Menace

Suzanna Danuta Walters

QUEER DEFINED (NOT!)

'Queer' is, in true postmodern fashion, a rather amorphous term and still emergent enough as to be vague and ill defined. Perhaps it makes sense to open, then, with my laundry list of the queer contemporary, a list admittedly more aware of the female manifestations of this 'queerness' and in no particular order:

Eve Sedgwick	Teresa de Lauretis	ball culture
Judith Butler	Queer Nation	kiss-ins
Madonna	lipstick lesbians	lesbian strippers
conferences at Santa Cruz, Rutgers, Iowa, etc.	drag	butch/femme
	piercing	Michelangelo Signorile
	Ru Paul	
'in your face activism'	tattoos	Sue-Ellen Case
	passing	dildos
Camille Paglia	queer zines	sadomasochism
go-go girls	outing	backrooms
men in skirts	cross-dressing	(for lesbians)
Riot Grrrls	male lesbians	Sandra Bernhard
Foucault	Annie Sprinkle	camp
On Our Backs	lesbians who sleep with men	bisexuality
Susie Bright		genderfuck

These signifiers (and others, of course) constitute what many have called the 'new queer sensibility'. There is no doubt that a new tide of gay visibility is sweeping the country – from *Time* magazine cover stories on the new chic lesbians, to k.d. lang's *Vanity Fair* dress up with supermodel Cindy Crawford, to gays in the military, drag queens on *Donahue*, outing, and our

6

little hypothalamuses and aberrant genes. As usual in our media-saturated/ structured culture, these (largely hetero) glam pieces intersect with unique developments, both intellectual and political, within various gay communities. So these shifting signifiers of 'queer' are never simply our own products, located solely in some subcultural netherworld (if they ever were – remember disco?), but instead they move uneasily in and out of the 'mainstream' as it recodes and cannibalizes these new images, icons, activisms. ...

HOMO POLITICUS, HOMO ACADEMICUS

The growth of queer theory and queer politics must be placed in a social and political context. The most important pieces of this are, of course, the AIDS crisis, the rise of postmodern/poststructural theory, the politics of academia, the sex debates,[1] and recent critiques of feminism. I want to go through each of these briefly to contextualize both the development of the term *queer* and my own criticisms of it as well.

As many writers have noted, the AIDS crisis not only prompted a renewed and reinvigorated gay and lesbian movement but radically opened up (or re-created) new ways of doing politics. Although this was surely not the first time gay men and women had worked together, AIDS activism brought us together in a time of crisis both from the disease itself and from the increasing attacks on gay and lesbian life from the religious Right and the Republican administrations. It encouraged a rethinking of gay politics in the light of this crisis but also in the light of the way in which gay men and women have learned more about each other and their various communities. So, we would want to recognize the specificity of queer politics as emerging with the crisis of AIDS and the development of groups such as ACT UP and Queer Nation: 'Many of these new gay militants reject the liberal value of privacy and the appeal to tolerance which dominate the agendas of more mainstream gay organizations. Instead, they emphasize publicity and self-assertion; confrontation and direct action top their list of tactical options; the rhetoric of difference replaces the more assimilationist liberal emphasis on similarity with other groups' (Duggan, 1992: 15). In addition, *queer* has developed as a way to broaden the definitions, so that the movement can be more inclusive (e.g., bisexual, transgendered, etc.): 'Queer culture ... in its openness and its non-specificity, potentially suggests the truly polymorphous nature of our difference, of difference within the gay and lesbian community. The minute you say "queer" you are necessarily calling into question exactly what you mean when you say it. There is always an implicit question about what constitutes "queerness" that attends the minute you say the word. So, it seems to me that queer includes within it a necessarily

expansive impulse that allows us to think about potential differences within
that rubric' (Harper, White and Cerullo, 1993: 30).

This has prompted no small amount of debate, as one might imagine.
On what basis are these different 'identities' (practices?) joined together
under the heading *queer*? Are queer politics simply a politics of the non-
normative, as this writer seems to suggest? 'An emergent lesbian politics
acknowledged the relative autonomy of gender and sexuality, sexism and
heterosexism. It suggested that lesbians shared with gay men a sense of
"queerness," a nonnormative sexuality which transcends the binary distinction homosexual/heterosexual to include all who feel disenfranchised by
dominant sexual norms – lesbians and gay men, as well as bisexuals and
transsexuals' (Stein, 1992: 50). Given this logic, could not the category *queer*
include paedophiles, incest perpetrators, hetero S/Mers, dissatisfied straights,
and so forth?[2] In other words, if all that we share is a non-normative
sexuality and a disenfranchisement, then why not be totally inclusive? This
reduces queer politics to a banal (and potentially dangerous) politics of
simple opposition, potentially affiliating groups, identities, and practices that
are explicitly and implicitly in opposition to each other. To link politically
and theoretically around a 'difference' from normative heterosexually
imposes a (false) unity around disparate practices and communities.
Politically, of course, these different groups/practices do not necessarily
share a progressive political agenda on sexuality; non-normativity is hardly a
banner around which to rally. However, for many writers and activists alike
(inspired, perhaps, by Michel Foucault's work), regulation itself is the
problem; the creation of norms is the fundamental act of repression. With
this logic, any unifying of the non-normative raises the political stakes
around regulation and thus opens the door to liberatory moves.

If, as bisexual writer Elisabeth Däumer writes, these new moves liberate
'the queer in all of us' (1992: 92), then what happens to any conception of
oppositional identity? Does this move of inclusivity (and the challenge to
notions of authentic identity that it entails) run the risk of setting up another
(albeit grander) opposition? And does it end up in a sort of meaningless
pluralism motivated only by a vague sense of dissent, as Lisa Duggan suggests: 'The notion of a "queer community" ... is often used to construct a
collectivity no longer defined solely by the gender of its members' sexual
partners. This new community is unified only by a shared dissent from the
dominant organization of sex and gender' (1992: 20).

The eighties and early nineties have also witnessed the rise of postmodernism and poststructuralism in social theory: the demise of the 'grand
narratives', a new suspicion of 'identity politics' as constructing a potential hegemony around the identity 'gay' or 'lesbian' as if that necessarily supposed a unified and coherent subjectivity: gay person. Identity is
critiqued here as supposing a unity, squeezing out difference, perpetuating

binarisms and dichotomous formations, and bordering on (if not instantiating) essentialism. So postmodern theory challenges the idea of gay identity as expressing 'true' – not constructed – gay sexuality.

Many feminists have produced trenchant critiques of postmodernism,[3] and even more find themselves (ourselves) in an admittedly ambiguous relation to the challenges offered by postmodern theorizing. While this is not the place to delve into *that* whole debate, suffice it to say that many feminists have been wary of the quick dismissal of 'the subject' and political agency just when it seemed that women were getting around to acquiring some. The critique of identity so central to postmodern theorizing seems to many to place feminist activism in a political straitjacket, unable to move (because moving requires reliance on identity concepts that are themselves suspect), yet needing desperately to organize women precisely around those newly suspect categories.

Postmodern theory, in addition, has been marked by its fetish of the margins. If postmodern theory finds resistance in the interstices of the body politic, in the marginal spaces, then queer theory takes up on that, dispersing resistance away from the locatable and specific body of the lesbian or the gay man and onto this more amorphous site of the 'queer body' (which may or may not be gay). Postmodern theory often tends toward a fetish of inconsistency, contradictions, and the ever-present 'difference'. This can degenerate into an assertion of the hipness or sexiness of contradiction. But progressives have long argued that *some* contradictions are not only *not* sexy but are actually reactionary and that there is indeed a relationship between how one lives one's life and the politics one espouses, so that living in a segregated neighbourhood or replicating the sexual division of labour in the home would not be 'sexy' contradictions for avowed antiracists and feminists but would instead be suspect to challenge. So this emphasis on the delight in inconsistency for its own sake seems to me foolhardy at best.

Queer theory in the academy is curiously placed. Clearly, most queer theory takes place in the context of women's studies and/or lesbian and gay studies, even as it attempts to move outside those parameters. And most queer theorists, I have no doubt, themselves embrace (albeit uneasily) the identity 'gay'. Nevertheless, there is a disturbing trend in which queer theory has become disassociated from gay identity. Indeed, this disassociation is often celebrated as the necessary adjunct to the disassociation of gender and sexuality. One of the interesting aspects of this phenomenon of queer theory in the academy is that you do not have to be gay to do it; in fact it is much better if you are not.[4] *Queer* (as opposed to *gay* or *lesbian*) lets you off the identity hook the way that gender studies has *vis-à-vis* women's studies, while cashing in on the trendiness of postmodernism. What are the implications of a queer theory disassociated from a gay and lesbian identity? This is not easy to answer, and I do not want to be claiming a sort of essentialist (god forbid!) idea that insists one must *be* something in order to teach it.[5] Clearly, non-gay scholars *must* teach gay 'subjects', as male professors must teach about women and whites must teach about people of colour. But the thorny issues of authenticity, experience, and co-operation are not resolved by an assertion that no identity is real. Are we really to evacuate the centrality of experience for vacuousness of positionality (positionality as indicating the always provisional and temporal nature of political location and action)? While compelling and suggestive, I fear that the concept of positionality tends toward a voluntarism that ignores the multiple, felt, structural determinations on people's everyday existence. If you are 'gay loving' (as Sedgwick often refers to it), is that synonymous with being gay? Does that difference not matter any more? Are gay and lesbian studies simply to become another academic commodity that anyone can buy in on, given the proper allegiances and fashion statements?

The straight white married man at my university who says he 'does' queer theory in his English classes is in a *structurally* different place than I am. Does this perhaps have some relevance? Should he not speak to this in some way? It is not to say that I (as a lesbian) can speak the 'truth' of lesbian life more than he can; it is to say that this difference needs to be acknowledged and reckoned with in the course of academic life. This means not only being explicit about the different risks implied in our positions but also acknowledging the different ways we know and present this knowledge and the effects that may have on our students. I know it is hopelessly retro to speak of structure these days, to insist that material conditions actually do impose real, felt and experienced limits on our lives in radically different ways. My straight colleague may or may not be well intentioned. But, while this does matter, it is not at all clear that his good intentions alter his power to speak and my relative powerlessness.

I suspect that these concerns about the politics of experience get lost in the radical disassociation of identity from embodied practices. This is not to say that oppression is the mark of truth or authenticity but that, given the hierarchies of power in academia, we cannot afford to lose sight of 'from where we speak'. The deconstruction of identity politics (the recognition that identity categories can be regulatory regimes) may have some merit, but it can also, in the world of academia as well as in other social spaces, become the vehicle for co-optation: the radical queer theorist as married heterosexual. It becomes a convenient way to avoid those questions of privilege. What are the implications involved in claiming 'queerness' when one is not gay or lesbian? And, would we tolerate this passing (indeed, it is even being celebrated!) in another context, say the context of race or ethnicity? If it is clearly co-optive and colonizing for the white person to claim blackness if she or he 'feels' black (or even feels aligned politically with the struggles against racism), then why is it so strangely legitimate for a heterosexual to claim queerness because she or he feels a disaffection from traditional definitions of heterosexuality? The white academic says she is *working on* antiracism and on issues of race and ethnicity; the straight (most often white) academic says she (or he, more often) *is* queer. There is a huge jump being made from studying/teaching gay and lesbian work to pronouncing oneself queer. That jump is, I believe, both intellectually and politically dangerous. Straight faculty can and must analyse and teach about the logics of compulsory heterosexuality, but they must explicitly recognize that, for example, they are more likely to be taken seriously and deemed legitimate because of that very system they are critiquing. In addition, they must acknowledge that the 'will to know' is different; 'knowing' lesbian and gay studies can never be simply or only an academic commodity for the gay or lesbian faculty member or student. It is not just a trope.

Queer theory, particularly in its more academic manifestations, is often posed as a response to a certain kind of feminist and lesbian theorizing that is now deemed hopelessly retro, boring, realist, modernist, about shoring up identity rather than its deconstruction. I will discuss this further below, but there has been a kind of reigning dogma in progressive and postmodern academic circles these days that constructs an 'old-time' feminism in order to point out how the sex debates, postmodernism, and queer theory have nicely superseded this outmoded, reformist, prudish, banal feminism of old. Is it possible that queer theory's unspoken Other is feminism, or even lesbianism, or lesbian-feminism?

Queer theory's relation to the politics and theorizing of racialized identities is no less fraught than its relation to feminism and feminist identities. It seems to me – in the little that has been published explicitly addressing this relationship (and this itself is a problem, because although there is a growing body of critique from white feminists, I have found little specifically addressing questions of race and queerness *per se*) – that lesbian and gay writers of colour are expressing both optimism with the new queer designations as well as trepidation. The optimism is located in the queer dethroning of gender and the (possible) opening up of queerness to articulations of 'otherness' beyond the gender divide. In other words, if queer can be seen to challenge successfully gender hegemony, then it can make both theoretical and political space for more substantive notions of multiplicity and intersectionality. However, queer can 'de-race' the homosexual of colour in much the same way 'old-time' gay studies often has, effectively erasing the specificity of 'raced' gay existence under a queer rubric in which whiteness is not problematized. Sagri Dhairyam, in 'Racing the Lesbian, Dodging White Critics', critiques the implicit whiteness of queerness while still attempting to instantiate the category 'queer women of colour'. ' "Queer theory" comes increasingly to be reckoned with as critical discourse, but concomitantly writes a queer whiteness over raced queerness; it domesticates race in its elaboration of sexual difference' (1994: 26). Gloria Anzaldúa makes a somewhat different point; she feels more affinity with *queer* as a term of more working-class and 'deviant' etymology than what she sees as the historically white and middle-class origins of the designations *lesbian* and *gay*. Cherríe Moraga and Amber Hollibaugh have made a similar argument in their use of the phrase *queer lesbian*, stressing their embrace of the term for its difference from middle-class lesbian feminist identities (1983). Yet Anzaldúa also accuses white academics of co-opting the term *queer* and using it to construct 'a false unifying umbrella which all "queers" of all races, ethnicities and classes are shoved under' (1991: 250).

In addition, I would also suspect that the inattention to material social relations (commodification, the fluctuations of international capital, shifting forms of familial life, rise in antigay activism, regressive social legislation, increasing disenfranchisement of people of colour, etc.) and the academicism of much of queer writing would be problems for a lesbian/gay praxis that is both class and race conscious. Marlon Riggs hinted at this when he deconstructed his own situation as 'black queer diva': 'Le Butch-Girl wonders, for instance, if her/his permission to say gender-fuck is contingent upon knowing and articulating Fanon, Foucault, Gates, Gilroy, hooks, Hall, West, and the rest as well' (1992: 102). To what extent does queerness embrace Ru Paul and *The Crying Game*'s Jaye Davidson as queer icons but effectively ignore the specific realities of lesbians and gays of colour?

THE CASE OF THE DISAPPEARING LESBIAN (OR, WHERE THE BOYS ARE)

My main critique of the new popularity of 'queer' (theory and, less so, politics) is that it often (and once again) erases lesbian specificity and the enormous difference that gender makes, evacuates the importance of feminism, and rewrites the history of lesbian feminism and feminism generally. Now this is not to say that strongly identified lesbians have not embraced queer theory and politics, or that those who do so are somehow acting in bad faith or are 'antifeminist'. Indeed, what makes queer theory so exciting in part is the way in which so many different kinds of theorists have been attracted to its promise. Many lesbians (including myself) have been attracted to queer theory out of frustration with a feminism that, they believe, either subsumes lesbianism under the generic category 'woman' or poses gender as the transcendent category of difference, thus making cross-gender gay alliances problematic. To a certain extent, I, too, share this excitement and embrace the queer move that can complicate an often too-easy feminist take on sexual identity that links lesbianism (in the worst-case scenario) to an almost primordial and timeless mother-bond or a hazy woman-identification. At the same time, however, I fear that many lesbians' engagement with queer theory is informed itself by a rudimentary and circumscribed (revisionist) history of feminism and gender-based theory that paints an unfair picture of feminism as rigid, homophobic, and sexless. As Biddy Martin notes, 'The work of complicating our theories has too often proceeded, however, by way of polemical and ultimately reductionist accounts of the varieties of feminist approaches to just one feminism, guilty of the humanist trap of making a self-same, universal category of "women" – defined as other than men – the subject of feminism. At its worst, feminism has been seen as more punitively policing than mainstream culture' (1994: 105).

The story, alluded to above, goes something like this: once upon a time there was this group of really boring ugly women who never had sex, walked a lot in the woods, read bad poetry about goddesses, wore flannel shirts, and hated men (even their gay brothers). They called themselves lesbians. Then, thankfully, along came these guys named Foucault, Derrida and Lacan dressed in girls' clothes, riding some very large white horses. They told these silly women that they were politically correct, rigid, frigid, sex-hating prudes who just did not GET IT – it was all a game anyway, all about words and images, all about mimicry and imitation, all a cacophony of signs leading back to nowhere. To have a politics around gender was silly, they were told, because gender was just a performance anyway, a costume one put on and, in drag performance, wore backward. And everyone knew boys were better at dressing up.

So, queerness is theorized as somehow beyond gender, a vision of a sort of transcendent, polymorphous perversity deconstructing as it slips from one desiring/desired object to the other. But this forgets the very real and felt experience of gender that women, particularly, live with quite explicitly. Indeed, one could argue that this is really the dividing line around different notions of queer; to what extent do theorists argue *queer* as a term beyond (or through) gender? 'Where de Lauretis retains the categories "gay" and "lesbian" and some notion of gender division as parts of her discussion of what "queerness" is (or might be), Judith Butler and Sue-Ellen Case have argued that queerness is something that is ultimately beyond gender – it is an attitude, a way of responding, that begins in a place not concerned with, or limited by, notions of a binary opposition of male and female or the homo versus hetero paradigm usually articulated as an extension of this gender binarism' (Doty, 1993: xv). But, again, this seems to assume that feminists (or gays and lesbians) have somehow created these binarisms.

Unlike the terms *gay* and *lesbian*, *queer* is not gender specific, and this of course has been one of its selling points, as it purports to speak to the diversity of the gay and lesbian community and to dethrone gender as the significant marker of sexual identity and sexual expression. Phillip Brian

Harper, in a piece adapted from a talk at the second OUTWrite Conference
in 1992, argues that it is precisely this attention to the diversity of gay and
lesbian culture that marks off *queer* from *lesbian* and *gay*: 'What I mean is
that the dichotomous formulation of gay and lesbian, that we've been
taught since the 1970s to use in politically correct contexts, is useful and has
been a very effective educational tool, but has at the same time suggested in
its dichotomy that there's only one relevant type of difference within our
culture, i.e., gender difference' (Harper, White and Cerullo, 1993: 29–30).

The point that gender is not the only significant marker of difference is an
important one and one that deserves development and reiteration.[6] This
point, of course, has been forcefully made in regard to both race and class.
But in a culture in which male is the default gender, in which *homosexual*
(a term that also does not specify gender) is all too often imaged as male,
and *gay* as both, to see queer as somehow gender *neutral* is ludicrous and
wilfully naive. Feminism has taught us that the idea of gender neutrality is
not only fictitious but a move of gender domination. I applaud queer
theory's expansion of the concept of difference but am concerned that, too
often, gender is not *complicated* but merely ignored, dismissed, or 'transcended'. In contradistinction, I would argue that the critique of gender
theory from the perspective of women of colour has done precisely what
the queer critique of gender is only partially and incompletely able to do.
In other words, gender in black feminist writing is not 'transcended' or
somehow deemed an 'enemy' concept. Rather, the concept of gender – and
feminist theory more generally – is complicated, expanded, deepened both
to challenge its 'privileged' status and to render it susceptible to theories of
intersectionality and multiplicity. The queer critique of the feminist mantra
of the separation of sex and gender (sex being the biological 'raw material'
and gender the socially constructed edifice that creates masculinity and
femininity) is helpful in complicating what has become a somewhat rote
recitation of social constructionist argument, an argument that too often
leaves the body and its various constructions unexamined. But in the light of
recently resurgent theories of biological determinism (see particularly the
firestorm of controversy generated by the determinist tract *The Bell Curve*
by Herrnstein and Murray, 1994), the insistence on a righteous social constructionism (women are made, not born; we are not simply an expression of
our biological make-up, etc.) might be important strategically and politically.
Too often in these queer challenges to this dichotomy, sex becomes the
grand force of excess that can offer more possibilities for liberatory culture,
and gender the constraint on that which would (naturally?) flow freely and
polymorphously if left to its own devices. Biddy Martin has made the
argument that, for Sedgwick and others, race and gender often assume a
fixity, a stability, a ground, whereas sexuality (typically thematized as male)
becomes the 'means of crossing' and the figure of mobility. In the process of

making the female body the 'drag' on the (male) play of sexuality, 'the female body appears to become its own trap, and the operations of misogyny disappear from view' (Martin, 1994: 104, 109–10).

But it is also not clear to me that this vision of a genderless non-normativity is a worthwhile goal. Is a degendered idea of sexual identity/sexual desire what we strive for? Is this just a postmodern version of a liberal pluralist 'if it feels good, do it' ethos? Also, the images/signifiers for this transcendence (of gender) are suspiciously male (why can't a woman be more like a fag?). If the phallus has been replaced by the dildo as the prime signifier of sexual transgression, of queerness, how far have we really come, so to speak?

Queer discourse sets up a universal (male) subject, or at least a universal gay male subject, as its implicit referent. (It is interesting to note in this regard that the 1993 summer special 'Queer Issue' of the *Village Voice* was called 'Faith Hope & Sodomy'.) We cannot deny the centrality of gay maleness to this reconstruction of queer as radical practice. For example, Sue-Ellen Case discusses her engagement with the word *queer* by saying that 'I became queer through my readerly identification with a male homosexual author' (1991: 1). This is not to say that it is not perfectly fine to 'identify' with gay men, but what this passage illustrates is a trend toward a giddy merger with gay men that is left relatively unproblematized. No one goes further with this identification than Sedgwick. I am reluctant to focus on her in this way, yet she herself has so foregrounded her own personal predilections that she seems rather fair game.[7] In a piece called 'A Poem Is Being Written', Sedgwick bemoans her 'failure ... to make the obvious swerve that would have connected my homosexual desire and identification with my need and love, as a woman, of women' (1993: 209). Indeed, she goes on to note that her 'identification as a gay person is a firmly male one, identification "as" a gay man' (209). In many ways, this does not even have the naive honesty of the fag hag who simply grooves on the panache of gay men. Sedgwick, the postmodern intellectual subject, must not only identify or sympathize or politically ally, she must *be*. And lesbianism here, in this 'tortured' self-study, simply becomes the unfortunate absence, not really the stuff of identities and identifications, merely the detritus of the grand narratives of male homosociality and homosexuality.

Although lesbians are occasionally mentioned (usually when speaking of S/M), gay men most assuredly have become the model for lesbian radical sex (e.g., the celebration of pornography, the 'reappropriation' of the phallus in the fascination with the dildo, the 'daddy' fantasies, and reverence for public sex of Pat Califia, etc.).[8] This has entailed a denigration of lesbian attempts to rethink sexuality within a feminist framework. Granted (and we do not need to go through this one more time), lesbian sexuality has suffered from both a discursive neglect and an idealization on the part of lesbians themselves. The image of hand-holding, eye-gazing, woodsy eroticism, however, is not wholly the creation of lesbians but part of the devaluation and stereotyping of all women's sexuality by male-dominant culture. Even in that haven of supposedly uptight, separatist nonsex (Northampton, Massachusetts, in the late 1970s and early 1980s), I seem to remember we were all doing the nasty fairly well, and, for all the talk of the 'lesbian sex police',[9] no girl ever banged down my door and stymied my sexual expression. The straight gaybashers, however, did. We should never forget this difference as we glibly use words like *police*.

Indeed, Vera Whisman criticizes those feminists who 'policed' other lesbians with charges of male identification and says that 'such charges of male-identification were rooted not only in anti-sex attitudes ... but also in essentialist understandings of womanhood' (1993: 55). Do we really want to relinquish a critique of male identification? After all, the feminist insight that a central impediment to women's liberation (yes, liberation) is an identification with and dependence on males and male approval, desire, status, and so on is so obvious as to be banal. Charges of male identification may have been spuriously made at times, but the *analysis* of male identification is central and important.

The construction of an old, bad, exclusive, policing lesbian feminism is necessary for the 'bad girl' (dildo in tow) to emerge as the knight in leather armour, ready to make the world safe for sexual democracy, as Terralee Bensinger argues: 'Any threat to the "unity" of the ideal feminist community (as well as to the more "general" lesbian community) is branded "outlaw" activity and purged from the networks of inclusion. In this case, pro-sex lesbian pornographers function as the expurged excess against which the illusion of community unity is maintained (in reified form). Lesbian feminism has a history of exclusion as much as anything else' (1992: 71).

In her history of this exclusion, Bensinger cites the political event known as the 'lavender menace' (the action to challenge the purge of lesbians in the National Organization for Women) to 'indicate how it stunted the historical "writing" of lesbian sexual identity and subsequent practice for years. The result of this group's strategic maneuver was a discursive/historical repression of the specificities of lesbian sexuality which was subsumed under the reified sign of Woman' (1992: 73). Gee, and I thought homophobia and antifeminism were the problem!

In an article on the 'decentering of lesbian feminism', Stein traces the history of the lesbian movement, from its early attempts to shift away from the medical models of sexual deviance to the construction of the 'woman-identified woman' and the development of a lesbian subculture and 'women's culture' in general. She takes us to the period of rupture – the 1980s – where 'a series of structural and ideological shifts conspired to decenter the lesbian-feminist model of identity. First, the predominantly white and middle-class women who comprised the base of the movement aged, underwent various life-cycle changes, and settled into careers and families of various stripes – often even heterosexual ones. Second, a growing revolt emerged from within: women of color, working-class women, and sexual minorities, three separate but overlapping groups, asserted their claims on lesbian identity politics' (Stein, 1992: 47).

But, in an otherwise astute and fair chronology, Stein engages in the kind of reductionist reading that has marred other similar narratives. In discussing the challenges of the 'sex debates' and the AIDS crisis as reintroducing sexuality and desire into lesbian discourse and identity, she engages in a simplistic substitution: 'As the withered body of the person with AIDS replaced the once-pervasive image of the all-powerful male oppressor, the sense of male threat which underlay lesbian-feminist politics diminished further' (Stein, 1992: 49). But, of course, 'male threat' (or even patriarchy) has hardly withered, although it has certainly changed. Curiously absent from this history is the rise of the religious Right, which brought with it an unprecedented backlash against feminism, women's rights, and poor people – along with its attacks on gays and lesbians. It is not that the image of the AIDS sufferer (and we will leave aside *that* iconography for the moment) has replaced the image of male oppressor; indeed, the images (and policies) of Reagan, Bush, Quayle, Helms, Robertson, Falwell, Terry (and now the new terror – Newt Gingrich), and others are vivid and imposing.

Even further, not only are those repressed and repressive lesbians responsible for putting a major damper on our nascent sexuality, but feminism itself is responsible for that horror of all horrors: THE BINARY. Bensinger indicts 'the binaries generated within feminist movement: feminism/patriarchy, inside/outside, and porn/erotica' (1992: 88). Certain strands of feminism might indeed have perpetuated some of these oppositions (and is feminism *not* opposed to patriarchy?), but, alas, they long pre-date second-wave feminism. Seventies feminism here becomes the ogre that haunts queer kids of today. 'By the seventies feminism had sanitized lesbianism. Lesbophobia forced lesbians to cling to feminism in an attempt to retain respectability. However, in the eighties, discussions of sadomasochism permanently altered the relationship of many lesbians to feminism' (Morgan, 1993: 39). I would have hoped most politically astute lesbians (and gay men, for that matter) were/are feminists; this should be a theory we embrace (not 'cling to') and, of course, transform and challenge in that embrace.

Many queer activists and theorists seem to believe the media fiction that feminism is either (*a*) dead because we lost or (*b*) dead because we won: '1988. So feminism is dead, or it has changed, or it is still meaningful to some of us but its political currency in the world is weak, its radical heart excised, its plodding middle-class moderation now an acceptable way of life. Feminism has been absorbed by the same generation that so proudly claims to reject it, and instead of women's liberation I hear, "Long live the Queer

nation!"' (Maggenti, 1993: 250). As Whisman notes, 'Today's "bad girls"
rebel as much against their feminist predecessors as against male power'
(1993: 48). In her review of the *differences* issue on queer theory, Hennessy
challenges those writers who set up feminism as the enemy, 'substitut[ing]
feminism (the Symbolic Mother) for patriarchy as the most notable
oppressive force that lesbian politics and eroticism must contend with.
For feminists this should seem a very disturbing perspective shift, especially
when feminism, among young people in particular, is more than ever a bad
word' (1993: 969).

This is not to deny the importance of the 'sex debates' and the new
discussions around lesbian sexuality that, I agree, are long overdue. The
open and volatile discussion of sexuality permanently altered feminist praxis
and allowed for a complex debate around the politics of passion and desire
that recognized that the simplistic rendering of women's sexuality was in
need of major revision. And this is not to say that some lesbians, and some
feminists, do not 'judge' and indeed condemn sexual practices that they have
deemed antithetical to the project of constructing a postpatriarchal world.
This censuring is to be heartily contested, as it has from numerous writers
and activists. But I simply suggest that we apply our own theories consistently: the narrative of 'sexless uptight dykes of the 1970s' is, after all, a
narrative, and as we have been so adept at deconstructing narrative for the
relations of power that inhere in the telling of history, we should be equally
able to 'read' this story with, well, a grain of salt at the very least.

Now gay male sex and *its* histories become the very model of radical chic:
the backroom replaces the consciousness-raising session as site of transformation. Feminist critiques of objectification, concern with abuse of
women, and desire to construct nonpatriarchal forms of intimacy become
belittled and denigrated as so much prudery and 'political correctness',
creating an ahistorical narrative that furthers the separation of feminism
from queer politics and theory.

In an article on her adventures in the new lesbian backrooms of the
Village, Donna Minkowitz sees sexual *and* political liberation in the construction of spaces for anonymous sex, never once questioning the male
model or her own location. She clearly envies the gay men of the pre-AIDS
days and bemoans her own teenage fate: 'I have a girlfriend, not a transgressive erotic world where I can do it with five strangers in an evening, or
suck off girl upon girl in the darkness of the meat district' (1992: 34). But
why is this practice deemed transgressive (and, consequently, a 'girlfriend'
deemed dreadfully banal and prudish)? The model of liberatory sex being
constructed here is one where 'sex ... is separate from the world outside –
it doesn't violate vows of monogamy or enter the partners into a "relationship"' (34). This may or may not be a liberatory practice (or it may just be
fun), but its transgressiveness is not self-evidently radical unless one sees

transgression itself as the supreme act of radical identity making. I fear, here, we have a real failure of imagination. Are lesbians unable to construct, envision, imagine, enact radical sexualities without relying so fundamentally on male paradigms? Must we look to the boys in the backroom as our Sapphic saviours? Why are 'gay male sluts' (as Minkowitz puts it) the model?

And why this (theoretical) obsession with the question of whether to call oneself a lesbian? In an article for the gay and lesbian anthology *Inside/Out*, Butler (1991) spends several pages pondering this puzzle, an analogous puzzle to that posed recently by feminists about whether there really are 'women' and whether our use of that category reinscribes its ability to construct us in power relations. Sure, to a certain extent, all categories are, as Butler and others have put it, 'regulatory regimes', but so what? How can resisting these regimes be anything other than an intellectual exercise, a game that can be reduced to that old canard 'don't categorize me' (as liberals and college students would put it)? Is this just an empty gesture or, rather, a gesture full with self-importance, postmodern hubris, rebellious nose thumbing? It is not to say there isn't much truth to the claim that homosexual identity, like all categorical identities, is a 'fiction' to a certain extent, is a collection of regulations and positions that can, perhaps, constrain as much as enable, impose as much as liberate, police as much as free. But I think that, in fact, the queer framework remains within the binarism it so desperately wants to explode, in that the assumption is that gay identities necessarily – in a structural sense – act like all the other identities.[10] All categories have rules, to be sure, but not all follow the same rules. The historical conditions of growing up 'gay' or 'lesbian' in a homophobic culture may, in fact, produce categories of identity that are more fluid, more flexible than the categories of other identities, such as heterosexuality. Why must we assume that all identities form around the same structural binarisms and with the same inherent rigidities? Is *that* not essentialist?

And does this difference not make a difference in how we 'think' identity? When Butler says that she is 'not at ease with "lesbian theories, gay theories"', referring to the title of the anthology, because 'identity categories tend to be instruments of regulatory regimes, whether as the normalizing categories of oppressive structures or as the rallying points for a liberatory contestation of that very oppression' (1991: 13–14), does she not want to stress the difference between these two moments – the moment of oppression and the moment of liberation? Are those different uses of identity categories just the surface that belies the 'deep meaning' of identity as 'really' about 'oppressive structures'? Or can we see these different uses and meanings of identity as radically different, not just somehow superficially different? Indeed, does it not actually sound a bit strange to heterosexual identity (or WASP identity, etc.) and should that r something about the differences in these two usages/meanings?

simply to argue that we need to adopt the terms *woman* or *lesbian* as a sort of 'strategic essentialism' as has been argued elsewhere, but rather to say let us think this concept *lesbian* through the historical developments of lesbian desires, bodies, passions, struggles, politics.

Butler goes on in the article to question not only identity as a lesbian but the process of 'coming out', as it further implicates the 'subject' in the subjection of being named and known: 'Is the "subject" who is "out" free of its subjection and finally in the clear? Or could it be that the subjection that subjectivates the gay or lesbian subject in some ways continues to oppress, or oppresses most insidiously, once "outness" is claimed?' (1991: 15). She further asks, 'Can sexuality even remain sexuality once it submits to a criterion of transparency and disclosure?' (15). Hmm, that old devil moon is back again. Sexuality, she must be, how you say, an enigma, hidden, dark, unconscious for her to be ... fun. Shhh, don't talk, don't know, don't even think you know, don't claim, don't reveal: desire needs dark curtains of mystery to be pleasurable.

Shane Phelan, writing in the *Signs* special issue on lesbianism, joins others in critiquing the prominence of the 'coming out' process for lesbian identity, asserting that the language of 'coming out' implies 'a process of discovery or admission rather than one of construction or choice' (1993: 773), thus producing an essentialist notion of a 'real' lesbian identity that exists beneath the layers of denial or hiding. But I am not sure coming out is as unitary and simple a process as these theorists make it out to be. Granted, for many it can be that sort of a revelatory move, revealing that which was 'really there' but hidden all along. But for others, coming out is, first, not a moment but rather a contradictory and complex process that involves (perhaps) self-revelation, construction, political strategy, choice, and so forth. Second, it seems ludicrous to pretend that internalized homophobia and the realities of heterosexism and heterosexual privilege are not operative in and around these 'coming out' processes. Phelan and others seem to write as if we 'come out' in a social and political vacuum. Phelan cites Barbara Ponse and Mark Blasius as arguing for a conception of coming out as a sort of 'becoming', learning the ways of being gay or lesbian (Phelan, 1993: 774). But, again, I do not see these as mutually exclusive. Of course 'coming out' implies a becoming, a construction of the self as gay, now not 'hidden' within the fiction of heterosexuality. But this 'becoming' is, for so many, also merged with a profound sense of 'revealing' a 'truth' that one had previously 'hidden'. That truth might indeed be a fiction (in that no identity is ever presocial, inhering in some untouched part of the soul or psyche or body), but it is a fiction that many live through, and in, quite deeply.

Steven Seidman also writes that he now feels more uneasy with the act of coming out and makes a similar leap that associates 'coming out' with a necessarily regulatory process:

To the extent that the positive effects of coming out have turned on announcing a respectable homosexuality, this politics has the negative effect of pathologizing all those desires, behaviors, and lives that deviate from a normalized homosexuality – or heterosexuality. Such a relentless politics of identity – 'homos are really no different from straights' – reinforces an equally relentless normalization of conventional sexual and gender codes. In other words, coming out is effective only if the homo made public is announced to be like the straight in every way but sexual orientation. Thus all the ways that homos may be queer – for example, those who like to cross-dress, role play, have multiple sex partners, or engage in commercial, rough, or public sex – are pathologized by the strategy of coming out as a respectable homo. (1994: 170)

This constructs a totalizing narrative of coming out that defies logic. Why does Seidman assume that all who come out do so as 'respectable homos'? Surely, that is part of the discourse but obviously not the whole of it. What, about the very act of 'coming out', *necessarily* implies the pathologizing of certain practices? It certainly can (as can everything), but I see no necessary relation unless one views any declaration of identity (however prefaced by caveats) as an immediate smoke signal to the forces of domination that all is clear. And what of our responsibility to others? If one less young person feels alone and vulnerable, one less colleague isolated and marginalized, is that not something – at the very least – to consider?

But queer theory gets its most Felliniesque when it starts mulling over the (exciting!) possibilities of the 'male lesbian'. Indeed, Jacquelyn Zita devotes an entire article to this subject. Zita proposes the male lesbian as radical gender bender, 'challenging the naturalness of "maleness" and "heterosexuality" by the bizarre-ness of his self-intending sex and gender attributions' (1992: 125). Once again, men in the front lines in the fight for equality and justice. Just like Tootsie!

3

Gay Men, Lesbians, and Sex: Doing It Together

Patrick Califia

I have sex with faggots. And I'm a lesbian. You think *you're* confused? How did this happen to a woman who maintained a spotless record as a militant lesbian separatist for eight years, a woman who had sex with only three men (once apiece) before coming out, a woman who gets called a dyke on the street at least once a week, a woman who has slept (and not stayed to sleep) with hundreds of other women?

To explain, I need to go back to 1977. Those of you who aren't ready for this have my permission to leave the room. But don't slam the door on your way out. Who knows who will be sitting on *your* face in 1984?

In 1977 when I bought my first dog collar, there was no such thing as a lesbian S/M community. There probably were a few isolated dykes who owned rope they never intended to string up for clothesline – but I couldn't find them. So when I heard about a women's S/M support group, I joined it even though most of the members were straight or bisexual. I was surprised to discover that most of them were honest, intelligent perverts – and feminists! One of them, a professional dominatrix, became my lover.

My lover found the straight S/M scene pretty joyless, so she hung out with a small group of gay men who were into fisting and S/M. She was especially attached to Steve McEachern, who ran private handballing parties in his extremely well-equipped basement. This club was called The Catacombs. The Christmas after we became lovers, she took me to a party at his house. About fifteen men were present. She and I were the only women. After a huge dinner, everybody just started taking off his clothes. I found myself sitting alone in a corner, wondering if I was going to spend the entire orgy feeling sorry for myself (my girlfriend had wandered off with Steve). A tall, handsome man (albeit a little skinny) sat down beside me and said, 'Hi, my name's Joe. How would you like to fist me?'

I took a deep breath and said, 'I'd like that, but you'll have to show me what to do.' That was fine with him. He got me an emery board and some nail clippers and showed me how to perform the very severe manicure handballing requires. He took for granted that a novice had to receive

22

detailed instructions, and he didn't expect me to dazzle him with a magic show of sexual expertise. This attitude was very reassuring and completely different from the way anybody else I'd met had approached sex. When Joe approved my hands, we went downstairs, located some towels and Crisco, and climbed onto the waterbed.

Joe lay on his back. He wrapped his arms around his thighs and held them apart. My first handful of grease melted right into his ass. It was like feeding a hungry animal – an animal that talked back. He gave me such careful instructions about when to push and when to pull back that I got into him easily, I can't remember how deep. It seemed like miles. I came to at one point and realized just how vulnerable he was, this big man clutching his thighs and groaning uncontrollably because I was so far into him. The walls of his gut hugged my hand and forearm, smoother and softer and more fragile than anything I'd ever touched before. I think I cried. I know I got wet.

Well, that's how it started. I've lost track of exactly how many men I've put my hand(s) into, and it still puts me in a trance. It's awesome to be that close to another human being. In between cans of Crisco, I've thought a lot about why it's possible to cross the 'gender line' in the context of this kind of sex. First of all, in fisting the emphasis is not on the genitals. Men at handballing parties don't usually cruise each other's dicks. They cruise each other's hands and forearms. It is not unusual for fisters to go all night without a hard-on. Tops with small hands are in demand, and my glove size is a popular one. Gay men who are into handballing usually think of themselves as sexually different from other gay men. They get a lot of attitude about being sick, kinky, and excessive. Hence some of them are willing to break a gay taboo and do it with a woman.

As I acquired more experience in the S/M community, I realized this, too, was a sexuality that allowed people to step outside the usually rigid boundaries of sexual orientation. I met lesbians who topped straight men for money (and did that myself for a while). I met straight men who would go down on other men or be fucked by them if their mistresses ordered them to do it. Since the acts took place under the authority of women, they thought of them as heterosexual behaviour. (I also met a lot of bisexuals who didn't need any excuses.)

These combined experiences have resulted in a lifestyle that doesn't fit the homosexual stereotype. I live with my woman lover of five years. I have lots of casual sex with women. Once in a while, I have casual sex with gay men. I have a three-year relationship with a homosexual man who doesn't use the term *gay*. And I call myself a lesbian.

Of course, I've modified my sexual pattern in the face of the AIDS crisis. I've become much more conscious of the need to maintain good general health by getting enough sleep, eating a nutritious diet, and reducing stress and recreational drug use. I've also quit having sex with strangers. I have the same amount of sex but with fewer people – and none of them are taking excessive risks with their health, either. I have not dropped fisting from my repertoire, I am simply more selective about whom I do it with. I have yet to be convinced that fisting exposes me or my partners to more danger than other kinds of sexual contact.

Why not identify as bi? That's a complicated question. For a while, I thought I was simply being biphobic. There's a lot of that going around in the gay community. Most of us had to struggle so hard to be exclusively homosexual that we resent people who don't make a similar commitment. A self-identified bisexual is saying, 'Men and women are of equal importance to me.' That's simply not true of me. I'm a Kinsey Five, and when I turn on to a man it's because he shares some aspect of my sexuality (like S/M or fisting) that turns me on *despite* his biological sex.

There's yet another twist. I have eroticized queerness, gayness, homosexuality – in men and women. The leatherman and the drag queen are sexy to me, along with the diesel dyke with greased-back hair, and the femme stalking across the bar in her miniskirt and high-heeled shoes. I'm a fag hag.

The gay community's attitude toward fag hags and dyke daddies has been pretty nasty and unkind. Fag hags are supposed to be frustrated, traditionally feminine, heterosexual women who never have sex with their handsome, slightly effeminate escorts – but desperately want to. Consequently, their nails tend to be long and sharp, and their lipstick runs to the bloodier shades of carmine. And They Drink. Dyke daddies are supposed to be beer-bellied rednecks who hang out at lesbian bars to sexually harass the female patrons. The nicer ones are suckers who get taken for drinks or loans that will never be repaid.

These stereotypes don't do justice to the complete range of modern faghaggotry and dyke daddydom. Today fag hags and dyke daddies are as likely to be gay themselves as the objects of their admiration.

I call myself a fag hag because sex with men outside the context of the gay community doesn't interest me at all. In a funny way, when two gay people of opposite sexes make it, it's still gay sex. No heterosexual couple brings the same experiences and attitudes to bed that we do. These generalizations aren't perfectly true, but more often than straight sex, gay sex assumes that the use of hands or the mouth is as important as genital-to-genital contact. Penetration is not assumed to be the only goal of a sexual encounter. When penetration does happen, dildos and fingers are as acceptable as (maybe even preferable to) cocks. During gay sex, more often than during straight sex, people think about things like lubrication and 'fit'. There's no such thing as 'foreplay'. There's good sex, which includes lots of touching, and there's bad sex, which is nonsensual. Sex roles are more flexible, so nobody is automatically on the top or the bottom. There's no stigma attached to masturbation, and gay people are much more accepting of porn, fantasies, and fetishes.

And, most importantly, there is no intention to 'cure' anybody. I know that a gay man who has sex with me is making an exception and that he's still gay after we come and clean up. In return I can make an exception for him because I know he isn't trying to convert me to heterosexuality.

I have no way of knowing how many lesbians and gay men are less than exclusively homosexual. But I do know I'm not the only one. Our actual behaviour (as opposed to the ideology that says homosexuality means being sexual only with members of the same sex) leads me to ask questions about the nature of sexual orientation, how people (especially gay people) define it, and how they choose to let those definitions control and limit their lives.

During one of our interminable discussions in Samois about whether or not to keep the group open to bi women, Gayle Rubin pointed out that a new, movement-oriented definition of lesbianism was in conflict with an older, bar-oriented definition. Membership in the old gay culture consisted of managing to locate a gay bar and making a place for yourself in bar society. Even today, nobody in a bar asks you how long you've been celibate with half the human race before they will check your coat and take your order for a drink. But in the movement, people insist on a kind of purity that has little to do with affection, lust, or even political commitment. Gayness becomes a state of sexual grace, like virginity. A fanatical insistence on one hundred percent exclusive, same-sex behaviour often sounds to me like superstitious fear of contamination or pollution. Gayness that has more to do with abhorrence for the other sex than with an appreciation of your own sex degenerates into a rabid and destructive separatism.

It is very odd that sexual orientation is defined solely in terms of the sex of one's partners. I don't think I can assume anything about another person simply because I've been told she or he is bisexual, heterosexual, or homosexual. A person's politics may be conservative, liberal, radical, or nonexistent, regardless of sexual orientation. In fact, a sexual orientation label tells you nothing about her or his sex life, for God's sake. There are lots of 'heterosexual' men who have plenty of anonymous sex with other men. There are celibate faggots and dykes. There are lesbians who've been married for thirty years and have six children. There are heterosexual women who frequently have sex with other women at swing parties. For many people, if a partner or a sexual situation has other desirable qualities it is possible to overlook the partner's sex. Some examples: a preference for group sex, for a particular socio-economic background, for paid sex, for S/M, for a specific age group, for a physical type or race, for anal or oral sex.

I no longer believe that there is some ahistorical entity called homosexuality. Sexuality is socially constructed within the limits imposed by physiology, and it changes over time with the surrounding culture. There was no such thing as a Castro clone, a lesbian-feminist, or a Kinsey Six a century ago, and one hundred years from now these types will be as extinct as *Urnings*.

This is not to say that in a sexual utopia we would all be bisexual. There is nothing wrong with having sex exclusively with members of your own sex (or the opposite sex). I simply question some of the assumptions or attitudes that have grown around the fact that some people have an erotic preference for same-sex behaviour. Gay people have responded to persecution and homophobia by creating our own mythology about homosexuality. Whenever desire and behaviour conflict with rhetoric, it's time to re-examine the rhetoric. Some lesbians and gay men are having opposite-sex experiences. Why? What are they learning?

Gay male friends and lovers have taught me things that I would never have learned in the lesbian community. I can't exaggerate my admiration for the well-developed technology, etiquette, attitudes and institutions that gay men have developed to express their sexuality. (Remember, this is from the perspective of a woman who can't go to the baths every night or answer fifty sex ads in the 'Pink Pages'.) There's a basic attitude that sex is good in and of itself and that people ought to get what they want and treat each other well while they pursue it. That includes taking responsibility for preventing and treating sexually transmitted diseases. There's certainly room for improvement, but gay men are better educated about STDs and deal with them more promptly than typical heterosexual swingers or nonmonogamous lesbians.

Having good sex with men also allowed me to confront some of my fears about what it might 'mean' to be a lesbian. You know, all that stuff about dykes being too unattractive to get a man and all the psychobabble about penis envy. I now feel that having sex with women really is a choice for me. I know that sexually active women are in demand in any straight sex environment, and I could walk into most of those joints and take my pick. I just don't want what they have to offer. I no longer feel threatened by sexual come-ons from men. Once you've had vice-presidents of large corporations on your leash, straight men lose a lot of their power to intimidate you.

As for penis envy, I often think it would be nice to have a cock. I love fucking people, and because there's all this cultural meaning assigned to getting fucked with a cock (as opposed to fingers or a dildo), I'd like to have that sexual power. But I'm better with a strap-on dildo than most straight boys are at using their own cocks, and besides, I can change sizes. Once you've gotten two hands up somebody's ass, you aren't likely to feel jealous of a penis. Nobody's cock is *that* big. So, while I wouldn't mind having one, I think after I was done using it, I'd want to be able to take it off and leave it on a shelf. I don't want to have to be adjusting it in my pants all the time. And *I like* sitting down to pee. It makes it easier to read, and if you're outdoors, the grass tickles your heinie.

It's been very nice to lose my phobia about cocks. Our culture's phallic mythology has given the male sex organ so much highly charged symbolic significance that anything powerful is a phallic symbol. A lot of feminist antiporn ideology puts out the idea that cocks are ugly weapons that do nothing but defile or murder women. This symbolic system is very harmful. If cocks really have an inherent power to pollute and damage women, the only solution is to forcibly excise them from the male body. Instead I'd like to see women become more phallic (i.e., more powerful). Cocks seem more fragile than thermonuclear to me. There's a vulnerability about getting an erection that I'm really grateful I don't have to experience before I can give someone a night to remember.

The last and most painful thing I've learned from my contacts with gay men is how the war between the sexes looks from the other side. As embarrassing as it is, I finally had to concede that women engage in a lot of behaviour that is homophobic or sexist, and that it is women who enforce much of the sexual repression of the children they raise. This doesn't mean that I think women are equally responsible for their own oppression. Men get most of the goodies from the system and have the highest investment in keeping it running. But I no longer feel that all women are innocent victims, and all men are misogynist monsters.

The information flows both ways. I don't remember how many times I've explained to a gay man what rape is and why women, being physically smaller, feel less safety and mobility on the streets than men do. Then there's economics. Many gay men really don't understand what kinds of jobs women can readily obtain and what these jobs pay.

And of course they get to learn a lot about things like menstrual cycles and multiple orgasms. I can still hear the quaver in the voice of the first gay man who ever went down on me. 'Let's see,' he said bravely, as he gently spread my labia apart, 'where's that famous clitoris I've heard so much about?'

In the midst of the craziness, hostility, ignorance, and angst that plague human relations and sexuality, I feel entitled to whatever comfort or gratification I can find. I'll be looking for some more tonight, in the company of a girlfriend of mine. We have a date to tie up a furry little number and show him a good time. If it bothers you to envision the details, consider it in the abstract. Think of it as a fine example of lesbian/gay solidarity ... just queers doing queer things together!

4

1,112 and Counting

Larry Kramer

If this article doesn't scare the shit out of you, we're in real trouble. If this article doesn't rouse you to anger, fury, rage, and action, gay men may have no future on this earth. Our continued existence depends on just how angry you can get.

I am writing this as Larry Kramer, and I am speaking for myself, and my views are not to be attributed to Gay Men's Health Crisis.

I repeat: Our continued existence as gay men upon the face of this earth is at stake. Unless we fight for our lives, we shall die. In all the history of homosexuality we have never before been so close to death and extinction. Many of us are dying or already dead.

Before I tell you what we must do, let me tell you what is happening to us.

There are now 1,112 cases of serious Acquired Immune Deficiency Syndrome. When we first became worried, there were only 41. In only twenty-eight days, from 13 January to 9 February [1983], there were 164 new cases – and 73 more dead. The total death tally is now 418. Twenty per cent of all cases were registered this January alone. There have been 195 dead in New York City from among 526 victims. Of all serious AIDS cases, 47.3 per cent are in the New York metropolitan area.

These are the serious cases of AIDS, which means Kaposi's sarcoma, *Pneumocystis carinii* pneumonia, and other deadly infections. These numbers do not include the thousands of us walking around with what is also being called AIDS: various forms of swollen lymph glands and fatigues that doctors don't know what to label or what they might portend.

The rise in these numbers is terrifying. Whatever is spreading is now spreading faster as more and more people come down with AIDS.

And, for the first time in this epidemic, leading doctors and researchers are finally admitting they don't know what's going on. I find this terrifying too – as terrifying as the alarming rise in numbers. For the first time, doctors are saying out loud and up front, 'I don't know.'

For two years they weren't talking like this. For two years we've heard a different theory every few weeks. We grasped at the straws of possible cause: promiscuity, poppers, back rooms, the baths, rimming, fisting, anal intercourse, urine, semen, shit, saliva, sweat, blood, blacks, a single virus, a new

28

virus, repeated exposure to a virus, amoebas carrying a virus, drugs, Haiti, voodoo, Flagyl, constant bouts of amebiasis, hepatitis A and B, syphilis, gonorrhea.

I have talked with the leading doctors treating us. One said to me, 'If I knew in 1981 what I know now, I would never have become involved with this disease.' Another said, 'The thing that upsets me the most in all of this is that at any given moment one of my patients is in the hospital and something is going on with him that I don't understand. And it's destroy-ing me because there's some craziness going on in him that's destroying him.' A third said to me, 'I'm very depressed. A doctor's job is to make patients well. And I can't. Too many of my patients die.'

After almost two years of an epidemic, there are still no answers. After almost two years of an epidemic, the cause of AIDS remains unknown. After almost two years of an epidemic, there is no cure.

Hospitals are now so filled with AIDS patients that there is often a waiting period of up to a month before admission, no matter how sick you are. And, once in, patients are now more and more being treated like lepers as hospital staffs become increasingly worried that AIDS is infectious.

Suicides are now being reported of men who would rather die than face such medical uncertainty, such uncertain therapies, such hospital treatment, and the appalling statistics that 86 per cent of all serious AIDS cases die after three years' time.

If all of this had been happening to any other community for two long years, there would have been, long ago, such an outcry from that com-munity and all its members that the government of this city and this country would not know what had hit them.

Why isn't every gay man in this city so scared shitless that he is screaming for action? Does every gay man in New York *want* to die?

Let's talk about a few things specifically.

• Let's talk about which gay men get AIDS.

No matter what you've heard, there is no single profile for all AIDS victims. There are drug users and non-drug users. There are the truly promiscuous and the almost monogamous. There are reported cases of single-contact infection.

All it seems to take is the one wrong fuck. That's not promiscuity – that's bad luck.

• Let's talk about AIDS happening in straight people.

We have been hearing from the beginning of this epidemic that it was only a question of time before the straight community came down with AIDS, and that when that happened AIDS would suddenly be high on all agendas for funding and research and then we would finally be looked after and all would then be well.

I myself thought, when AIDS occurred in the first baby, that would be the break-through point. It was. For one day the media paid an enormous amount of attention. And that was it, kids.

There have been no confirmed cases of AIDS in straight, white, non-intravenous-drug-using, middle-class Americans. The only confirmed straights struck down by AIDS are members of groups just as disenfranchised as gay men: intravenous drug users, Haitians, eleven haemophiliacs (up from eight), black and Hispanic babies, and wives or partners of IV drug users and bisexual men.

If there have been – and there may have been – any cases in straight, white non-intravenous-drug-using, middle-class Americans, the Centers for Disease Control (CDC) isn't telling anyone about them. When pressed, the CDC says there are 'a number of cases that don't fall into any of the other categories'. The CDC says it's impossible to fully investigate most of these 'other category' cases; most of them are dead. The CDC also tends not to believe living, white, middle-class male victims when they say they're straight, or female victims when they say their husbands are straight and don't take drugs.

Why isn't AIDS happening to more straights? Maybe it's because gay men don't have sex with them.

Of all serious AIDS cases, 72.4 per cent are in gay and bisexual men.

• Let's talk about 'surveillance'.

The Centers for Disease Control is charged by our government to fully monitor all epidemics and unusual diseases.

To learn something from an epidemic, you have to keep records and statistics. Statistics come from interviewing victims and getting as much information from them as you can. Before they die. To get the best information, you have to ask the right questions.

There have been so many AIDS victims that the CDC is no longer able to get to them fast enough. It has given up. (The CDC also had been using a questionnaire that was fairly insensitive to the lives of gay men, and thus the data collected from its early study of us have been disputed by gay epidemiologists. The National Institutes of Health is also fielding a very naive questionnaire.)

Important, vital case histories are now being lost because of this cessation of CDC interviewing. This is a woeful waste with as terrifying implications for us as the alarming rise in case numbers and doctors finally admitting they don't know what's going on. As each man dies, as one or both sets of men who had interacted with each other come down with AIDS, yet more information that might reveal patterns of transmissibility is not being monitored and collected and studied. We are being denied perhaps the easiest and fastest research tool available at this moment.

It will require at least $200,000 to prepare a new questionnaire to study the next important question that must be answered: *How* is AIDS being transmitted? (In which bodily fluids, by which sexual behaviours, in what social environments?)

For months the CDC has been asked to begin such preparations for continued surveillance. The CDC is stretched to its limits and is dreadfully underfunded for what it's being asked, in all areas, to do.

● Let's talk about various forms of treatment.

It is very difficult for a patient to find out which hospital to go to or which doctor to go to or which mode of treatment to attempt.

Hospitals and doctors are reluctant to reveal how well they're doing with each type of treatment. They may, if you press them, give you a general idea. Most will not show you their precise number of how many patients are doing well on what and how many failed to respond adequately.

Because of the ludicrous requirements of the medical journals, doctors are prohibited from revealing publicly the specific data they are gathering from their treatments of our bodies. Doctors and hospitals need money for research, and this money (from the National Institutes of Health, from cancer research funding organizations, from rich patrons) comes based on the performance of their work (i.e., their tabulations of the results of their treatment of our bodies); this performance is written up as 'papers' that must be submitted to and accepted by such 'distinguished' medical publications as the *New England Journal of Medicine*. Most of these 'distinguished' publications, however, will not publish anything that has been spoken of, leaked, announced, or intimated publicly in advance. Even after acceptance, the doctors must hold their tongues until the article is actually published. Dr Bijan Safai of Sloan-Kettering has been waiting over six months for the *New England Journal*, which has accepted his interferon study, to publish it. Until that happens, he is only permitted to speak in the most general terms of how interferon is or is not working.

Priorities in this area appear to be peculiarly out of kilter at this moment of life or death.

● Let's talk about hospitals.

Everybody's full up, fellows. No room in the inn.

Part of this is simply overcrowding. Part of this is cruel. Sloan-Kettering still enforces a regulation from pre-AIDS days that only one dermatology patient per week can be admitted to that hospital. (Kaposi's sarcoma falls under dermatology at Sloan-Kettering.) But Sloan-Kettering is also the second-largest treatment centre for AIDS patients in New York. You can be near death and still not get into Sloan-Kettering.

Additionally, Sloan-Kettering (and the Food and Drug Administration) require patients to receive their initial shots of interferon while they are hospitalized. A lot of men want to try interferon at Sloan-Kettering before they try chemotherapy elsewhere.

It's not hard to see why there is such a waiting list to get into Sloan-Kettering.

Most hospital staffs are still so badly educated about AIDS that they don't know much about it, except that they've heard it's infectious. (There still have been no cases in hospital staff or among the very doctors who have been treating AIDS victims for two years.) Hence, as I said earlier, AIDS patients are often treated like lepers.

For various reasons, I would not like to be a patient at the Veterans Administration Hospital on East 24th Street or at New York Hospital. (Incidents involving AIDS patients at these two hospitals have been reported in news stories in the *Native*.)

I believe it falls to this city's Department of Health, under Commissioner David Spencer, and the Health and Hospitals Corporation, under Commissioner Stanley Brezenoff, to educate this city, its citizens, and its hospital workers about all areas of a public health emergency. Well, they have done an appalling job of educating our citizens, our hospital workers, and even, in some instances, our doctors. Almost everything this city knows about AIDS has come to it, in one way or another, through Gay Men's Health Crisis, and that includes television programmes, magazine articles, radio commercials, newsletters, health-recommendation brochures, open forums, and sending speakers everywhere, including – when asked – into hospitals. If three out of four AIDS cases were occurring in straight men instead of gay men, you can bet all hospitals and staff would know what was happening. And it would be this city's Health Department and Health and Hospitals Corporation who would be telling them.

• Let's talk about what gay tax dollars are buying for gay men.

Now we're arriving at the truly scandalous.

For over a year and a half the National Institutes of Health (NIH) has been 'reviewing' which from among some $55 million worth of grant applications for AIDS research money it will eventually fund.

It's not even a question of NIH having to ask Congress for money. It's already there. Waiting. NIH has almost $8 million already appropriated that it has yet to release into usefulness.

There is no question that if this epidemic was happening to the straight, white, non-intravenous-drug-using middle class, that money would have been put into use almost two years ago, when the first alarming signs of this epidemic were noticed by Dr Alvin Friedman-Kien and Dr Linda Lauben-stein at New York University Hospitals (NYU).

During the first *two weeks* of the Tylenol scare, the United States Government spent $10 million to find out what was happening.

Every hospital in New York that's involved in AIDS research has used up every bit of the money it could find for researching AIDS while waiting for NIH grants to come through. These hospitals have been working on AIDS for up to two years and are now desperate for replenishing funds. Important studies that began last year, such as Dr Michael Lange's at St Luke's-Roosevelt, are now going under for lack of money. Important leads that were and are developing cannot be pursued. (For instance, few hospitals can afford plasmapheresis machines, and few patients can afford this experimental treatment either, since few insurance policies will cover the $16,600 bill.) New York University Hospital, the largest treatment centre for AIDS patients in the world, has had its grant application pending at NIH for a year and a half. Even if the application is successful, the earliest time that NYU could receive any money would be late summer.

The NIH would probably reply that it's foolish just to throw money away, that that hasn't worked before. And, NIH would say, if nobody knows what's happening, what's to study?

Any good administrator with half a brain could survey the entire AIDS mess and come up with twenty leads that merit further investigation. I could do so myself. In any research, in any investigation, you have to start somewhere. You can't just not start anywhere at all.

But then, AIDS is happening mostly to gay men, isn't it?

All of this is indeed ironic. For within AIDS, as most researchers have been trying to convey to the NIH, perhaps may reside the answer to the question of what it is that causes cancer itself. If straights had more brains, or were less bigoted against gays, they would see that, as with hepatitis B, gay men are again doing their suffering for them, revealing this disease to them. They can use us as guinea pigs to discover the cure for AIDS before it hits them, which most medical authorities are still convinced will be happening shortly in increasing numbers.

(As if it had not been malevolent enough, the NIH is now, for unspecified reasons, also turning away AIDS patients from its hospital in Bethesda, Maryland. The hospital, which had been treating anyone and everyone with AIDS free of charge, now will only take AIDS patients if they fit into their current investigating protocol. Whatever that is. The NIH publishes 'papers', too.)

Gay men pay taxes just like everyone else. NIH money should be paying for our research just like everyone else's. We desperately need something from our government to save our lives, and we're not getting it.

- Let's talk about health insurance and welfare problems.

Many of the ways of treating AIDS are experimental, and many health insurance policies do not cover most of them. Blue Cross is particularly bad about accepting anything unusual.

Many serious victims of AIDS have been unable to qualify, for increasing numbers of men are unable to work and unable to claim welfare because AIDS is not on the list of qualifying disability illnesses. (Immune deficiency is an acceptable determining factor for welfare among children, but not adults. Figure that one out.) There are also increasing numbers of men unable to pay their rent, men thrown out on the street with nowhere to live and no money to live with, and men who have been asked by roommates to leave because of their illnesses. And men with serious AIDS are being fired from certain jobs.

The horror stories in this area, of those suddenly found destitute, of those facing this illness with insufficient insurance, continue to mount. (One man who'd had no success on other therapies was forced to beg from his friends the $16,600 he needed to try, as a last resort, plasmapheresis.)

- Finally, let's talk about our mayor, Ed Koch.

Our mayor, Ed Koch, appears to have chosen, for whatever reason, not to allow himself to be perceived by the non-gay world as visibly helping us in this emergency.

Repeated requests to meet with him have been denied us. Repeated attempts to have him make a very necessary public announcement about this crisis and public health emergency have been refused by his staff ...

On 28 October 1982, Mayor Koch was implored to make a public announcement about our emergency. If he had done so then, and if he was only to do so now, the following would be put into action:

1. The community at large would be alerted (you would be amazed at how many people, including gay men, still don't know enough about the AIDS danger).
2. Hospital staffs and public assistance offices would also be alerted and their education commenced.
3. The country, President Reagan, and the National Institutes of Health, as well as Congress, would be alerted, and these constitute the most important ears of all.

If the mayor doesn't think it's important enough to talk up AIDS, none of these people is going to, either.

The Mayor of New York has an enormous amount of power – when he wants to use it. When he wants to help his people. With the failure yet again of our civil rights bill, I'd guess our mayor doesn't want to use his power to help us.

With his silence on AIDS, the Mayor of New York is helping to kill us.

I am sick of our electing officials who in no way represent us. I am sick of our stupidity in believing candidates who promise us everything for our support and promptly forget us and insult us after we have given them our votes. Koch is the prime example, but not the only one. [Senator] Daniel Patrick Moynihan isn't looking very good at this moment, either. Moynihan was requested by gay leaders to ask Margaret Heckler publicly at her confirmation hearing for Secretary of Health and Human Services if she could be fair to gays in view of her voting record of definite anti-gay bias. (Among other horrors, she voted to retain the sodomy law in Washington, DC, at Jerry Falwell's request.) Moynihan refused to ask this question, as he has refused to meet with us about AIDS, despite our repeated requests. Margaret Heckler will have important jurisdiction over the CDC, over the NIH, over the Public Health Service, over the Food and Drug Administration – indeed, over all areas of AIDS concerns. Thank you, Daniel Patrick Moynihan. I am sick of our not realizing we have enough votes to defeat these people, and I am sick of our not electing our own openly gay officials in the first place. Moynihan doesn't even have an openly gay person on his staff, and he represents the city with the largest gay population in America.

I am sick of closeted gay doctors who won't come out to help us fight to rectify any of what I'm writing about. Doctors – the very letters 'MD' – have enormous clout, particularly when they fight in groups. Can you imagine what gay doctors could accomplish, banded together in a network, petitioning local and federal governments, straight colleagues, and the American Medical Association? I am sick of the passivity or nonparticipation or half-hearted protestation of all the gay medical associations (American Physicians for Human Rights, Bay Area Physicians for Human Rights, Gay Psychiatrists of New York, etc., etc.), and particularly our own New York Physicians for Human Rights, a group of 175 of our gay doctors who have, as a group, done *nothing*. You can count on one hand the number of our doctors who have really worked for us.

I am sick of the *Advocate*, one of this country's largest gay publications, which has yet to quite acknowledge that there's anything going on. That newspaper's recent AIDS issue was so innocuous you'd have thought all we were going through was little worse than a rage of the latest designer flu. And their own associate editor, Brent Harris, died from AIDS. Figure that one out.

With the exception of the *New York Native* and a few, very few, other gay publications, the gay press has been useless. If we can't get our own papers and magazines to tell us what's really happening to us, and this negligence is added to the negligent non-interest of the straight press (the *New York Times* took a leisurely year and a half between its major pieces, and the *Village Voice* took a year and a half to write anything at all), how are we going to get the word around that we're dying? Gay men in smaller towns and cities everywhere must be educated, too. Has the *Times* or the *Advocate* told you that twenty-nine cases have been reported from Paris?

I am sick of gay men who won't support gay charities. Go give your bucks to straight charities, fellows, while we die. Gay Men's Health Crisis is going crazy trying to accomplish everything it does – printing and distributing hundreds of thousands of educational items, taking care of several hundred AIDS victims (some of them straight) in and out of hospitals, arranging community forums and speakers all over this country, getting media attention, fighting bad hospital care, on and on and on, fighting for you and us in two thousand ways, *and* trying to sell 17,600 circus tickets, too. Is the Red Cross doing this for you? Is the American Cancer Society? Your college alumni fund? The United Jewish Appeal? Catholic Charities? The United Way? The Lenox Hill Neighborhood Association, or any of the other fancy straight charities for which faggots put on black ties and dance at the Plaza? The National Gay Task Force – our only hope for national leadership, with its new and splendid leader, Virginia Apuzzo – which is spending more and more time fighting for the AIDS issue, is broke. Senior Action in a Gay Environment and Gay Men's Health Crisis are, within a few months, going to be without office space they can afford, and thus will be out on the street. The St Mark's Clinic, held together by some of the few devoted gay doctors in this city who aren't interested in becoming rich, lives in constant terror of even higher rent and eviction. This community is desperate for the services these organizations are providing for it. And these organizations are all desperate for money, which is certainly not coming from straight people or President Reagan or Mayor Koch. (If every gay man within a 250-mile radius of Manhattan isn't in Madison Square Garden on the night of 30 April to help Gay Men's Health Crisis make enough money to get through the next horrible year of fighting against AIDS, I shall lose all hope that we have any future whatsoever.)

I am sick of closeted gays. It's 1983 already, guys, when are you going to come out? By 1984 you could be dead. Every gay man who is unable to come forward now and fight to save his own life is truly helping to kill the rest of us. There is only one thing that's going to save some of us, and this is *numbers* and pressure and our being perceived as united and a threat. As more and more of my friends die, I have less and less sympathy for men who are afraid their mommies will find out or afraid their bosses will find out or afraid their fellow doctors or professional associates will find out. Unless we can generate, visibly, numbers, masses, we are going to die.

I am sick of everyone in this community who tells me to stop creating a panic. How many of us have to die before *you* get scared off your ass and into action? Aren't 195 dead New Yorkers enough? Every straight person who is knowledgeable about the AIDS epidemic can't understand why gay men aren't marching on the White House. Over and over again I hear from them, 'Why aren't you guys doing anything?' Every politician I have spoken to has said to me confidentially, 'You guys aren't making enough noise. Bureaucracy only responds to pressure.'

I am sick of people who say 'it's no worse than statistics for smokers and lung cancer' or 'considering how many homosexuals there are in the United States, AIDS is really statistically affecting only a very few'. That would wash if there weren't 164 cases in twenty-eight days. That would wash if case numbers hadn't jumped from 41 to 1,112 in eighteen months. That would wash if cases in one city – New York – hadn't jumped to cases in fifteen countries and thirty-five states (up from thirty-four last week). That would wash if cases weren't coming in at more than four a day nationally and over two a day locally. That would wash if the mortality rate didn't start at 38 per cent the first year of diagnosis and climb to a grotesque 86 per cent after three years. Get your stupid heads out of the sand, you turkeys!

I am sick of guys who moan that giving up careless sex until this blows over is worse than death. How can they value life so little and cocks and asses so much? Come with me, guys, while I visit a few of our friends in intensive Care at NYU. Notice the looks in their eyes, guys. They'd give up sex forever if you could promise them life.

I am sick of guys who think that all being gay means is sex in the first place. I am sick of guys who can only think with their cocks.

I am sick of 'men' who say, 'We've got to keep quiet or *they* will do such and such.' *They* usually means the straight majority, the 'Moral' Majority, or similarly perceived representatives of *them*. Okay, you 'men' – be my guests: You can march off now to the gas chambers; just get right in line.

We shall always have enemies. Nothing we can ever do will remove them. Southern newspapers and Jerry Falwell's publications are already printing editorials proclaiming AIDS as God's deserved punishments on homosexuals. So what? Nasty words make poor little sissy pansy wilt and die?

And I am very sick and saddened by every gay man who does not get behind this issue totally and with commitment – to fight for his life.

I don't want to die. I can only assume you don't want to die. Can we fight together?

For the past few weeks, about fifty community leaders and organization representatives have been meeting at Beth Simchat Torah, the gay synagogue, to prepare action. We call ourselves the AIDS Network. We come from all areas of health concern: doctors, social workers, psychologists, psychiatrists, nurses; we come from Gay Men's Health Crisis, from the National Gay Health Education Foundation, from New York Physicians for Human Rights, the St Mark's Clinic, the Gay Men's Health Project; we come from the gay synagogue, the Gay Men's Chorus, from the Greater Gotham Business Council, SAGE, Lambda Legal Defense, Gay Fathers, the Christopher Street Festival Committee, Dignity, Integrity; we are lawyers, actors, dancers, architects, writers, citizens; we come from many component organizations of the Gay and Lesbian Community Council.

We have a leader. Indeed, for the first time our community appears to have a true leader. Her name is Virginia Apuzzo, she is head of the National Gay Task Force, and, as I have said, so far she has proved to be magnificent.

The AIDS Network has sent a letter to Mayor Koch. It contains twelve points that are urged for his consideration and action.

This letter to Mayor Koch also contains the following paragraph:

It must be stated at the outset that the gay community is growing increasingly aroused and concerned and angry. Should our avenues to the mayor of our city and the members of the Board of Estimate not be available, it is our feeling that the level of frustration is such that it will manifest itself in a manner heretofore not associated with this community and the gay population at large. It should be stated, too, at the outset, that as of February 25th, there were 526 cases of serious AIDS in New York's metropolitan area and 195 deaths (and 1,112 cases nationally and 418 deaths) and it is the sad and sorry fact that most gay men in our city now have close friends and lovers who have either been stricken with or died from this disease. It is against this background that this letter is addressed. It is this issue that has, ironically, united our community in a way not heretofore thought possible.

Further, a number of AIDS Network members have been studying civil disobedience with one of the experts from Dr Martin Luther King's old team. We are learning how. Gay men are the strongest, toughest people I know. We are perhaps shortly to get an opportunity to show it.

I'm sick of hearing that Mayor Koch doesn't respond to pressures and threats from the disenfranchised, that he walks away from confrontations. Maybe he does. But we have *tried* to make contact with him, we are *dying*, so what other choice but confrontation has he left us?

I hope we don't have to conduct sit-ins or tie up traffic or get arrested. I hope our city and our country will start to do something to help start saving us. But it is time for us to be perceived for what we truly are: an angry community and a strong community, and therefore *a threat*. Such are the realities of politics. Nationally we are 24 million strong, which is more than there are Jews or blacks or Hispanics in this country.

I want to make a point about what happens if we *don't* get angry about AIDS. There are the obvious losses, of course: little of what I've written about here is likely to be rectified with the speed necessary to help the growing number of victims. But something worse will happen, and is already happening. Increasingly, we are being *blamed* for AIDS, for this epidemic; we are being called its perpetrators, through our blood, through our 'promiscuity', through just being the gay men so much of the rest of the world has learned to hate. We can point out until we are blue in the face that we are not the cause of AIDS but its victims, that AIDS has landed among us first, as it could have landed among them first. But other frightened populations are going to drown out these truths by playing on the worst bigoted fears of the straight world, and send the status of gays right back to the Dark Ages. Not all Jews are blamed for Meyer Lansky, Rabbis Bergman and Kahane, or for money-lending. All Chinese aren't blamed for the recent Seattle slaughters. But all gays are blamed for John Gacy, the North American Man/Boy Love Association, and AIDS.

Enough. I am told this is one of the longest articles the *Native* has ever run. I hope I have not been guilty of saying ineffectively in five thousand words what I could have said in five: we must fight to live.

I am angry and frustrated almost beyond the bound my skin and bones and body and brain can encompass. My sleep is tormented by nightmares and visions of lost friends, and my days are flooded by the tears of funerals and memorial services and seeing my sick friends. How many of us must die before *all* of us living fight back?

I know that unless I fight with every ounce of my energy I will hate myself. I hope, I pray, I implore you to feel the same.

I am going to close by doing what Dr Ron Grossman did at GMHC's second Open Forum last November at Julia Richman High School. He listed the names of the patients he had lost to AIDS. Here is a list of twenty dead men I knew:

Nick Rock, Rick Wellikoff, Jack Nau, Shelly, Donald Krintzman, Jerry Green, Michael Maletta, Paul Graham, Toby, Harry Blumenthal, Stephen Sperry, Brian O'Hara, Barry, David, Jeffrey Croland, Z., David Jackson, Tony Rappa, Robert Christian, Ron Doud.
And one more, who will be dead by the time these words appear in print.

If we don't act immediately, then we face our approaching doom.

5

The Leather Daddy and the Femme

Carol Queen

AFTER THE LIGHT CHANGED

I was looking pretty boyish that evening. Maybe that's why he looked twice at the stoplight when my car pulled up next to his motorcycle. Usually guys like that are moving, you just see a gleaming blur of black and silver. But here at the light was a real done-up daddy, sitting stock-still, except for his head, which turned in response to my eyes fixed on him and found what he saw noticeable enough to make him turn again. When boy-energy gets into me I look like an effete young Cambridge faggot looking to go bad: round spectacles framing inquisitive eyes and a shock of hair falling down over one. Not classically Daddy's Boy, something a little different. Maybe tonight this daddy was looking for a new kind of ride.

A real done-up daddy, yeah. His leathers were immaculate, carried that dull gleam that well-kept black leather picks up under streetlights. Black leather cap, high boots, everything on him black and silver except the well-worn blue denim at his crotch, bulging invitingly out of a pair of chaps. I eyed that denimed expanse quite deliberately; he noticed. He had steely blue Daddy-eyes and a well-trimmed beard. I couldn't see his hands under the riding gloves, but they looked big, and from the looks of him I bet they were manicured. I love these impeccable daddies. They appeal to the femme in me.

And his bike! A huge shiny animal, a Harley, of course, nothing but classic for this daddy. The chrome gleamed like he did the fine polish with his tongue – or rather, used the tongue of some lucky boy. I'm more for polishing leather, myself, but if this stone-hot daddy told me to do his bike, of course I'd get right to it.

Ooh, he was looking right into my eyes, taking in my angelic Vienna-Choirboy face and my leather jacket, much rattier than his with all its ACT UP and Queer Nation stickers. Does he think I'm cute enough for a walk on the wild side? I could hear it as he dished me to all the other daddies: 'Yeah, this hot little schoolboy, looked real innocent but he cruised me like he knew what I had and wanted it, so I let him follow me home.'

40

On the cross-street the light turned yellow. I *did* want what he had. This was it. I leaned out the window and said, just loud enough to be heard, careful to keep my voice low-pitched, 'Daddy, can I come too?'

The daddy grinned. When the light turned green he gunned the Harley, took the space in front of my car, and signalled for me to follow.

An apartment South of Market – oh, this was perfect. At three a.m. on any given night he could probably open his bedroom window and find a willing mouth down here to piss in – I've heard about *this* alley. The entryway was dark. Good. I parked my car and caught up with him there. I fell to my knees as he pulled his keys from his belt. By the time he had his door unlocked I was chewing on his balls through the denim. He let me go on that way for a minute and then he collared me and hauled me into the dark foyer. I barely had time to grab my rucksack, which I'd let fall beside me so I could get both hands on his hard, leather-clad thighs.

Inside, I pulled off my glasses and tucked them away safely in my jacket. Daddy pushed me back onto my knees, and I scrambled to open the buttons of his Levi's. I wanted his cock, wanted it big, wanted it down my throat with his hands fisting the hair at the nape of my neck, giving it to me hard and rhythmic. I wanted to suck both his balls into my mouth while he slapped his dick against my cheeks. Cock worship in the dark, *Use me, Daddy, no, don't come yet – I have a surprise for you.*

I don't know how long I went on. I get lost in cock sucking sometimes, it's like a ritual, it disconnects me from my head, and when it's anonymous all the more so. I hadn't even seen this cock I was sucking, and that made me feel I could be anyone, even an adventurous gay boy in a South-of-Market alley, sucking Daddy's big hard dick. Any second now he could realize that I was no ordinary boy, and that gave me a great rush of adrenaline, a lust to have it down my throat. Until he discovered me I could believe this illusion myself, and with most men this was all I could expect, a cocksucker until they turned the lights on.

Daddy was moaning; guess as a cocksucker I got a passing grade. I felt the seam of my Levi's, wet where they pressed into my cunt. Jesus, I wanted it, I wanted it from him, I wanted him not to care. The scents of leather and sweat filled my head. Finally I pulled my mouth away from his dick, no problem speaking in a low voice now, shit, I was hoarse from his pounding. 'Daddy, please, I want you to fuck me.'

He pulled me up at once, kissed me, hard. That was a surprise. I was swooning, not feeling like a boy now, whatever a boy feels like, but all womanly, my brain in my cunt. And I was about to be discovered. His hand was sliding into my jacket; any second now it would fall upon the swell of my breast. This was where most guys freaked out and sent me home to beat off. That was okay, usually, but God, it would kill me to break this kiss.

But the kiss went on even when his fingers grazed first one breast, then the other ... when his other hand followed the first under my jacket, then under my shirt, as if for corroboration, and he felt my nipples go hard under his touch. He squeezed them, eliciting a very un-boyish moan, thrusting his tongue deep down where his cock had been, so that even when he twisted my nipples into the shape of morning glories, furled around themselves, I couldn't cry out.

The kiss went on even when one hand slid down my belly and started undoing the buttons of my jeans until there was room for him to slip a finger down between my pussy-lips, root its way, almost roughly, all the way into my cunt, pull the slick finger out again and thrust it into my mouth, where our tongues sucked it clean. The kiss lasted until he'd slid his fingers back in and fucked me all slow and juicy and excruciating and I finally broke away to beg, 'Oh, Jesus, please, make me come!' He stroked in faster, then; I came like a fountain into his hand. He rubbed the juice all over my face, licked some of it off kissing me again, then pulled me down the hall into a lit room. I felt weak-kneed and wildly dishevelled; he was immaculate yet, but his cock was out and it was still hard. For me.

Those steel blue eyes were lit with more than amusement, and when he spoke, in a soft, low, almost-drawl, I realized it was the first time I'd heard his voice.

'Well, little boy, I must say you had me tricked.' He laughed; I guess I looked a little proud. 'Do you make a habit of fooling guys like me?'

'Not very often,' I managed. 'And most men don't want what they get.'

'No, I would imagine not. A little too much pussy under that boy-drag. A man wouldn't want to get himself ... *confused*. Hey, where'd you learn to suck cock? A bathhouse?'

'My brother taught me. He's gay.'

'Shit, bring him with you the next time you visit,' said the daddy. 'I'll die and go to heaven.' He pushed me back on the bed then and knelt above me. His big cock dangled above my face and at first he held me down, teasing me with it, but I begged and he lowered it to my lips, letting me have just enough to suck on like a baby dreams over a tit. 'Good girl,' he said, smiling a little, running his fingertips over my skin in a most enticing way. The boy-energy was gone, but I didn't want to stay a little girl with a man this hot. Anyway, he wasn't acting like a leather daddy anymore.

I don't know what gets into me. When I cruise gay men as a boy, I know full well that I have to stay a boy the whole time. Unless they send me out at the first touch of curves, the first smell of pussy, they only want to play with me if I can keep up the fantasy. I lick Daddy's boots and suck his cock and get on my face for him, raise my ass up at the first brush of his cock on my cheeks. I beg Daddy to fuck my ass and promise I'll be his good boy, always. But deep inside, even as he's slam-fucking my ass and I'm screaming from the deep pounding pleasure of it, even though I love being a faggot for him, I secretly wish he'd slip and bury his meat all the way deep in my cunt. I love being the boy, but I don't like having to be two separate people to get what I want. I really want the men I fuck to turn me over and see the whole me: the woman in the boy, the boy in the woman. This daddy, this leatherman whose name I didn't even know, was the first one with whom that seemed possible – and I wanted to make sure. I wanted to know if he would really play with me.

So again I let his cock slip from my lips. 'Daddy, will you let me up for a minute? I want to play a new game, and I really want you to like it.' He released me, looking at me quizzically as I reached for my bag and pulled the last of my clothes off. There. A femme hates having pants bagging around her ankles.

Feeling sleeker already, I took the bag into the bathroom, promising I'd be right back. Everything there, shoes, clothes, makeup. It was time to grow up.

The dress was red and tight and hugged my small breasts into cleavage. Its backline plunged down almost to the swell of my ass. Black stockings and garters (the dress was too tight to wear a belt under, only a black G-string), and red leather pumps with high, high heels. The kind of shoes drag queens named so aptly 'come-fuck-me pumps'. You're not supposed to walk in them, you're supposed to offer the toe to a worshipful tongue, or lock them around a neck while you get pounded. Which is what I hoped would be happening to me shortly.

With some gel and a brush my hair went from boyish to chic. Powder on my face, then blush. I darkened my eyebrows and lashes, lined and shaded my eyes with green and violet, and brushed deep crimson onto my lips. An amazingly changed face, all angles and shadows and eyes and cheekbones, looked back at me from the mirror. One last glance: I was sufficiently stunning. In fact, the sight, combined with the knowledge that I was about to emerge from the little room into the leather daddy's view, had me soaked, my heart pounding, my clit buzzing. I get so very narcissistic when I'm femmed out. I want to reach for my image in the mirror, take her apart, and fuck her. No doubt I'd be riding this energy into the girl-bars tomorrow night, looking for my image stepped through the looking glass, out looking for me.

One last flourish, a long sheer black scarf, sheer as my stockings, flung around my shoulders, hiding nothing. I stepped back into the leather daddy's room.

He'd taken his jeans off from beneath the chaps. His jacket was off, too, hung carefully over a chair. His dick was in his hand. He'd been stroking it, staying hard. Bands of leather drew my gaze to the hard curves of his biceps. Silver rings gleamed in his nipples. I felt like a *Vogue* model who'd stumbled into a Tom of Finland painting. He was gorgeous. He was every bit the spectacle I was, body modified and presented to evoke heat, to attract sex.

He looked at me hard, taking in the transformation. I saw his cock jump; good.

'So, Daddy, do you still want to play?' I said 'Daddy' in a different voice this time, let it be lush with irony, like a '40s burlesque queen. A well-educated faggot ought to pick up on that.

There was a touch of wonder in his voice. 'God damn. I don't believe I've ever picked up anything quite like *you.*' Then suspicion. 'So what's your trip? Trying to turn the heathens into hets? No wonder all those other guys threw you out.'

I experienced a new rush of adrenaline. I thought to myself, *Go ahead, be uncomfortable, baby, but don't stop wanting it.* I took a couple of steps, nearing the bed enough that I could put one foot up on it. I moved into his territory, gave him a view of the tops of my stockings and the wet, pussy-redolent G-string. I narrowed my eyes. 'Did I suck your cock like a het? You think I can't take it now that I have a dress on?'

He persisted. 'Why waste this on gay men? Straight boys must fall over for you.'

'Straight boys don't know how to give me what I want.' I ran my eyes down his body. 'Besides, your cock says I'm not wasting this on you.'

He made no move to try to hide the hard-on. His voice was more curious than accusatory when he said, 'You get a perverse charge out of this, don't you?'

'Yeah, I do. But I really want *you* to get a perverse charge out of it.' I moved to him, knelt over him so that only the insides of my knees touched the smooth leather of the chaps. He was close enough to touch; I had to stop from reaching. This was it, the last obstacle. His hard cock almost touched me. 'I'm no ordinary boy Daddy, and I'm no ordinary woman. Do you want it? Just take it.'

There is so much power in being open and accessible and ready. So much power in wanting it. That's what other women don't understand. You'll never get what you want if you make it too hard for someone to give it to you. He proved it: he lifted his hands to me, ran them once over my body, bringing the nipples up hard through the clinging dress, pinned my arms at my sides, and brought me down into a kiss that seared and melted, a kiss I felt like a tongue in my cunt. I felt myself sliding along his body till his cock head rested against the soaked silk of my G-string, hard and hot, and he stroked against my clit over and over and over. When he released my arms, one big hand held my ass, keeping me pushed against him. The other hand was fisted in my hair. He held me fast, and once again my cries of orgasm were muffled on his tongue.

When his mouth left mine it went to my ear, talking low.

'Pretty girl, I want your cunt so hot you go crazy. You got all dressed up for me, didn't you? Pretty bitch, you want it rough, you like it like that?'

'Yes!' I gasped, still riding the last waves of come, wanting more.

'Then tell me. Ask for it. Beg me!'

He pulled the scarf from around my neck, threw me easily onto my back. He pinned my arms over my head, bound my wrists with the scarf, talking in his low daddy-voice, playing my game:

'You want it, pretty bitch? You're going to get it, Miss Special. Think your cunt is good enough for my meat, do you? Can't get what you need from straight boys? You're gonna need it bad before you get an inch of it, baby ... Spread 'em, that's right, spread for me, show it to me, let me have a good look. I haven't seen one of these in a long time ... You know what I usually do with this cock, don't you? Is that what you want, is that what straight boys don't give you? Want it in your ass, make you be Daddy's boy again, hmmmm? ... No, you want it in your pussy, baby, I can feel it. Just shove it all inside you, you want to feel it open you up, can you take it?'

Now he was reddening my ass with slaps, the dress pulled up to my waist, and from nowhere he clicked open a knife. I gasped and whimpered, but he just used it to cut the G-string off and it disappeared again. He slapped my pussy with his cock, scattering drops of my wetness, stopping short before I came, whispering, 'Want it, pretty bitch? Want it all?' And I writhed against him and begged him:

'Jesus, please, give it to me, Daddy! Please ... please!'

He was a consummate tease, this daddy; I wondered dimly if his boys tried to wiggle their assholes onto his just-out-of-reach cock the way I was trying to capture it with my hungry cunt. Not so much difference between one hunger and another, after all.

He reached for a rubber, worked it over his cock head, and rolled it down the shaft. The encasement made his big cock strain harder. As he knelt between my spread-wide legs, I murmured, 'Give it to me, give it to me, give ...' And in a long plunge, he did.

It felt so good to be filled so full, with the smell of hot leather and cock and pussy and the feel of the chaps against my legs. The second thrust came harder than the first, and a look of sexy concentration played across my leather-daddy's face as he settled in for a long, hard, pounding ride.

It was my turn to talk to him as I met his strokes with thrusts of my own, letting my pinned-down body fill with the delicious tensions that would build up to even more intense peaks.

'... Oh, yeah, just like that, give me your cock, baby, fill up my pussy, yeah ... Give it to me, give it to me, you know I can take it, hard, yeah, come on ... Fuck my cunt like you fuck your boys' asses, make me take it from you, yeah, don't stop, don't ever stop, just try to outlast me, Daddy, you can fuck me all night, fill that rubber with a big hot load and I'll come just thinking about you, just give it to me ... Just give it to me, make me, make me ... come ...'

And it was all lost in cries and sobs and breath taking over. Somehow he'd untied my hands and I held him and came and came and came, and the wild ride was over with half a dozen bucking thrusts. I heard his yells mingle with mine, and I reached down to pull cock and rubber free of my cunt and feel the heft of jism in my hand as we lay together in a tangle of sweaty limbs, not man and woman, just animals, two sated animals.

I drifted off to sleep and woke again as he was working the tight, sweaty dress over my head and off. My red leather shoes glowed against the white sheets.

'Hellion,' he said as my eyes opened, 'faggot in a woman's body, bitch-goddess, do you intend to sleep in your exquisite red shoes?'

I held them up for him to take off, one and then the other, and he placed respectful kisses on each toe before he set them on the bed.

'No,' I said, 'that's too femmy, even for me.'

'And what does a man need to do with you around,' he continued, pulling off my stockings, 'to get fucked? Call your brother?'

He hadn't seen all the contents of my trick bag. I reached for it and spilled it onto the floor: three dildos, a harness, and a pair of long rubber gloves fell out. I promised that in the morning he could take his pick. I was dying to show Daddy what else a femme can do.

THE NEXT MORNING

I woke to the sound of shower spray hitting tile, and for a minute I stayed groggy, listening to the hum of water in the pipes, not entirely sure where I was. I was drifting in and out of a dream, something about Harleys and red leather shoes. I heard a motorcycle rev and catch outside, and it twined itself into my dream, not waking me. But when the bike gunned and roared away, it shocked me into alertness and I remembered where I was, recognized the leather daddy's spare, neat room, and his face swam into my consciousness: I saw him pulling my pumps off and kissing each toe.

He wasn't next to me, though the bed was tousled as if two people had fucked here and shared it later in sleep. For a minute I was afraid the bike I'd heard outside was his, that he'd gone off and left me to wake in his bed and let myself out of his alley apartment. Well, maybe he'd only gone out to get us coffee and croissants or something. I wasn't sure he looked like the kind of guy who made his own coffee.

But no, the water was running in the next room. He must be in the shower, and thinking about him naked and wet in a steamy room was giving me ideas. I hoped he had lots of hot water.

I stretched like a just-roused cat and rolled out of bed. My red dress and red shoes were neatly laid over the arm of the room's one chair. The other arm, like a tireless valet, held his chaps. I remembered he had taken them off, along with his wrist and biceps cuffs, before he returned to bed and allowed me to curl up under his musky-scented armpit. The cuffs lay with his worn leather riding gloves on the dresser-top. I picked the gloves up and drew in a long breath of the leather, redolent of his man-smell and the machine-smell of the bike, and placed them carefully back where he'd put them when he took them off.

Over the dresser hung an old silver-backed mirror with a simple, polished wooden frame, the kind of mirror his granddad had probably had. With my fingers I combed my hair into some semblance of presentability, and I rubbed away the mascara that overnight had migrated into a raccoon-mask around my eyes. That was really the most embarrassing part of being a femme, I reflected; the desire to be fucked into a stupor was definitely incompatible with wearing make-up, at least when the fucking happened right before bed.

I was not concerned with resurrecting my femme look now, however. The leather daddy already knew who I was, in that respect at least. In the whole room the only thing out of place, besides the rumpled bedclothes, was my upended trick bag. I picked up my harness and strapped it on, then chose a dildo from the three in my bag, a big one. If everything went as well as it had last night, the daddy was about to get his morning fuck. In the full-length mirror on the closet door I surveyed myself. Very much a woman, and a big latex dick curving up where you'd expect a clit to be. I rolled a condom onto the dick and opened the bathroom door.

He was there, all right; I saw his silhouette through the opaque glass of the shower door. The glass diffused the image of the moving man inside. I watched him for a minute before I moved any closer, tightening the straps of the harness, a nylon one unlike the leather I usually wore. I'd just bought it on a lark, thinking maybe I'd want to fuck somebody in a hot tub someday and would need something waterproof – now the day was here. Reflexively I stroked the dildo, my cock now, feeling its heft. It pressed tight against my clit, and stroking it sent little waves of pleasure through me. I jacked off for a few minutes, wondering if he'd jack off to *my* silhouette in a shower. Then I decided it was time to step inside. I had butterflies; I always do before fucking somebody new. This was different from spreading my legs to someone's hand or cock, this was scarier. Strapping on a cock means strapping on a new kind of responsibility. I'm glad I don't have it all the time.

He was aware of my presence the minute my hand touched the door, and it was like he'd been waiting for me, waiting to see if I'd take the initiative by coming in to find him. His skin shone in the water and the rivulets that streamed down his body looked like sweat on a hot, hot day. His hair was wettened down, sleek as a seal's. Seeing him naked I caught my breath; seeing my cock he caught his.

He pulled me to him to kiss me and I felt the beat of the water and his mouth at the same time. His hand was on my cock already, the shower rained down warm on us, and every stroke of his hand pressed the dildo into my clit. My cunt was as hot and wet as all the rest of me.

The shower was big, twice the size of an ordinary one. It was tiled with small gray flagstones, dark as wet pavement under the shower spray. It had a tiled bench. It also had a fancy showerhead, and he reached up and switched the spray to a fine mist, fine enough to breathe through, like a San Francisco fog but hot. Then he knelt to me and took the head of my cock in his lips.

He sucked it like it was real, and I could feel each tug of his mouth on my clit; and I could have sworn I remembered how it felt, from another life nearly forgotten, exactly how it felt to have a dick that could feel lips and tongue and teeth. I felt the amazement, the miracle I'd felt the night before: I'd found a man who would *play* with me.

The daddy had my ass cheeks in his hands, kneeling to me, and he was throating my dick. The latex gave me a dim reflection of the sensations a flesh-and-blood cock would: I felt the cock head pop in and out of the ring of muscle at his throat. No gag reflex at all, Jesus – this man was impressive. He growled around the dick, bit it, used my ass to pull me down his throat. I rested my hands on his hard shoulders and let him control the pace, and felt orgasm simmering from the rhythm of the dildo on my clit and the pressure of his big hands squeezing and parting my cheeks. He was sucking it just a little too slow to make me come – maybe on purpose. I got lost in the building sensation just as I had the night before when it had been his cock in my throat.

Gradually he picked up the pace. I laced my hands around the back of his head, just to make sure he wasn't going to stop on me, but he showed no signs of flagging. Pushing me back 'til I was supported by the warm wet tile, he tumbled me into a blinding orgasm, and my first awareness when I came to was his voice in my ear, low: 'Yeah, come for me, shoot it, baby, I want that load, I want it all ...'

'My cock's still hard, Daddy,' I said, and ran my hands down his belly and grasped his dick, harder still. 'It's hard for you – are you gonna get back on your knees for me? Are you gonna let me slide my big cock deep into you?'

That got his attention. He made a sound that fell somewhere between his cock-sucking growl and a whimper, and he reached past me and came up with a tube of K-Y.

'Lube it, baby. Lube my cock, that's right, get it slick. I'm gonna slide my cock up your ass. I'm gonna fuck you, Daddy.'

My cunt was humming, and I felt the foreshadow of another orgasm just from talking to him that way, just from reading the hungry energy of his response. I had the feeling I'd finally found someone with as complicated a sexuality as mine, for it was clear that he wanted it as badly from me now as I'd wanted it from him the night before.

He didn't lube it right away. He went for my dick with his mouth again, sucking so hard on it that I came again just from the insistent, rhythmic throb of the dildo's base on my clit. I yelled this time, and the sound reverberated, mixed with the hissing sound the water made on the wall of the shower cubicle. My dick was shiny with the thick saliva from his throat. It glittered on the black rubber.

I liked how surreal it looked, shiny black like that, but suddenly wished I'd brought the realistic-looking dick. Would that make it hotter for him, seeing veins and skin-like latex, Jeff Stryker's movable balls to squeeze? For a man in love with cock, how could this stylized one do the trick?

But he was growling in his throat again and I saw him stroking his own meat, the veins on it pulsing a little with each new hot gush of blood they let in, and I relaxed, remembered the time my last lover undid her 501s to reveal a dildo tucked in and covered by her shirt-tail. I had been in the bar with her for an hour and hadn't even noticed, 'til she came into the restroom cubicle with me, stood before me as I peed, and loosed each button 'til the dick popped out and ever so delicately she took my chin in her hand and brought my lips to the head of the thing. It was lavender silicone and not shaped like a cock at all. It wasn't even *meant* to be a cock, on her. She never was all that turned on to cocks, but strapping on something to fuck with, something that let her pin me to a bed or a wall and let her cunt-energy come exploding out of her and into my cunt or asshole, she liked *that* just fine. Still pissing, I took her dildo between my teeth, sucked it in deep so the slime from my throat would make it slick enough to shove into me hard when she raised me, turned my face to the wall, my skirt up around my waist, her fingers finding my clit and rubbing it with the last drops of my piss.

She didn't think of it as a cock so I didn't either, but I sure did take it seriously ... so maybe the daddy, reaching for the lube now, *really* wanted this cock, my cock, even if I wasn't hung like Jeff Stryker.

So I told him to get on his knees; I told him to give me his ass. He anointed my cock and it glistened in the hot fog of the shower. He took a high crouch, bracing himself with his hands on the low bench. He growled one more time, rubbed his ass up and down my thighs, trying to capture the dildo just like I'd tried to grab his cock with my pussy the night before. The growl turned to words: he was saying, 'C'mon. Put it in. *Fuck* me.' My sleek daddy had metamorphosed into a horny weasel with a voracious asshole – and I knew just how he felt. I didn't have the heart to tease him, and besides, I was horny myself for the feeling of his asshole smoothly beginning to open for my dick.

I angled my cock toward his ass. The next sweep he made against me slid his hole right up against my cock head, just where I wanted him. He stopped moving, with a shudder and a moan, and leaned back against the lubed rubber dick. The pressure was beginning to open his asshole – no surprise, he was easy.

I pulled back just a little. He actually whimpered, thought I was teasing him, but I grabbed his hips and started pulling him against me, pumping him fast but not hard enough for the tip of the dildo to pop all the way in. A couple of minutes of that will drive any fuck-starved man or woman insane; *I* ought to know. He was still trying to thrust back onto my cock, but I held his hips harder, told him with my body that even as I had given him control to fuck me last night, I would take it now, take it when and how I wanted him. A fuck is almost always better for that kind of energy; I just wanted him off balance enough to really *need* it. That was a gamble – until now I'd only known him as a topman, and a consummate one at that. I was already hoping he played rougher games and that I'd have the chance to give myself over to his will again. The only indication I'd had that he might be willing to bottom at all – much less to a strange, gender-schitzed boy-girl from out of nowhere – was the sight of him kissing the toes of my shoes as he undressed me and laid me down to share his bed.

But the daddy had responded so immediately when I signalled my willingness to play, took me so smoothly, met me so completely, that I had a feeling he'd like being flipped – it would be just as hot to be taken as to take. I'd never tried this with a man, much less a gay one. But I'd met a couple of butch women whose *savoir faire* was really an open invitation to lay them down and fist them. Besides, I was trusting my intuition, and right now my intuition was operating out of the head of my dick. My intuition was about to sink balls-deep into his ass.

In one fast motion, on the back thrust, I released my hold on his hips. By the time I was thrusting forward I had thrown my arms around his chest and gotten him by the tits. I pulled him against me and my dick sank home.

That one long stroke, the one he'd been waiting for, made him come – I felt his asshole pulse around my cock, buried deep in him now, and he moaned and gasped as I slowly, slowly started to fuck him, hardly pulling out at all, a slow deep fuck while I worked his nipples and began to whisper how good he was, how good he could take it, how good I was gonna give it to him, how fine he was with my big cock in his butt, taking it from me so nice and slow.

Then I got my footing and pulled almost all the way out. He swallowed hard, braced.

'That's right, baby,' I said, almost a croon, 'you know what comes next, don't you? What am I gonna do with my cock, Daddy? What am I going to do to you?'

'Fuck me,' he said in his cock-sucking voice, 'you're going to fuck me.' His ass was in the air. My black rubber dick shone in the water-diffused light. He was the most gorgeous fucking thing I'd ever seen, a strong nasty man impaled on my cock. If only I could give it to him right. If only I could fuck him as perfectly as he had fucked me. Before I went any further I ran my hands down his belly, over his cock. Still straining hard – he hadn't shot yet, only orgasmed with pulses of his cock and asshole and pelvic muscles – just like me, he could come without shooting. He didn't know it yet, but I could also come and shoot, just like him, spray my lighter jizz in a scented gush.

My touch made him shudder. I had the sudden thought, accompanied by a hot pulse in my cunt, that he would take anything from me now. Fuck sex differences, fuck 'men are . . .' and 'women are . . .'. He was giving himself to me just like I had given myself to him. Penetrated, in submission, ass poised and open to me, he was mine.

I took him, not slow, not soft. I knew what he wanted. I wanted to give it to him so bad I could taste the adrenaline. I slammed my cock into his ass. I spread his cheeks with my hands, watched, mesmerizing myself, as my hips took hold of a rhythm so primal it seemed my brain had nothing at all to do with it. I pumped him as hard as I could, pumped him 'til we were both growling. I was chanting, 'Take it! Take it!' and he interrupted his alley-cat-getting-fucked noise only with an occasional guttural 'Yeah! *Fuck!*'

I had him by the throat. One of my feet was braced on the bench. He was thrusting his body back as hard and fast as I was thrusting in. I knew I wasn't strong enough to strangle him, but I had him just right: I could throttle him into dizziness, almost to passing out, into a vast, almost-orgasmic plane where he would feel like he was getting butt-fucked on a cloud in heaven. I could keep him there or bring him back just by varying the pressure. The powerful feeling of having him in my hands was filling my heart as well as my cunt.

Suddenly I was acutely aware that I did not know his name. We were so raw with each other, so right, too – so *intimate* – even if he *did* sex like this with all his tricks. But nameless. That was hot and frightening in equal measure. It gave me both more power and less.

I changed my stroke. I angled my cock so it pumped over his prostate, and under my hands and through my dick I felt him soar up toward orgasm. I moved my hands from his throat back to his rampant cock, and my touch triggered him. With a guttural cry he shot five long, wrenching pulses into my hands, and I sank into him deeply, teeth holding the back of his neck like a cat does when it's fucking. His asshole clenched on my cock, his skin and muscle between my teeth, I thought about bringing my hand full of his jism to my lips, thought of licking the cream off my fingers – *can't* – and so I brought the hand to his mouth instead, thrust four fingers in for him to suck his own juice off me – and the hot suction of mouth on fingers triggered me into a come so strong I thought I was going to cry. I held him tightly from behind and we collapsed onto the shower floor. I became aware again, slowly, of the hot mist.

We lay all tangled the way we had the night before, a long time, silent except for our breathing returning to normal and the shower's hiss. At last he moved his hand away from where it had been resting on my thigh and pulled my dildo free of his ass. I loosed the harness's buckles with one hand and slipped it off, my pussy returning to nestle tightly against his ass, my hand reaching around to rest on his softening cock. The silence felt neither uncomfortable nor natural, for we both were looking for a way past the fact that we did not know each other. I was tempted to pull his hand to my cunt, start us sexing again, just so we wouldn't have to talk, just to avoid breaking the spell. He closed his big hand around my hand, the one that held his dick. With the pressure I became aware of my pulse, beating fast. His thumb and forefinger closed around my wrist – he was feeling it too. That or he was measuring to see how well it would fit in his ass.

My mind was racing in the silence. I was developing a case of nerves, which seemed stupid, since five minutes before I'd been playing *Realm of the Senses* with a man who I now couldn't think of a way to talk to. Opening lines spun through my head, but I was feeling too nervous to use them.

He shifted onto his back and pulled me on top of him. Seeing his big-dicked alley-cat girl in a lather of shyness he laughed and wrapped his arms around me and, mercifully, let me off the hook.

'We should probably have gotten introductions out of the way last night, little hellion,' he said. 'I didn't quite bargain on having this kind of a morning. I didn't bargain on ever meeting up with anything like you, in fact. I'm not even sure you're real, except my asshole's still pulsing. Do you have a name?'

'I have two names,' I said. 'The one you picked up last night is Randy. The one you fucked is Miranda.'

'Which one is with me now?'

I shook my head. 'Not sure. I'm off-centre right now. Maybe I'm in transition from one to the other. You're not supposed to be real either, you know.'

'If you're doubting my existence after fucking me into the middle of next week I guess I'd really better introduce myself. I'm Jack Prosper, and I assure you I am real, but you can keep calling me Daddy for as long as you want, dear, and I must say I *never* wind up on the floor of the shower with my tricks. Did your brother teach you to fuck ass, too?'

I giggled and nodded. 'But I've had a little practice elsewhere. Girls like to get butt-fucked too, you know. *Some* girls.'

Jack shook his head. 'Until last night, I hadn't given much thought to what girls like – not for a lot of years. But I don't think you bear much resemblance to the girls I used to know. You're queer as a three-dollar bill, for one thing. Are there more out there like you?'

I frowned a little. 'Some. Not very many.'

'Must be frustrating to be the weirdest gal on the block.'

'Jack ... Daddy ... I don't want to talk about this right now.' I'd turned almost petulant, buried my nose in his armpit to try to keep from thinking how unlikely it was that Jack and I would be able to relate in broad daylight, with our clothes on. Boys and girls, what a mess. Girls and girls were almost as bad. It was true that I had a hard time finding lovers willing to follow me all over the gender-and-sex landscape. If I wasn't too queer I was too kinky. If I wasn't too kinky I was too insatiable. If I wasn't that I was too slutty or even too serious. All of a sudden I was worried that Jack would realize who he'd stuck his butt in the air for, have an episode of heterosexual panic, and throw me out.

He was kind of psychic, though. 'You're too much for most people, aren't you, Randy-Miranda? Just too queer. What do you think, I'm gonna decide I don't want my dick to smell like fish?' I glared at him, then frowned and nodded. 'Child, any faggot who'd kick a love goddess with a big dick out of bed is insane, I don't care what anybody says. I don't give a fuck that you're a girl. Last I checked, you creatures were receiving far different socialization. I'll just consider this a little science project.'

I burst out laughing at that, couldn't help it.

'Besides, I believe you implied earlier that you could fist me. I've never been fisted by a woman before, and none of my friends have either. I don't think. And I *will* try anything once. You're such a complicated little animal, I might have to try you more than once. In the interests of science, you understand. Miss Miranda, how about another date?'

He rolled me onto my back and kissed me, just like the first kiss last night that undid me.

'I'm a leather daddy's science project,' I thought fuzzily as my hands found his nipple rings and tugged on them. I would crawl on my belly like a human reptile straight through the flames of hell for kisses like this. He sucked on my lower lip and my cunt started to involuntarily spasm. When we came up for breath, only for a second, I whispered, 'I don't think *this* date is over yet, Daddy,' and pulled him back down.

6

The Return to Biology

Marjorie Garber

Whether or not we find what we are seeking
Is idle, biologically speaking.

Edna St Vincent Millay, 'I Shall Forget You Presently'

OVER SEXED

'Dear Ann Landers,' wrote 'A Concerned Father in Ukiah, California',

> My teenage son came home the other day with a story that floored me.
> One of his high school teachers is teaching the students that there are five
> sexes in the human race – male, female, homosexual, bisexual, and
> asexual. ...
> I told my son that the teacher is wrong, that there are only TWO sexes,
> male and female, and the other categories are sexual practices.
> Ann, I'm disturbed by this misinformation. ... What do the experts say
> about this? Do they claim there are five sexes nowadays? Things are
> changing so fast that it's hard to keep up.

Rising to the occasion, Ann Landers hastened to set the record straight:
'There are only two sexes – male and female. Recent studies indicate that
homosexuality, bisexuality and asexuality are not the result of something
that has gone wrong with the sex organs, but rather a biochemical–genetic
alteration that no one has been able to explain.'[1]

This exchange, printed under the pedagogically disturbing but culturally
reassuring headline 'Teacher Needs to Learn Lesson – There Aren't Five
Sexes', is a fairly characteristic signpost of the increasing desire to categorize
and 'explain' the vagaries of human sexuality in popular terms. What is
sometimes called sexual preference (implying a choice) and sometimes called
sexual orientation (implying a destiny) are in this schoolroom example – at
least as reported, third hand, by the teenager's father – equated with 'sex'.
'Sex' (biology) and 'gender' (sociology, anthropology, and culture) are here

silently and unhelpfully conflated. The result is to 'save' heterosexuality, pointedly not listed as one of the 'sexes', as the 'natural' province of the first two delineated 'sexes', male and female. Ann Landers's reply, addressing in telescoped terms both the list of five sexes and the implied critique, asserts that bi-, homo-, and asexuality are not 'wrong' but different. They aren't wrong; but they aren't sexes.

This would seem perfectly straightforward, so to speak, in the everyday commerce of the newspaper advice page and perhaps even self-evident, if there had not appeared three months later in the respected journal *The Sciences* an article by geneticist Anne Fausto-Sterling, called 'The Five Sexes', with the provocative subhead, 'Why Male and Female Are Not Enough'.[2]

Fausto-Sterling describes the legal erasure and medical reassignment of intersexed persons, those whose bodies are, biologically, anatomically, or chemically, a mixture of male and female.

The deep commitment of Western culture to the idea that there are only two sexes, exemplified in the limitations of language (Fausto-Sterling has to have recourse to *s/he* and *his/her* to describe some of her subjects) and law (over the past century, rights and obligations like the vote, the military draft, marriage, and private, consensual sex have all been governed by state or national laws about males and females), has led to a cultural resistance to openly intersexed individuals, called by Fausto-Sterling 'herms' (true hermaphrodites, with one testis and one ovary), 'merms' (male pseudohermaphrodites, with testes, some aspects of female genitalia, but no ovaries), and 'ferms' (female pseudohermaphrodites, with ovaries and some aspects of male genitalia but no testes).

Doctors have translated the bodies of such persons into some semblance of 'normality', reclassifying children who, as they grew older, developed sexual characteristics (an organ on a 'female' that looks more like a penis than a clitoris; a 'male' with an X and Y chromosome who develops breasts and begins to menstruate) that marked them as other than they had at first been regarded. 'The aims of the policy', she stresses, 'are genuinely humanitarian, reflecting the wish that people be able to "fit in" both physically and psychologically. In the medical community, however, the assumptions behind the wish – that there be only two sexes, that heterosexuality alone is normal, that there is one true model of psychological health – have gone virtually unexamined.'[3]

It is almost as if, in the story of the Ugly Duckling, veterinary intervention (and concomitant counselling) had translated the undiagnosed cygnet into a cosmetic mallard for his (or her?) own good.

'Hermaphrodites', Fausto-Sterling asserts with eloquence, 'have unruly bodies. They do not fall naturally into a binary classification; only a surgical shoehorn can put them there. But why should we care if a "woman," defined as one who has breasts, a vagina, a uterus and ovaries and who menstruates, also has a clitoris large enough to penetrate the vagina of another woman? Why should we care if there are people whose biological equipment enables them to have sex "naturally" with both men and women? The answers seem to lie in a cultural need to maintain clear distinctions between the sexes. Society mandates the control of intersexual bodies because they blur and bridge the great divide. Inasmuch as hermaphrodites literally embody both sexes, they challenge traditional beliefs about sexual difference: they possess the irritating ability to live sometimes as one sex and sometimes as another, and they raise the spectre of homosexuality.'[4]

Of homosexuality – or of bisexuality? 'To have sex "naturally" with both men and women.' This geneticist's fearless and provocative vision of a society, perhaps many generations from now, in which 'sexuality is something to be celebrated for its subtleties and not something to be feared or ridiculed' opens the door not only to a fuller acceptance of homosexuality but also to the inclusion of bisexuals, transgenderists, and others who do not neatly fit into older preconceptions of social 'normality'.

Needless to say, such a visionary view of science and society did not go unchallenged. A briefer version of Fausto-Sterling's article appeared on the op-ed page of the *New York Times* under the title 'How Many Sexes Are There?' and elicited a predictable range of commentary. One letter writer asked, plaintively, 'What is it about human sexuality that leads people to engage in extraordinarily fuzzy thinking?'[5] British geneticist Winston Holt's book on *The Sexual Continuum* was cited to suggest that 'each of us to some degree is both heterosexual and homosexual, and therefore bisexual', and Alfred Kinsey was quoted as saying that 'The only abnormal sex act is the one you can't do.'[6] *Times* readers were also reminded that 'Native Americans believe that there are four sexes: men who love women, men who love men, women who love women and women who love men; and since men who love men and women who love women are fewer in number, they must be blessed by the gods.'[7] (This cross-cultural point is one often made in bisexual 'zines and newsletters.)

What is especially striking about this cultural moment, however, is the way in which the 1990s seem to be re-creating the 1890s. Biologistic arguments explaining homosexuality are again in force, in contention, and in vogue; studies of hereditary family linkages are once again being undertaken, as they were a hundred years ago, in quest of an answer to the riddle of human sexuality that can be grounded in ascertainable 'fact' – in science rather than in cultural influence. And once again, as was the case a hundred years ago, the quest for the biological truth of homosexuality, and thus of heterosexuality, is foundering on another inconvenient 'fact' – the fact of bisexuality as a mode of human behaviour. For bisexuality queers the pitch, messes up the neat double columns of figures: straight and gay.

Bi for biology, from *bios*, life. Bi for bisexuality, from *bis*, two.

THE QUESTION OF BIOLOGY

Biology is back. After decades of disfavour as an explanation for homosexual behaviour (what used to be called, with finger-pointing disparagement, 'homosexual tendencies'), biology is now making a major comeback. The 'gay gene', the 'gay brain', and the biological imperative – not a 'lifestyle choice' but a DNA blueprint, a 'fact' of life – are now the focus of studies by clinicians and investigators.[8] The politics of these new (or rather, renewed) claims has, in effect, come full circle. As the *Wall Street Journal* noted, 'the discovery of a definitive biological cause of homosexuality could go a long way toward advancing the gay-rights cause. If homosexuality were found to be an immutable trait, like skin color, then laws criminalizing homosexual sex might be overturned.'[9] Same-sex marriage, job protection, antidiscrimination in housing laws – all of these could hinge on the redefinition of homosexuality as biologically caused rather than socially and culturally chosen.

Dr Paul Cameron, the chairman of the Family Research Institute, a conservative lobbying group that sails under the slogan 'Scientists Defending Traditional Family Values', offered the following political advice to gay-rights activists: 'If I were a gay-rights manager, I'd say, "Guys, whatever we do, we have to make them believe we were born that way." If they can get a majority of Americans believing it, they're home free.'

But the political stakes for gays and lesbians are complex: If science can 'prove' that homosexuality isn't a choice, what is to prevent its being repathologized and either 'cured' or therapeutically aborted after prenatal testing discloses the presence of the gay gene? Tying the rights discourse to science opens the possibility of devaluing choice as somehow illegitimate. It also tacitly reaffirms the either/or nature of the heterosexual–homosexual split. What would happen if the 'gay gene' were detected in routine testing of heretofore impeccably heterosexual men and women? Would that mean they were 'really' gay? Would it suggest that they should be therapeutically resocialized as gay in order to be true to their genes?

'A biological explanation of homosexuality simultaneously explains heterosexuality,' write Michael Bailey and Richard Pillard in an article welcoming Simon LeVay's research on the brain as good news for gays and lesbians. They note that 'homophobia remains the one form of bigotry that respectable people can express in public', and suggest that the scientific study of the origins of sexual orientation will open up public debate and lead to breakthroughs of 'self-discovery'.[10] To track the genetic origins of homosexuality, they claim, is no more stigmatizing than to seek out the genetic causes of traits like extroversion or intelligence, which are regarded as positive rather than negative qualities. (How dubiously uncontroversial such other quests would prove was demonstrated by the clamorous reception of Richard Herrnstein and Charles Murray's *The Bell Curve*.)

The quest for a 'scientific' explanation (or should that be scientific 'explanation'?) of homo- and heterosexuality has been much on the minds of gender critics, as well as of biological scientists, in recent years. 'Nobody knows how sexual orientation is in fact determined', Mariana Valverde observed in 1987, insisting that one reason for this failure was that almost all research to date had concentrated on finding 'the causes' of homosexuality 'as if heterosexuality had no cause'.[11] Research like that of Bailey and Pillard, LeVay, and Dean H. Hamer attempts to redress that unequal balance, but in doing so it creates a new one. By seeking to resist ambiguity, their research models inevitably write out bisexuality.

The old biology of nineteenth-century sexologists (and, subsequently, the racial 'hygienics' of Nazism, a 'scientific' view that saw homosexuals as genetically flawed and logically subject to extermination) had maintained that homosexuals could be recognized by certain stigmata, from beard-lessness and 'limp wrists' in men to enlarged clitorises and short haircuts in women. By this biological logic, Jewish men, for example, were associated with women and with homosexuals; they were 'oriental', 'soft', high-voiced, degenerate, circumcised (and thus already self-castrated), and extravagant of gesture. According to sexologist Richard von Krafft-Ebing, the most identifiable 'sexual inverts' were congenital, and could be recognized by the high voice, small waist, and wide pelvis in men, or, conversely, by the low voice, small breasts, and narrow pelvis in women.[12] Thus the form of the body represented the 'inverted' desire: If a man desired a man, he would, according to this theory of 'ideal' congenital sexual inversion, look not like a man but like a woman. Heterosexuality was thereby retained as the model. A male–female pair was envisaged, even if the 'male' was a lesbian in trousers or the 'female' a man in skirts.

The diagnosis of homosexuality as a perversion with biological roots and clinical and behavioural symptoms (women who wore trousers, smoked, chose not to marry; men who as children played with dolls and grew up to be hairdressers, ballet dancers, or interior decorators) was set aside by liberal psychology and psychoanalysis.

Thus Freud's initial insistence on the 'bisexual disposition' of all human beings was grounded in an early faith in biology. By 'bisexual', Freud meant a wide range of things, from what we would call explicit homosexuality to same-sex friendship, identification with the 'opposite sex', cross-gender behaviour (men acting 'effeminate'; 'masculine' women), the undifferentiated tissues of the embryo, and the vestigial presence in the adult of tissues and organs of what, once again, he and his successors would call the 'opposite sex'. But Freud's early attempts to find a biological and anatomical basis for what he variously characterized as the 'bisexual disposition', the 'bisexual constitution', and the 'bisexual organization' of all human beings bears a striking resemblance to recent claims, almost a hundred years later, that again seek an answer in biology.

'We're mixed bags, all of us', declared a professor directing research on androgens and women's health.[13] Yet even when modern science confronts the fact that 'the borders between classic maleness and femaleness are much grayer than people realized', with the increasing awareness that male sex hormones like testosterone play a crucial part in women's bodies, the implications go unexplored. 'Male Hormone Molds Women, Too, in Mind and Body', announced the *New York Times*. 'What society says is normal and what is normal for women can be very different', observes another medical researcher. 'Women can have a full beard and still be breast-feeding.'[14]

But though the debate about how androgens affect the brains as well as the bodies of women has begun to heat up – are androgenized women in fact 'more mathematical, more aggressive, more sexually active, more enamored of guns and computers'?[15] – it does not seem to include the suggestion that the 'mixed bags' might (bio)logically include 'mixed' desires. That is to say, bisexual desires.

'The theory of bisexuality', Freud wrote, 'has been expressed in its crudest form by a spokesman of the male inverts: "a feminine brain in a masculine body". But we are ignorant of what characterizes a feminine brain.' Krafft-Ebing, he says, also puts forward such a theory, one perhaps not quite so crude: that 'every individual's bisexual disposition endows him with masculine and feminine brain centres as well as with somatic organs of sex'. And here, too, Freud is sceptical: 'But what has just been said of masculine and feminine brains applies equally to masculine and feminine "centres"' within the brain.[16]

Later gender theorists, like the psychoanalyst Robert J. Stoller, would challenge this on the basis of new scientific research even as they praised Freud's vision: 'the brain is female', Stoller asserted, 'in that *in both sexes* feminine behavior results if male hormones are not added'.[17] And the media fanfare surrounding Simon LeVay's 1991 research on the hypothalamus revisits this territory of the 'sexual brain' with the object of demonstrating that homosexuality is biologically produced.

According to LeVay – who examined the brains of forty-one men and women, many of them gay men who died of AIDS, and included no lesbian women in his research sample – the hypothalamus, the 'part of the brain that produces sexual feelings', is much smaller in gay men than in straight men. As a result, he claims, it is possible to argue for a genetic and biological basis to male homosexuality. Gay men may after all be born rather than made. Even hairdressers and flower arrangers, he provocatively told the gay and lesbian newsmagazine *The Advocate*, might be biologically determined, identifiable by the size of their hypothalamic nuclei.[18] (Questions of larger and smaller size are not unfamiliar in sex discourse, as the *Advocate* headline 'And How Big Is Yours?' wryly conceded.)

What advantage was there in grounding sexuality in biology? Hadn't some gay people objected to the idea that they were programmed for life by their brain structure? LeVay, himself a gay man, offered a by now familiar political analogy with the civil rights movement of the sixties. If gay identity were innate rather than chosen, genetic rather than optional and capricious, biological rather than behavioural, laws restricting equal opportunity for homosexuals would be prohibited by the courts. Surveys had shown, LeVay noted, that people were more tolerant of gays and lesbians when they thought they 'were born that way' than when they thought it was 'a lifestyle choice'.

LeVay returns not only to biology but, in fact, to sociobiology. His remarks are characteristically full of analogies to male lions, lesbian seagulls, and the evolutionary strategies of the mammalian male animal, whose promiscuity is seen as ensuring the propagation of the species; hence gay men are living out a biological dictum for multiple partners which is inhibited in straight men by 'the reluctance of women to be promiscuous'. Thus, with the return to biology, the liberal move of Freud and his followers appears to have come full circle.

But what place has *bisexuality* in a medical research project like Simon LeVay's? If the hypothalamus of gay men is smaller than that of straight men, what size hypothalamus should bisexuals have? Are they to be imagined, like the furnishings of Goldilocks's third bear, to be neither too big nor too small, but just right – middle-sized glands for the excluded middle of sexual orientation? Might bisexuals have even smaller hypothalamuses than gay men – or larger ones, even, than straights? Or would medical science support the convictions of those psychologists and psychiatrists who think bisexuality is a mirage? Are all hypothalamuses either gay or straight? Is there such a thing as a 'bi brain'? And if not, how do we account for bisexuality? The many political critiques of LeVay's study, which took him to task for everything from removing sexual desire from the realm of culturally constructed behaviour to facilitating a eugenic campaign to eliminate homosexuals *in utero*, do not focus on this key question.

Critics of LeVay's research pointed out that (1) his hypothesis claimed a symmetry based upon the object of attraction, with those attracted to men (gay men and heterosexual women) having smaller hypothalamic nuclei than those attracted to women (heterosexual men and lesbians), but because his study contained no brain tissue from lesbians he was unable to test that part of his hypothesis; that (2) according to his own data the *range* of sizes of hypothalamic nuclei was virtually the same for homosexuals and heterosexuals, with some homosexuals having larger nuclei than many heterosexuals, and some heterosexuals having smaller nuclei than many homosexuals, so that 'though the groups showed some difference as groups, there was no way to tell anything about an individual's sexual orientation by looking at his hypothalamus';[19] and that (3) since all his subjects were cadavers, there was no way of verifying the range or extent of their sexual behaviours.

This last point is the most relevant to charting bisexuality. LeVay describes his subjects as follows: '[N]ineteen subjects were homosexual men who died of complications of acquired immunodeficiency syndrome (AIDS) (one bisexual man was included in this group). Sixteen subjects were presumed heterosexual men; six of these subjects died of AIDS and ten of other causes. Six subjects were presumed heterosexual women. One of these women died of AIDS and five of other causes.'[20]

The word 'presumed' in the phrase 'presumed heterosexual men' is marked by a footnote: 'Two of these subjects (both AIDS patients) had denied homosexual activity. The records of the remaining 14 patients contained no information about their sexual orientation; they are assumed to have been mostly or all heterosexual on the basis of the numerical preponderance of heterosexual men in the population [A. C. Kinsey, W. B. Pomeroy, C. E. Martin, *Sexual Behavior in the Human Male* (Saunder, Philadelphia, 1948)].'

This strikes me as extraordinary 'scientific' information. LeVay's category of 'heterosexual men', the functional basis of his comparison study ('A Difference ... Between Heterosexual and Homosexual Men') turns out to be almost entirely based on inference, guesswork, or statistical percentages drawn from a social science study which, however prestigious or canonical in the field, was completed more than forty years ago. To 'presume' that the percentages remain the same over time, and that Kinsey's percentages are authoritative enough in 1991 to allow the 'assumption' of heterosexuality in fourteen men about whose sexual orientation in fact nothing is known, seems not only stunningly inexact but also to be positing the very thing that LeVay wants to prove: namely, that homosexuality and heterosexuality are biological, perhaps innate, rather than social and cultural. For if 'homosexuality' and 'heterosexuality' – or, to use Kinsey's much less problematic terms, homosexual and heterosexual *behaviour* – were in fact substantially produced or altered by cultural factors, we would have no reason to think that 1948's 'numerical preponderance' would hold today.

Then there is the matter of the AIDS patients who 'had denied homosexual activity' – itself a phrase of some interest, since it seems to imply that the investigators or doctors attending on the case initially 'presumed' them homosexual – and of the 'one bisexual man' who was included, by LeVay, in his homosexual sample. Why not include him, with equal logic, in the *heterosexual* group? Or indeed in *both* groups? 'Homosexual' here becomes in effect a 'default' category meaning 'anything but straight'.

Either LeVay regarded bisexuality as a euphemistic cover for gay identity, so that a 'bisexual' in the terms of his study was really a gay man who had not come out to himself or to others, or else he hypothesized that having any sexual interest in men, even if he also had a sexual interest in women, would affect a man's hypothalamus in ways that would make him look, under the microscope, more gay than straight. In either case, bisexuality as a scientifically determinable category once again disappears, is subsumed. The 'bisexual individual' is counted among the homosexual men 'for statistical purposes', while the 'presumed heterosexuals', about whose sex lives in fact nothing is known, are counted among the straights.

LeVay begins his paper in *Science* by noting that sexual orientation has traditionally been studied on the level of psychology, anthropology, or ethics,[21] with the clear implication that he is going to move the discourse in the direction of biological evidence, of ascertainable scientific fact. He ends it by reviewing problems in interpreting his data, including the fact, already noted above, that his 'ability to make correlations between brain structure and the diversity of sexual behavior that undoubtedly exists within the homosexual and the heterosexual populations' was limited – one might use a stronger word – by the 'use of postmortem material'. Dead men tell no tales.

The telltale word here is 'undoubtedly' ('the diversity of sexual behavior that undoubtedly exists'), a word that, casually introduced into the text, becomes in effect the paper's bisexual ghost (here, there, and everywhere) – or, if you like, the bisexual skeleton in its half-opened closet. For what can this undoubted diversity of behaviour be, in the context of an article that is only concerned with the sexual object (men or women) and not with the sexual aim (oral, anal, or genital sex)[22] – what can this 'diversity' be except bisexuality? How much 'diversity' makes a straight into a gay, or a gay into a straight, according to the either/or logic of LeVay's classification?

LeVay himself, challenged to explain how 'a 40-year-old guy who's married and with children' can one day come out as gay, compares the gayness of such men to other genetic traits, like that for adult diabetes, that do not manifest themselves until later in life. 'Their sexuality is probably just as genetically loaded as are kids' who realize they are gay when they are 12 years old.'[23] Thus, for LeVay, such instances of sequential bisexuality are indices of a kind of latency; these men are genetically homosexual, not bisexual, although their homosexuality may not be apparent to them early on. Bisexuality here disappears into a kind of genetic false consciousness.

In the contrary case, that of a person who had early sexual experiences with same-sex partners and then switched to exclusive other-sex relations (the 'it's a phase' or boys-will-be-boys theory of bisexuality, Freud's 'contingent inverts'), should we expect that the hypothalamus would give the answer 'straight'? And what is to be said about the individual, male or female, who is genetically programmed for gayness but dies before the program kicks in? Would the gland of such a person disclose this future identity? Would he or she be 'really' *potentially* gay? LeVay's study had at least six variables: gay/straight, male/female, died of AIDS/died of other causes. Bisexuality here would be an inconvenient further complication, whether the size of the hypothalamus is a product of innate genetic design or, as has also been conjectured, a result of lived experience as a gay – or straight – person.

Furthermore, the absence of lesbians from his study makes the question of bisexuality's place even more acute. LeVay subsequently apologized for perpetuating 'the tradition of ignoring women in biomedical research', explaining that he couldn't find 'brains of women whose sexual orientation is known', since that information doesn't usually appear on medical charts. Because so many of his subjects were gay men with AIDS, their sexuality became part of their etiology of disease. They were 'known' to be gay. The women, by contrast, were apparently 'known' to be straight. But how do we 'know'? How much gay sex, or straight sex, makes a person gay or straight? Bear in mind the spectre of the 'bisexual AIDS carrier', that bogeyman of the eighties, whose secret life was said to be itself a cause of infection, and whose personality was conjectured to be duplicitous, cowardly, self-indulgent, or self-hating. Were any of them among the AIDS casualties in LeVay's study? If so – or even if not – would he mark them down as 'gay'?

'This way of categorizing people obscure[s] the hitherto accepted fact that many people do not have sexual relations exclusively with one or the other sex', biologist Ruth Hubbard observes trenchantly, reflecting on the nineteenth-century turn of inquiry by which 'homosexuality stopped being what people did and became who they were'.[24] At what point does the politics of identity, necessary for the attainment of equal rights, come into conflict with the political incorrectness of human desire?

Some people are only attracted to redheads, or to people with muscular bodies, or to rich people. Do we call them roussophiles, or biceptophiles, or plutophiles? Do we examine their brains or their genes for the cause? When a young and beautiful woman marries an elderly and wealthy husband we may call her a fortune-hunter or a trophy wife or a society matron, but we do not, usually, describe her as having a perversion, or as choosing a way of life contrary to the will of God – at least not to her face. Indeed, the Bible might well be called in as evidence for sanctioning just such an arrangement. What if the same woman has previously been married to a man her own age, or if a woman who marries a blond had previously married a man with black hair? Is she to be questioned closely about why she has changed her mind?

But blond hair and black hair do not affect the economic structure, it will be objected. They do not enforce the institution of marriage and patriarchy, so there is no real analogy to be made. Well, then, what if a white woman marries a black man? We used to have a name for this unlawful practice – miscegenation. But black–white marriages are no longer against the law, at least in the United States, and while many people, black and white, may privately question it even today, 'intermarriage' – between blacks and whites, between Christians and Jews – has become a much more culturally accepted practice now than it was fifty years ago. The term for such arrangements these days is not 'intermarriage' or 'mixed marriage' or 'miscegenation' but 'marriage'.

Why do we resist the idea that erotic life is all part of the same set of pleasures, that there is only one sexuality, of which the 'sexualities' we have so effectively and efficiently defined are equally permissible and gratifying aspects?

Because to do so would threaten the social structures on which 'civilization' and 'society' are built. And because much modern eroticism depends, in part, precisely upon transgression, upon the sensation or perception of daring, of breaking a law or flauting a taboo. Like Robert Frost's famous definition of free verse as 'playing tennis with the net down', what used to be called 'free love' (extramarital, nonmonogamous, ambisexual) needs rules to break.

GAY GENES

Simon LeVay, who has now given up science for a career in adult education at the West Hollywood Institute of Gay and Lesbian Education, gave the media the 'gay gland'. Other researchers – Michael Bailey and Richard Pillard in one study, Dean H. Hamer and associates at the National Cancer Institute in another – have given us the 'gay gene'. Hamer's investigation, results of which were published in *Science* in July 1993 (two years after LeVay's research appeared in the same journal), examined forty pairs of gay brothers and determined that identical pieces of the end tip of the X chromosome (inherited from the mother) appeared in thirty-three pairs to predispose them genetically to homosexuality. Again, the immediate non-scientific fallout was political, and the findings were once more appropriated to a discourse of rights.

If homosexuality was proved to be largely inborn, gay people would be protected by the courts from discrimination. The same fears – of experimentation to eliminate potential homosexuals from the population, in this case by gene therapy – and the same doubts – about drawing a firm distinction between gay and straight – were voiced. Anne Fausto-Sterling, who had been critical of earlier attempts to study human behaviour through genetic research, praised the caution of Hamer's conclusions, which allowed for an interplay of the genes, the brain, and the environment in the moulding of human behaviour. As for LeVay, the *New York Times* described him as 'ecstatic'. He was quoted as calling Hamer's results 'the most important scientific finding ever made in sexual orientation'.[25]

Once again, though, the question of bisexuality might be said to complicate the equation, if not to queer the results. What Hamer's team did was to scrutinize the life histories of 114 men who identified themselves as homosexual. They then discovered a surprising number of homosexual males on the maternal side of the family, and, turning to brothers as most likely to be genetically linked, scrutinized their X chromosomes through a procedure known as linkage mapping. It was this procedure that revealed the surprising consonance of DNA markers on the tip of the X chromosome.

How did the study know these men were gay? Because they said so. No men who said they were heterosexual – or bisexual – were included, and although a parallel study of lesbians (again, self-identified) is under way, no results have yet appeared. 'Sexual orientation is too complex to be determined by a single gene', said Hamer. But if the presence or absence of this genetic marker indicates either a direct relationship to sexual object choice or (as is also conjectured) a 'temperamental' predisposition to homosexuality, what is the status of the bisexual? Is he to be thought of as resisting (heroically or perversely) the message of his genes when he has relationships with women? Should genetic factors be thought of as options or as limits? We are once again here on the terrain of the 'natural' and the 'original'.

Hamer and his team of researchers at the National Cancer Institute begin their paper on genetics and male homosexuality with a stylish reference to homosexuality as a 'naturally occurring variation', thus whisking it under the big tent of Darwinism. Their study of forty pairs of homosexual brothers, like Michael Bailey and Richard Pillard's earlier twins study, 'recruited' subjects 'through advertisements in local and national homophile publications'.[26]

They end with a cautionary note on medical ethics that looks forward to Jonathan Tolins's play *The Twilight of the Golds*, in which a couple is told that genetic testing has proved their unborn child will be gay. Should they have the child or abort it and try again for a straight one?

'We believe', writes Hamer and his colleagues with admirable directness, 'that it would be fundamentally unethical to use such information to try to assess or alter a person's current or future sexual orientation, either heterosexual or homosexual or other normal attributes of human behavior.'[27] The zinger here is 'other normal attributes', which closes the parentheses begun by 'naturally occurring variation' to establish that both in the language of biology and in the language of psychology homosexuals are as 'normal' and 'natural' as hets.

But who are Hamer's either/or homo- and heterosexuals? Using the Kinsey scale of 0 to 6, Hamer finds that his straights are very straight (Kinsey 0s and 1s) and his gays are very gay (Kinsey 5s and 6s) in self-identification, attraction, and fantasy. 'Only the sexual *behavior* scale gave a small overlap between the two groups largely because of adolescent and early adult experiences' (my emphasis).[28] So at least a small number of persons said one thing about their sexuality(ies) and did another. Yet by discounting these early experiences as insignificant, the researchers were able to conclude that sexual orientation was a 'dimorphic rather than a continuously variable trait'. That is, they were able to omit consideration of bisexuality. ('Dimorphic' means existing or occurring in two distinct forms.) 'Heterosexuals' who had sex with men, and 'homosexuals' who had sex with women, were part of this 'dimorphic' sample.

Furthermore, when participants were asked about their family histories, they were requested to rate their male relatives as either 'definitely homosexual' or 'not definitely known to be homosexual (heterosexual, bisexual, or unclear)'. Checking with the relatives in question, researchers confirmed these opinions, except for one person who said he was asexual and two who refused to answer. (The total number of participants and relatives in the study was 166.) In this context, then, bisexual was determined to mean, for statistical purposes, 'not homosexual', rather than 'homosexual'. Thus, while the default category for LeVay was homosexual, for Hamer it is 'not homosexual'.

Hamer et al. were, perhaps deservedly, rather defensive about this flattening out of the sample: '[D]escribing individuals as either homosexual or nonhomosexual,' they declare, 'while undoubtedly overly simplistic, appears to represent a reliable categorization of the population under study.' Here is the word 'undoubtedly' again, a word that in the narrative of LeVay's hypothalamic study played the role of the bisexual ghost. We could say that it does the same in Hamer's gene study, for what is 'undoubtedly overly simplistic' is in fact the elimination of bisexuality as a category of analysis. To prove a point about the scientific relationship of homosexuality to genetics it is apparently necessary to remove distractions like 'bisexual', 'asexual', or the extremely provocative 'unclear'.

In other words, in the interests of science, bisexuality has been made to disappear. But not completely.

In their peroration, which we have already noted to be both hortatory and political in tone, Hamer et al. suggest a broadening of linkage studies beyond 'males who self-identified as predominantly or exclusively homosexual' to include 'individuals who identity as bisexual or ambisexual'. Self-identification rather than behaviour thus becomes the key to the scientific analysis of sexual orientation. What does this tell us about the relationship of ideas to acts?

By taking self-description as the ground of fact, rather than tracing sexual contacts as systematically as it traced family trees and DNA markers, Hamer's study may be said to repeat what it finds: that men who say they are gay are gay. The *Times* qualifies its own noncommittal response to the news ('Report Suggests Homosexuality is Linked to Genes') by raising the question of 'ambiguity', but in what might be regarded as the wrong place. 'So far the study has been limited to men who said they were gay, eliminating the ambiguity that would come from considering the genes of men who called themselves heterosexual.' The real 'ambiguity' here is, we may say, itself ambiguous, doubly located in the careful phrasing of 'men who *said* they were gay ... men who *called themselves* heterosexual' and in the intrinsic ambiguity of sexuality and eroticism especially when regarded over the span of a lifetime. The 'bi' at the centre of 'ambiguity' is more than just a coincidental felicity for my argument; rather, it is a linguistic tag, like the genetic tag at the end tip of the chromosome, indicating a potential and posing a question. Is it possible to 'eliminate ambiguity', or desirable to do so? What does science mean when it claims to know the truth about sexual desire? Does X really mark the spot?

Many of the scientists who are conducting studies on genetics and gay identity are, like Simon LeVay, themselves gay. This should not in itself suggest bias, any more than does the heterosexual identity of past sex researchers, but it does suggest a certain overdetermination of interest. Like so many researchers, in any discipline, scientific or humanistic, they are looking to find themselves. The popular response to their work has been a response consonant with identity politics. Whether 'good news' or 'bad news' for gays, it affirms essential identities rather than fluid constructions. Should we now look forward to a cadre of bisexual scientists searching for a bi gland, a bi gene, or, perhaps, a bisexually identified male research subject with a small hypothalamus and an unmarked X chromosome? Or vice versa?

OFF THE CHARTS

The social scientists' quest to locate sexualities on a quantifiable continuum and the geneticists' attempt to fix and determine gay identity through the microscope have in common a desire to *see*: to see clearly who is gay, who is straight, and who might cross those boundaries without showing or knowing it. Since the discourse of rights, at least in the United States, depends upon the identity of personhood – the US constitution protects only persons, not acts – bisexuals have, following the lead of gays and lesbians in quest of civil rights, sought to establish themselves as a visible and definable group. Just as some gays believe that scientific evidence of their existence will aid them in their quest for equal treatment under the law, so some bisexuals seek a parallel equality through visibility: the model here clearly is identity politics, which has enabled not only interest-group lobbying but also historical self-awareness and individual pride for African Americans; women; Asian, Latino, and Native Americans; and, in the past decade, gays and lesbians.

But bisexuality will not readily fit this model. Defining the set as broadly as possible for both political and humane reasons as those who have or have had any degree of attraction to men and to women, bisexual activists and organizers come up, for example, against the real differences between what social scientists call 'concurrent' and 'sequential' bisexual behaviour.

If 'sequential' bisexuals are categorized as 'really' gay or 'really' straight depending on the nature of their present relationships ('coming out to themselves' on the one hand or 'going straight' and getting beyond an adolescent 'phase' on the other) then not only the definition of 'bisexuality' but also those of 'homosexuality' and 'heterosexuality' are at stake.

For 'homo' and 'hetero' define themselves as opposites, however social science instruments like the Kinsey scale and the Klein grid keep demonstrating that such 'purity' is a cultural artefact. And identity politics as well as science has an interest in keeping them opposite. To add 'bisexuality' as a third category here is not in fact to refine the terms of analysis but instead to expose the radical limitations of rights-based arguments when linked to a concept of fixed identity. This is one reason why 'reclaiming' historical personages and contemporary celebrities as bisexual rather than gay – Oscar Wilde, Virginia Woolf, David Bowie, Martina Navratilova – has stirred such a fuss in both the gay and the bisexual communities.

Biologists don't see bisexuality through their instruments and social scientists only see it as a composite of elements. Yet it exists, in other mammals as well as in humans, in ordinary people as well as in the famous, in adults as well as in children. If the subjects of social science analysis come uncannily to life in the talk-show medium, provoking the inevitable discussion of whether they are being used by the media or are using it for their own ends, the dispassionate categories of the Kinsey scale have likewise been taken over by today's gay and bisexual activists.

As bisexual writer Amanda Udis-Kessler notes, 'phrases such as "one in ten" and "Kinsey 6" are probably as ingrained in queer culture as Judy Garland, Oscar Wilde, leather, *Desert Hearts*, Provincetown and Ferron'.[29] In choosing 'Kinsey 6' (or 'Kinsey 3', defined as 'equally heterosexual and homosexual') as a T-shirt slogan mode of self-identification, the successors of Kinsey's abstract 'males' and 'females' reclaim the territory of the survey, infusing it with personality, irony, and wit. But in giving life to these abstractions they also give them reality. To think in terms of categories is to categorize. It is no accident that gay and lesbian visibility gave rise to 'gay and lesbian chic' as well as to campaigns to liberalize or repress gay and lesbian rights.

Thus, when a scale making use of the terms 'concurrent' and 'sequential' bisexuality came to the attention of a bisexual feminist writer, she was quick to 'predict' that this 'new jargon' would 'find its way into many a bi circle'.[30] No matter that the terms were not new;[31] a new use would be found for them in mirroring and 'scientifically' validating their existence. Like Rock Hudson reading the Kinsey Report, like Simon LeVay charting the biology of gay identity, bisexuals also seek to read the face of nature, to find themselves already written there.

Ultimately, however, the object of scrutiny will escape even the most vigilant and searching eyes. Bisexuality undoes statistics, confounds dimorphism, creates a volatile set of subjects who will not stay put in neat and stable categories. No calipers will fit the shape of desire, which remains, thankfully, unquantifiable by even the most finely tested instruments.

7
Intersex Activism, Feminism and Psychology
Peter Hegarty in conversation with Cheryl Chase

INTRODUCTION

In the 1950s John Money and his colleagues at Johns Hopkins University developed protocols for the treatment of infants born with genitalia that deviate from social norms for acceptable male and female bodies.[1] In 1990 psychologist Suzanne Kessler commented that Money's theory of intersexuality was 'so strongly endorsed that it has taken on the character of gospel' among medical professionals.[2] Since that time intersexed persons have begun to protest the violent and stigmatizing effects of those medical protocols on their lives. On 10 June 1999, I interviewed Cheryl Chase, the founder of the Intersex Society of North America (ISNA), the largest organization of intersexed persons in the world, at her home in northern California. We discussed the surgeries that Cheryl was subjected to as an infant, her discovery that she was intersexed, the formation of ISNA, and the relationships between intersex activism, feminism, and lesbian and gay politics. I transcribed our two-hour conversation and what follows is an edited version that Cheryl has read and commented on. [Interviewer]

INTERVIEWER (hereafter INT):   Let's start by talking about your own story, and how you learned you were intersexed.

CC: When I was eight my parents admitted me to the hospital. All they said was 'Remember you used to have stomach aches? We are going to look and see if everything is OK.' I just remember that the surgery was extraordinarily uncomfortable and painful. Then when I was 10, my parents told me that I had been born with an 'enlarged' clitoris. You could hear the quotes on 'enlarged' when they said it. They said a clitoris was 'something that might have been a penis if you were a boy but you are a girl and so you don't need one'.

INT: 'You don't need one'?

70

CC: Yes. They said 'and since yours was "enlarged" doctors removed it when you were born. The surgery was just to check everything was OK. But don't tell anyone about this.'

INT: They wanted to cover up the medical procedures?

CC: Yes. And they explained it all in terms that I had no understanding of. Then when I was about 12 I started reading books about sex. I understood there was supposed to be some focus of pleasurable sensation in your genitals but I couldn't find it. By the time I was 19 I understood that I couldn't masturbate and I wasn't having orgasms. But until well into my 30s I held contradictory beliefs. I knew that my parents had had my clitoris removed, yet I believed that eventually I would figure out where it was on my body.

INT: Did you get any psychological care as a child?

CC: My parents took me to a psychiatrist when I was 10. She gave me IQ tests and tried to interest me in having children. She gave me a plastic toy model called 'The Visible Woman', which had abdominal organs that you could replace with pregnant ones. I guess she was trying to prepare me for a future role as wife and mother.

INT: Did she know that you were intersexed?

CC: She never mentioned it directly, but she told me that I was 'medically famous', and that I was in a lot of textbooks. When I was about 19 I decided to find out who had done the clitorectomy and why. Because that psychiatrist had said I was 'medically famous', I started reading medical journals; I came away with the hypothesis of progestin virilization.

INT: Can you explain that?

CC: Progestin is a synthetic form of progesterone; a hormone that is produced during pregnancy that maintains the uterine lining. The synthetic progestin, given to pregnant women back in the 1950s and 1960s, isn't identical to natural progesterone and sometimes it has virilizing effects on female infants. Quite a few genetic females born at that time had large clitorises and even relatively male-looking genitals because their mothers were given progestin. The solution was for the doctor to remove the clitoris. DES, a kind of synthetic oestrogen, was also marketed at that time. Then in the 1970s large numbers of cases of a rare kind of cervical cancer in young women began to appear. It turns out that DES given to pregnant women causes their daughters to have cervical cancer 20 years later. I confused DES and progestin in my mind at this time and concluded that I was at risk for cervical cancer. Anyway, I saw a gynaecologist and told him I wanted my records. When I talked to him again he told me the hospital had ignored his request and he couldn't understand why. He instructed me to ask for the records in person and gave me an undated letter to that effect. But when I went to the hospital records department in New York City they wouldn't show them to me nor explain why. I told them that I had a legal right to those records and they said, 'so, sue us'. I broke down completely. Later I got hold of that gynaecologist's correspondence and learned that they did send him the records and he had lied to me.

INT: Your gynaecologist lied to you?

CC: Yes. They sent him the records twice. I think he lied to me because he saw how distressed I already was. He didn't want what was going to happen to me to happen in his office. He wanted it to happen on their watch.

INT: It seems like more than one person tried to deny you this information.

CC: Everyone I turned to did. Next I found that psychiatrist I had seen as a child. I asked for her help in getting the records. She said: 'You don't need them.' Then she asked me if I had a boyfriend.

INT: Sounds like she was only interested in normalizing you.

CC: I told her I didn't have a clitoris and couldn't orgasm and she said 'Oh that's childish. Adult women prefer vaginal orgasms.'

INT: This was in the 1970s, even after Masters and Johnson?

CC: Oh yes. This is post-, post lots of women's writings about sex. So I retreated from that interaction in tears too. Around that time I decided to move to San Francisco because I heard there were lesbians there and I had understood I was lesbian from quite a young age. A couple of years later in San Francisco I consulted a female gynaecologist, told her what I knew, and asked for her help in getting the records. She obtained a three-page summary and gave it to me, saying 'It seems as if your parents at first weren't sure if you were a boy or a girl.' The records showed that I was actually legally and socially a boy for the first *year and a half* of my life.

INT: Was that the first time you learned of this?

CC: Yes. There was a name I had never heard before in the records, 'Charlie', with my parents' names and address, and with my date of birth. That boy was admitted at a year and a half to the hospital for 'sex determination', and Cheryl was dismissed. The records say things like 'true hermaphrodite' and 'pseudo hermaphrodite' and 'ovo-testes' and 'clitorectomy' and 'phallus'; things that were utterly shocking to me. That was in the 1970s in San Francisco. There was a lesbian community, but lesbian separatism was popular and men were supposed to be evil. In that context I wasn't about to explain to another lesbian that I didn't have a clitoris because I had been a *boy* for a year and a half! No way! I got those records when I was about 21. I didn't talk about it again until I was 35.

INT: So that female gynaecologist gave you the information but didn't help you deal with it.

CC: She discounted the meaning of it. She pretended that it wasn't going to hurt. Later I got hold of her correspondence with the hospital. After she saw me, she wrote to tell them they should be really proud and that I was doing great as my 'true sex, i.e., female'.

INT: It seems that doctors are very unprepared to deal with intersexed adults.

CC: Doctors refer to adults as 'formerly intersexed'. Once they have done the surgery, intersexuality is over. There are no sequelae. One member of ISNA, Angela Moreno, had her clitoris chopped off when she was 12.[3] Afterwards her parents asked the doctors explicitly, 'Shouldn't we go and get her some counselling about this?' The doctors said: 'Don't do that because then she'll find out she has a Y chromosome and she'll commit suicide.' That's only 10 years ago. The doctors believe that your experience is so horrible, nobody could possibly own it. That's their position.

INT: If people are kept so much in the dark about their own bodies, how did you come to form this organization and meet people with such similar histories?

CC: I spent the next dozen or more years occupying myself with work. I studied at MIT and Harvard; I moved to Japan and started a high-tech company there. I was successful, but I was terribly depressed and I realized that my life wouldn't have meaning without a radical change. So I volunteered for a telephone counselling service in Tokyo. They had an intensive training with role-playing and speakers talking about personal emotional crises. The more that I did the training, the more I fell apart completely in my personal life. Eventually I told part of the story to the person in charge and she sent me to see their professional therapist, but this psychologist couldn't even deal with the fact that I was lesbian! I told her how I didn't feel like a woman; I said that when I went to buy gloves that women's gloves didn't fit me. She said, 'Well you know, I'm small and they're all too big for me.' But she didn't understand that she doesn't have a history of sex change for her small hands to remind her of. I told her I was unable to masturbate, that sex is always emotionally difficult, and that my partners always leave me. 'Well, everybody has their ups and downs', she said.

INT and CC: [Laugh]

CC: Eventually I decided to fire her. I also decided to confront some of the intersex doctors, based, in part, on what I had learned in the counselling class. Those three pages of medical records were in an ex-girlfriend's basement. I asked her to send me the records and they came the day after I broke off with my therapist. When I looked at the papers and saw this boy again and 'true hermaphrodite' and 'clitorectomy', I realized that those papers had much more power to hurt me than I had realized. I saw

another therapist once but she was way over her head too. I didn't know
what I was going to do. I thought about killing myself. I thought about
cutting my throat and planned just how to make the cut. Then I decided
that if I was going to have such a messy death, at least I wanted to do it
in the office of the surgeon who had mutilated me. At that point I
decided that I needed to work harder at getting help. So I talked to some
therapists in the US and eventually was referred to someone trained in
sexuality, who practised in Japan. I saw him several times a week for
some months, and it helped. He didn't know anything specifically about
intersexuality, but he didn't deny my experience, that my parents and
doctors had defaulted on their responsibility to take care of me.
I decided to find out everything I could about what happened. The
records didn't describe how people thought and felt about me, or how
they made decisions about me. I flew to the US to see my mother and I
asked her lots of questions. She answered me in a way that was
incredibly frustrating. She said that it hadn't been painful, it wasn't
shocking or embarrassing, she hadn't had anything to do with any of it,
the doctors had been completely in charge, and she had never given any
of it a second thought. I believe that it was still so painful for her that
she couldn't stand to acknowledge it.

INT: Are you in contact with your family now?

CC: No. My mother's dead; she broke off contact with me after that.
My father is also dead and my sisters don't talk to me. After that I
realized that the US would be a better place to get help than Japan so
I moved back to San Francisco. I knew that what doctors did to me in
the 1950s was barbaric, but I assumed that what they do to intersexed
kids now has to be very different. So I looked for doctors who dealt
with intersexed children.

INT: You still thought there must be a logic in this system somewhere?

CC: Yes. Back in the US I got in touch with intersex specialists, but they
were shockingly ignorant. One woman surgeon said to me, 'My good-
ness, you have received really excellent care.'

INT: What did she mean?

CC: The only thing she could hear was that they didn't remove my ovaries.
I asked another doctor, one of the most famous men in the whole field,
if he knew any therapists. He said: 'No, but if you find a good one . . .'

INT: '. . . let me know?'

CC: No, he didn't even say 'let me know?' he just said 'hang on to him'.
He didn't want to know about providing therapy for intersexed adults.
Plus they couldn't tell me anything about sexual function. I realized
that doctors were still no smarter than they had been in the 1950s. I was
lucky enough to find a great therapist, a man who is himself intersexed.

And I started talking about my history to everybody, indiscriminately and badly, but within a year I found six others.

INT: And the stories are like yours?

CC: Yes. That's when I decided to start the Intersex Society. I came across Anne Fausto-Sterling's *Myths of Gender*. Anne had mentioned this girl who was about to be clitorectomized to make her 'look like other girls'. And she wrote: 'If the surgery results in genitalia that looks like those shown in Money and Erhardt's book, then these particular psychologists are in need of an anatomy lesson!'[4]

INT: [Laughs]

CC: She also had written that males impregnate; females gestate and lactate and menstruate. So I called and told her that I thought that was wrong because intersex was a complex phenomenon, and that there are counter-examples to any binarizing definition that she can come up with. 'You are right,' she said, 'and since I wrote that I have changed my mind.'

INT: Great.

CC: She had an article in press in *The Sciences* called 'The Five Sexes', where she wrote about this stuff.[5] She sent it to me and I wrote a letter to the editor talking about my experience, because there weren't first-person narratives of medicalized people out there. The letter came out in *The Sciences* two issues later and announced the formation of the Intersex Society. Right away the mailbox started to fill up with letters from people whose stories are very much like mine. Not in the exact details, but in terms of being treated as shameful, lied to and being subjected to surgeries which they, as adults, deeply regret happening.

INT: How big is the membership now?

CC: Our mailing list is about 1500 and we are six years old.

INT: And there are other intersex organizations too?

CC: Yes, there are more than a dozen now around the world, and all have pretty similar things to say.[6]

INTERSEX ACTIVISM AND FEMINIST POLITICS

INT: ISNA is somewhat of a success story. Relatively quickly the organization has grown, gained some media attention, and even had an impact on the medical establishment. What lessons do you think other feminist activists could learn from ISNA?

CC: Don't bother with feminism!

INT: Tell me more.

CC: Back in 1991 or 1992, there was a lot of media attention about African clitorectomies. I figured, 'great, the press is going to be all over this'.

So I tried to talk to feminists who worked on that issue and they
wouldn't speak to me or cover what we were doing.

INT: Have you been in touch with any African feminists?

CC: I've talked to some Africans working in the US who were much more
receptive. Soraya Mire is a Somali filmmaker working in the US. She
told me, 'Alice Walker's been helping me and we're going to get her to
help you too.' Soraya and I had met, had looked at each other's
genitals, talked about sex and cried together. She spoke to Alice Walker
about me, but Walker still won't talk to me. Walker has never
acknowledged that clitorectomy continues in the US.

INT: In a recent article you pointed out how Western doctors used to make
analogies between intersex clitorectomy and African clitorectomy.[7]

CC: Yes. There was a medical article on intersex from the 1960s which
described how to do a very deep clitorectomy. The article editorializes
that clitorectomy doesn't harm sexual function, as evidenced by the fact
that it is performed universally in parts of Africa.[8] Up until the early
1970s Western doctors always called it 'clitorectomy'. Now they call it
'clitoral reduction' or 'clitoral recession' or 'clitoroplasty' because the
word 'clitorectomy' has come to be equated with barbarism, child abuse
and mutilation. However, doctors still remove extensive clitoral tissue.
'-Ectomy' means 'to cut' – if you cut on something, it's an -ectomy,
whether you remove 100 per cent of the tissue or less. Clitorectomies in
Africa do not remove 100 per cent of the structure, nor do most
surgeries performed on intersex children. The distinction between
African 'clitorectomy' and Western 'clitoroplasty' is purely political.

INT: Is there anything in feminist thinking that you have found helpful or
useful?

CC: There is, but it's often not practised in feminism. Feminist theory
prides itself on politicizing personal experience. But the first article I
wrote about intersex, I sent to the journal *Signs* and they rejected it
without review because it contained some personal narrative.[9]

INT: So that is quite the opposite of 'the personal is political'.

CC: Right, the personal is ... is prohibited!

CC and INT: [Laugh]

INT: What stake do feminists have in changing the medical treatment of
intersex infants?

CC: The surgeries are incredibly sexist. They're based on the idea that men
have sex; women are penetrated by men and have babies. For instance,
when doctors are presented with a boy whose penis is very small and
pees from the underside rather than from the tip, they ask themselves:
'What can we do about this boy's pain? That's going to be an
emotionally painful thing to live with.' And I agree that's going to be
painful to live with. Then they say: 'We'll chop off his dick and cut out

his balls and tell everybody he's a girl and give him oestrogen and then stitch a piece of colon into his crotch and have him live as a woman. That will be less painful.' What you produce is somebody who has a body that is vaguely female, is infertile, doesn't menstruate, probably doesn't have any sexual function, might have genital pain, and has been lied to and shamed. That is supposed to be less painful than having a small dick? I think it is taken to be less painful because female pain is discounted. Once it has been transformed into female pain it doesn't bother us so much.

INT: Do most intersexed kids end up being sexed as female?

CC: Doctors acknowledge that they make nine out of ten kids with ambiguous genitals females because 'you can dig a hole but you can't build a pole'.[10]

INT: So femaleness is defined as the absence of maleness.

CC: Their idea is that if you have somebody who is not a good enough male and you cut off enough parts, whatever's left is female. The Former Surgeon General of the United States, Joycelyn Elders, is a paediatric endocrinologist and has this done to her patients. She says, 'I always teach my students you can't make a good male but you can make a pretty good female. Just take everything out and make a pouch.'[11] That was quoted in the *New Yorker*, and you know where the feminist outrage was?

INT: Where?

CC: Nowhere. Nobody even noticed it. Alice Dreger has written about 'monster ethics'. She argues that the ethics that have been applied to dealing with children who have atypical anatomies are ones that we would think of as ludicrous if we didn't think of the child as a monster.[12]

INT: Yes. We're strongly invested in the belief that categories like 'male' and 'female' are based in nature. When natural bodies come along that trouble the categories, there's nothing rational about people's reactions at all.

CC: So we fix the person instead of the category.

INT: It sounds as if, politically, intersexed people are caught between two poles. According to the doctors, there are no intersexed adults and so your concerns are not important. But according to some feminists, intersexed persons are not real women and so your concerns about clitorectomy are not important to them either.

CC: A good example of that last point is Germaine Greer's new book, which devotes an entire chapter, titled 'Pantomime Dames', to arguing that women with complete AIS are really just boys that doctors have made into girls like transsexuals.[13] She also says that they develop a 'masculine figure – broad shoulders, narrow hips, no waist, short legs – and progressive baldness and heavy facial hair'. All of which is utterly untrue.[14]

INT: Even if it were true, so what?

CC: Yes, but women with AIS are the most physically feminine of intersexed people: they lack the androgen receptor which produces masculine proportions, baldness, facial hair and so on. Greer says that because doctors have been using 'woman' as a trash category, feminists should not accept people with AIS as real women.

INTERSEX ACTIVISM AND LESBIAN AND GAY ISSUES

INT: How do you see the relationship between the treatment of intersexed infants and homophobia?

CC: The treatment is deeply homophobic. When a child is born with unusual sex anatomy parents get freaked out that the child is going to be homosexual. Even in medical writings the homophobia is explicit. Doctors are advised in journals and textbooks to tell the parents that with surgery, their child will be normal, happy and heterosexual.

INT: It's taken as a failure of surgery if the child grows up gay or lesbian?

CC: It's assumed to be a likely outcome if there isn't any surgery.

INT: Homophobia is used to motivate the surgery?

CC: Absolutely. Yet lots of intersexed people end up homosexual, by which I mean sexually attracted to people of the social sex that they were assigned to. In other words, they are likely to be harassed and stigmatized as queer. They are vulnerable to homophobia. It would be caring to help parents deal with their own homophobia before the child grows up. Right now doctors validate the parents' homophobia by encouraging them to pray that their anxiety that the child will turn out to be queer will not come true.

INT: So lesbian, gay and bisexual folk have a stake in the treatment of these infants.

CC: Yes. Normalizing medical treatments deepen parents' homophobia, making it harder for those intersexed children who do end up gay.

INT: Around the same time that medical protocols were being developed for dealing with intersexed infants, psychologists and psychiatrists claimed that it was the parents' fault when their child grew up gay or lesbian, and that sexual orientation could be changed through therapy.

CC: Yes, they were attempting to change sexual orientations with therapy, lobotomies, shock treatments ...

INT: ... and clitorectomies.

CC: Yes.

INT: In reaction to that kind of psychology, some people argue that, if sexual orientation was recognized as something biological, that homophobia would be ameliorated; straight people would then think that it's not a person's fault if they are gay or lesbian. But intersexed infants are believed to be biologically preprogrammed to be gay or lesbian and yet homophobia pervades their lives.

CC: There's an even simpler way to put it. The notion that if we could prove that sexual orientation is biologically determined then homosexuals would be granted greater civil rights is terribly naive. For most intersexed conditions, the biological basis is pretty well understood, and yet intersexuals are stigmatized and punished by the enormously powerful mechanism of the medical establishment. Why should it be any different with gay men and lesbians? One of the things that I understood on that night when I was contemplating suicide was that, as hard as it was for me to accept the body that I was born with, it was impossible for that body to have been shameful. It was my knowledge of the history of the gay and lesbian civil rights movement that brought me to understand that the shame was socially imposed, not intrinsic to my anatomy.

INT: For some lesbian and gay folk it would be easy to see a parallel between protests against the psychiatric diagnosis of homosexuality in the early 1970s and some of the actions that ISNA has taken recently.

CC: Yes. Some sexologists tell me 'Good science will provide answers, will right these wrongs.' I think that's bullshit. They need to read Ronald Bayer's book *Homosexuality and American Psychiatry* on the history of how activism – not science – changed the psychiatric treatment of homosexuality![15]

INT: It's more likely that intersexed people will change science, right?

CC: Yes. When I started ISNA I resisted people who told me to do radical things like picket and demonstrate. I believed that doctors wouldn't listen to us if we did that. Then the US Congress passed legislation prohibiting clitorectomy that was drafted in a way that tried to avoid protecting intersexed children.[16] Then I said: 'OK, now we're picketing.' It turns out that my original understanding was naive. Doctors will change last, not first. Only after we change public opinion and bring pressure on doctors from the margins of their own profession will they change.

INT: Would you say that intersexed politics are 'queer'?

CC: Yes, absolutely.

INT: That term, 'queer', has been used in many ways. What does it mean to you?

CC: The value of the word 'queer' is that it talks about difference that's stigmatized or transgressive without defining exactly what that difference is. That's how it is different from 'gay and lesbian'. When intersexed people say 'my body is OK like this' and 'my identity is OK like this', those are queer things to do and to think. Intersexed children's bodies are queer because they elicit homophobic responses in parents and doctors.

INT: The categories 'gay' and 'lesbian' depend on a binary gender system. 'Homo-' and 'hetero-' mean 'the same as' and 'different from'.

CC: And if you think about it, those terms don't mean much if the gender or the sex of either of the two people is at all in question.

8

Axiomatic

Eve Kosofsky Sedgwick

Anyone working in gay and lesbian studies, in a culture where same-sex desire is still structured by its distinctive public/private status, at once marginal and central, as *the* open secret, discovers that the line between straining at truths that prove to be imbecilically self-evident, on the one hand, and on the other hand tossing off commonplaces that turn out to retain their power to galvanize and divide, is weirdly unpredictable. In dealing with an open-secret structure, it's only by being shameless about risking the obvious that we happen into the vicinity of the transformative. In this Introduction I shall have methodically to sweep into one little heap some of the otherwise unarticulated assumptions and conclusions from a long-term project of antihomophobic analysis. These nails, these scraps of wiring: will they bore or will they shock?

Under the rule that most privileges the most obvious:

AXIOM 1: PEOPLE ARE DIFFERENT FROM EACH OTHER.

It is astonishing how few respectable conceptual tools we have for dealing with this self-evident fact. A tiny number of inconceivably coarse axes of categorization have been painstakingly inscribed in current critical and political thought: gender, race, class, nationality, sexual orientation are pretty much the available distinctions. They, with the associated demonstrations of the mechanisms by which they are constructed and reproduced, are indispensable, and they may indeed override all or some other forms of difference and similarity. But the sister or brother, the best friend, the classmate, the parent, the child, the lover, the ex-: our families, loves, and enmities alike, not to mention the strange relations of our work, play, and activism, prove that even people who share all or most of our own positionings along these crude axes may still be different enough from us, and from each other, to seem like all but different species. ...

In the particular area of sexuality, for instance, I assume that most of us know the following things that can differentiate even people of identical gender, race, nationality, class, and 'sexual orientation' – each one of which, however, if taken seriously as pure *difference*, retains the unaccounted-for potential to disrupt many forms of the available thinking about sexuality.

- Even identical genital acts mean very different things to different people.
- To some people, the nimbus of 'the sexual' seems scarcely to extend beyond the boundaries of discrete genital acts; to others, it enfolds them loosely or floats virtually free of them.
- Sexuality makes up a large share of the self-perceived identity of some people, a small share of others'.
- Some people spend a lot of time thinking about sex, others little.
- Some people like to have a lot of sex, others little or none.
- Many people have their richest mental/emotional involvement with sexual acts that they don't do, or even don't *want* to do.
- For some people, it is important that sexual acts be embedded in contexts resonant with meaning, narrative, and connectedness with other aspects of their life; for other people, it is important that they not be; to others it doesn't occur that they might be.
- For some people, the preference for a certain sexual object, act, role, zone, or scenario is so immemorial and durable that it can only be experienced as innate; for others, it appears to come late or to feel aleatory or discretionary.
- For some people, the possibility of bad sex is aversive enough that their lives are strongly marked by its avoidance; for others, it isn't.
- For some people, sexuality provides a needed space of heightened discovery and cognitive hyperstimulation. For others, sexuality provides a needed space of routinized habituation and cognitive hiatus.
- Some people like spontaneous sexual scenes, others like highly scripted ones, others like spontaneous-sounding ones that are none the less totally predictable.
- Some people's sexual orientation is intensely marked by autoerotic pleasures and histories – sometimes more so than by any aspect of alloerotic object choice. For others the autoerotic possibility seems secondary or fragile, if it exists at all.
- Some people, homo-, hetero-, and bisexual, experience their sexuality as deeply embedded in a matrix of gender meanings and gender differentials. Others of each sexuality do not.

The list of individual differences could easily be extended. That many of them could differentiate one from another period of the same person's life as well as one person's totality from another's, or that many of them record differentia that can circulate from one person to another, does not, I believe, lessen their authority to demarcate; they demarcate at more than one site and on more than one scale. The impact of such a list may seem to depend radically on a trust in the self-perception, self-knowledge, or self-report of individuals, in an area that is if anything notoriously resistant to the claims of common sense and introspection: where would the whole, astonishing and metamorphic Western romance tradition (I include psychoanalysis) be if people's sexual desire, of all things, were even momentarily assumed to be transparent to themselves? Yet I am even more impressed by the leap of presumptuousness necessary to dismiss such a list of differences than by the leap of faith necessary to entertain it. To alienate conclusively, *definitionally*, from anyone on any theoretical ground the authority to describe and name their own sexual desire is a terribly consequential seizure. In this century, in which sexuality has been made expressive of the essence of both identity and knowledge, it may represent the most intimate violence possible. It is also an act replete with the most disempowering mundane institutional effects and potentials. It is, of course, central to the modern history of homophobic oppression. ...

Repeatedly to ask how certain categorizations work, what enactments they are performing and what relations they are creating, rather than what they essentially *mean*, has been my principal strategy.

AXIOM 2: THE STUDY OF SEXUALITY IS NOT CO-EXTENSIVE WITH THE STUDY OF GENDER; CORRESPONDINGLY, ANTIHOMOPHOBIC INQUIRY IS NOT CO-EXTENSIVE WITH FEMINIST INQUIRY. BUT WE CAN'T KNOW IN ADVANCE HOW THEY WILL BE DIFFERENT.

Sex, gender, sexuality: three terms whose usage relations and analytical relations are almost irremediably slippery. The charting of a space between something called 'sex' and something called 'gender' has been one of the most influential and successful undertakings of feminist thought. For the purposes of that undertaking, 'sex' has had the meaning of a certain group of irreducible, biological differentiations between members of the species *Homo sapiens* who have XX and those who have XY chromosomes. These include (or are ordinarily thought to include) more or less marked dimorphisms of genital formation, hair growth (in populations that have body hair), fat distribution, hormonal function, and reproductive capacity. 'Sex' in this sense – what I'll demarcate as 'chromosomal sex' – is seen as the relatively minimal raw material on which is then based the social construction of *gender*. Gender, then, is the far more elaborated, more fully and rigidly dichotomized social production and reproduction of male and female identities and behaviours – of male and female *persons* – in a cultural system for which 'male/female' functions as a primary and perhaps model binarism affecting the structure and meaning of many, many other binarisms whose apparent connection to chromosomal sex will often be exiguous or non-existent. Compared to chromosomal sex, which is seen (by these definitions) as tending to be immutable, immanent in the individual, and biologically based, the meaning of gender is seen as culturally mutable and variable, highly relational (in the sense that each of the binarized genders is defined primarily by its relation to the other), and inextricable from a history of power differentials between genders. This feminist charting of what Gayle Rubin refers to as a 'sex/gender system',[1] the system by which chromosomal sex is turned into, and processed as, cultural gender, has tended to minimize the attribution of people's various behaviours and identities to chromosomal sex and to maximize their attribution to socialized gender constructs. The purpose of that strategy has been to gain analytic and critical leverage on the female-disadvantaging social arrangements that prevail at a given time in a given society, by throwing into question their legitimative ideological grounding in biologically based narratives of the 'natural'.

'Sex' is, however, a term that extends indefinitely beyond chromosomal sex. That its history of usage often overlaps with what might, now, more properly be called 'gender' is only one problem. ('I can only love someone of my own sex.' Shouldn't 'sex' be 'gender' in such a sentence? 'M saw that the person who approached was of the opposite sex.' Genders – insofar as there are two and they are defined in contradistinction to one another – may be said to be opposite; but in what sense is XX the opposite of XY?) Beyond chromosomes, however, the association of 'sex', precisely through the physical body, with reproduction and with genital activity and sensation keeps offering new challenges to the conceptual clarity or even possibility of sex/gender differentiation. There is a powerful argument to be made that a primary (or *the* primary) issue in gender differentiation and gender struggle is the question of who is to have control of women's (biologically) distinctive reproductive capability. Indeed, the intimacy of the association between several of the most signal forms of gender oppression and 'the facts' of women's bodies and women's reproductive activity has led some radical feminists to question, more or less explicitly, the usefulness of insisting on a sex/gender distinction. For these reasons, even usages involving the 'sex/gender system' within feminist theory are able to use 'sex/gender' only to delineate a problematical *space* rather than a crisp distinction. My own loose usage in this book will be to denominate that problematized space of the sex/gender system, the whole package of physical and cultural distinctions between women and men, more simply under the rubric 'gender'. I do this in order to reduce the likelihood of confusion between 'sex' in the sense of 'the space of differences between male and female' (what I'll be grouping under 'gender') and 'sex' in the sense of sexuality.

For meanwhile the whole realm of what modern culture refers to as 'sexuality' and *also* calls 'sex' – the array of acts, expectations, narratives, pleasures, identity-formations, and knowledges, in both women and men, that tends to cluster most densely around certain genital sensations but is not adequately defined by them – that realm is virtually impossible to situate on a map delimited by the feminist-defined sex/gender distinction. To the degree that it has a centre or starting point in certain physical sites, acts, and rhythms associated (however contingently) with procreation or the potential for it, 'sexuality' in this sense may seem to be of a piece with 'chromosomal sex': biologically necessary to species survival, tending toward the individually immanent, the socially immutable, the given. But to the extent that, as Freud argued and Foucault assumed, the distinctively sexual nature of human sexuality has to do precisely with its excess over or potential difference from the bare choreographies of procreation, 'sexuality' might be the very opposite of what we originally referred to as (chromosomal-based) sex: it could occupy, instead, even more than 'gender' the polar position of the relational, the social/symbolic, the constructed, the variable, the representational (see Figure 1). To note that, according to these different findings, *something* legitimately called sex or sexuality is all over the experiential and conceptual map is to record a problem less resolvable than a necessary choice of analytic paradigms or a determinate slippage of semantic meaning; it is rather, I would say, true to quite a range of contemporary worldviews and intuitions to find that sex/sexuality *does* tend to represent the full spectrum of positions between the most intimate and the most social, the most predetermined and the most aleatory, the most physically rooted and the most symbolically infused, the most innate and the most learned, the most autonomous and the most relational traits of being.

Biological	Cultural
Essential	Constructed
Individually immanent	Relational

Constructivist Feminist Analysis

chromosomal sex ——————————————— gender
gender inequality

Radical Feminist Analysis

chromosomal sex
reproductive relations ——————————— reproductive relations
sexual inequality sexual inequality

Foucault-influenced Analysis

chromosomal sex ——————— reproduction ——————— sexuality

Figure 1 *Some mappings of sex, gender and sexuality*

If all this is true of the definitional nexus between sex and sexuality, how much less simple, even, must be that between sexuality and gender. It will be an assumption of this study that there is always at least the potential for an analytic distance between gender and sexuality, even if particular manifestations or features of particular sexualities are among the things that plunge women and men most ineluctably into the discursive, institutional, and bodily enmeshments of gender definition, gender relation, and gender inequality. This, too, has been posed by Gayle Rubin:

> I want to challenge the assumption that feminism is or should be the privileged site of a theory of sexuality. Feminism is the theory of gender oppression. . . . Gender affects the operation of the sexual system, and the sexual system has had gender-specific manifestations. But although sex and gender are related, they are not the same thing.[2]

This book will hypothesize, with Rubin, that the question of gender and the question of sexuality, inextricable from one another though they are in that each can be expressed only in the terms of the other, are none the less not the same question, that in twentieth-century Western culture gender and sexuality represent two analytic axes that may productively be imagined as being as distinct from one another as, say, gender and class, or class and race. Distinct, that is to say, no more than minimally, but none the less usefully.

Under this hypothesis, then, just as one has learned to assume that every issue of racial meaning must be embodied through the specificity of a particular class position – and every issue of class, for instance, through the specificity of a particular gender position – so every issue of gender would necessarily be embodied through the specificity of a particular sexuality, and vice versa; but none the less there could be use in keeping the analytic axes distinct.

An objection to this analogy might be that gender is *definitionally* built into determinations of sexuality, in a way that neither of them is definitionally intertwined with, for instance, determinations of class or race. It is certainly true that without a concept of gender there could be, quite simply, no concept of homo- or heterosexuality. But many other dimensions of sexual choice (auto- or alloerotic, within or between generations, species, etc.) have no such distinctive, explicit definitional connection with gender; indeed, some dimensions of sexuality might be tied, not to gender, but *instead* to differences or similarities of race or class. The definitional narrowing-down in this century of sexuality as a whole to a binarized calculus of *homo-* or *hetero*sexuality is a weighty fact but an entirely historical one. To use that *fait accompli* as a reason for analytically conflating sexuality *per se* with gender would obscure the degree to which the fact itself requires explanation. It would also, I think, risk obscuring yet again the extreme intimacy with which all these available analytic axes do after all mutually constitute one another: to assume the distinctiveness of the *intimacy* between sexuality and gender might well risk assuming too much about the definitional *separability* of either of them from determinations of, say, class or race. . . .

Even given the imperative of constructing an account of sexuality irreducible to gender, however, it should already be clear that there are certain distortions necessarily built into the relation of gay/lesbian and antihomophobic theory to a larger project of conceiving a theory of sexuality as a whole. The two can after all scarcely be co-extensive. And this is true not because 'gay/lesbian and antihomophobic theory' would fail to cover heterosexual as well as same-sex object choice (any more than 'feminist theory' would fail to cover men as well as women), but rather because, as we have noted, sexuality extends along so many dimensions that aren't well described in terms of the gender of object choice at all. Some of these dimensions are habitually condensed under the rubrics of object choice, so that certain discriminations of (for instance) *act* or of (for another instance) *erotic localization* come into play, however implicitly and however incoherently, when categories of object choice are mobilized. One used to hear a lot, for instance, about a high developmental stage called 'heterosexual genitality', as though cross-gender object choice automatically erased desires attaching to mouth, anus, breasts, feet, etc.; a certain anal-erotic salience of male homosexuality is if anything increasingly strong under the glare of heterosexist AIDS-phobia; and several different historical influences have led to the de-genitalization and bodily diffusion of many popular, and indeed many lesbian, understandings of lesbian sexuality. Other dimensions of sexuality, however, distinguish object choice quite differently (e.g., human/animal, adult/child, singular/plural, autoerotic/ alloerotic) or are not even about object choice (e.g., orgasmic/nonorgasmic, noncommercial/commercial, using bodies only/using manufactured objects, in private/in public, spontaneous/scripted).[3] Some of these other dimensions of sexuality have had high diacritical importance in different historical contexts (e.g., human/animal, autoerotic/alloerotic). Others, like adult/child object choice, visibly do have such importance today, but without being very fully subsumed under the hetero/homosexual binarism. Still others, including a host of them I haven't mentioned or couldn't think of, subsist in this culture as nondiacritical differences, differences that seem to make little difference beyond themselves – except that the hyperintensive structuring of sexuality in our culture sets several of them, for instance, at the exact border between legal and illegal. What I mean at any rate to emphasize is that the implicit condensation of 'sexual theory' into 'gay/lesbian and antihomophobic theory', which corresponds roughly to our by now unquestioned reading of the phrase 'sexual orientation' to mean 'gender of object choice', is at the very least damagingly skewed by the specificity of its historical placement.

AXIOM 3: THERE CAN'T BE AN *A PRIORI* DECISION ABOUT
HOW FAR IT WILL MAKE SENSE TO CONCEPTUALIZE
LESBIAN AND GAY MALE IDENTITIES TOGETHER.
OR SEPARATELY.

Although it was clear from the beginning of this book project that its central
focus would be on male sexual definition, the theoretical tools for drawing a
circumferential boundary around that centre have been elusive. They have
changed perceptibly even during the period of this writing. In particular, the
interpretive frameworks within which lesbian writers, readers and inter-
locutors are likely to process male-centred reflections on homo/heterosexual
issues are in a phase of destabilizing flux and promise. . . .

Thus, it can no longer make sense, if it ever did, simply to assume that a
male-centred analysis of homo/heterosexual definition will have no lesbian
relevance or interest. At the same time, there are no algorithms for assuming
a priori what its lesbian relevance could be or how far its lesbian interest
might extend. It seems inevitable to me that the work of defining the
circumferential boundaries, *vis-à-vis* lesbian experience and identity, of any
gay male-centred theoretical articulation can be done only from the point of
view of an alternative, feminocentric theoretical space, not from the heart
of the male-centred project itself.

However interested I am in understanding those boundaries and their
important consequences, therefore, the project of this particular book, just
as it will not *assume* their geography, is not the one that can trace them.
That limitation seems a damaging one chiefly insofar as it echoes and
prolongs an already scandalously extended eclipse: the extent to which
women's sexual, and specifically homosexual, experience and definition tend
to be subsumed by men's during the turn-of-the-century period most
focused on in my discussion, and are liable once again to be subsumed *in*
such discussion. If one could demarcate the extent of the subsumption
precisely, it would be less destructive, but 'subsumption' is not a structure
that makes precision easy. The problem is obvious even at the level of
nomenclature and affects, of course, that of this book no less than any
other; I have discussed, above, the particular choices of usage made here.
Corresponding to those choices, the 'gay theory' I have been comparing
with feminist theory doesn't mean exclusively gay male theory, but for the
purpose of this comparison it includes lesbian theory insofar as that (*a*) isn't
simply co-extensive with feminist theory (i.e., doesn't subsume sexuality
fully under gender) and (*b*) doesn't *a priori* deny all theoretical continuity
between male homosexuality and lesbianism. But, again, the extent,
construction and meaning, and especially the history of any such theoretical
continuity – not to mention its consequences for practical politics – must be
open to every interrogation. That gay theory, falling under this definition

and centring insistently on lesbian experience, can still include strongly feminist thought would be demonstrated by works as different as those of Gayle Rubin, Audre Lorde, Katie King and Cherríe Moraga.

AXIOM 4: THE IMMEMORIAL, SEEMINGLY RITUALIZED DEBATES ON NATURE VERSUS NURTURE TAKE PLACE AGAINST A VERY UNSTABLE BACKGROUND OF TACIT ASSUMPTIONS AND FANTASIES ABOUT BOTH NURTURE AND NATURE.

If there is one compulsory set piece for the Introduction to any gay-oriented book written in the late 1980s, it must be the meditation on and attempted adjudication of constructivist versus essentialist views of homosexuality. The present study is hardly the first to demur vigorously from such a task, although I can only wish that its demurral might be vigorous enough to make it one of the last to need to do so. My demurral has two grounds. The first, as I have mentioned, is that any such adjudication is impossible to the degree that a conceptual deadlock between the two opposing views has by now been built into the very structure of every theoretical tool we have for undertaking it. The second one is already implicit in a terminological choice I have been making: to refer to 'minoritizing' versus 'universalizing' rather than to essentialist versus constructivist understandings of homosexuality. I prefer the former terminology because it seems to record and respond to the question, 'In whose lives is homo/heterosexual definition an issue of continuing centrality and difficulty?' rather than either of the questions that seem to have become conflated in the constructivist/essentialist debate: on the one hand what one might call the question of phylogeny, 'How fully are the meaning and experience of sexual activity and identity contingent on their mutual structuring with other, historically and culturally variable aspects of a given society?'; and on the other what one might call that of ontogeny, 'What is the cause of homo- [or of hetero-] sexuality in the individual?' I am specifically offering minoritizing/universalizing as an *alternative* (though not an equivalent) to essentialist/constructivist, in the sense that I think it can do some of the same analytic work as the latter binarism, and rather more tellingly. ...

In particular, my fear is that there currently exists no framework in which to ask about the origins or development of individual gay identity that is not already structured by an implicit, trans-individual Western project or fantasy of eradicating that identity. It seems ominously symptomatic that, under the dire homophobic pressures of the last few years, and in the name of Christianity, the subtle constructivist argument that sexual aim is, at least for many people, not a hard-wired biological given but, rather, a social fact

deeply embedded in the cultural and linguistic forms of many, many decades
is being degraded to the blithe *ukase* that people are 'free at any moment to'
(i.e., must immediately) 'choose' to adhere to a particular sexual identity
(say, at a random hazard, the heterosexual) rather than to its other. (Here
we see the disastrously unmarked crossing of phylogenetic with ontogenetic
narratives.) To the degree – and it is significantly large – that the gay
essentialist/constructivist debate takes its form and premises from, and insistently refers to, a whole history of other nature/nurture or nature/culture
debates, it partakes of a tradition of viewing culture as malleable relative to
nature: that is, culture, unlike nature, is assumed to be the thing that can be
changed; the thing in which 'humanity' has, furthermore, a right or even an
obligation to intervene. This has certainly been the grounding of, for
instance, the feminist formulation of the sex/gender system described above,
whose implication is that the more fully gender inequality can be shown to
inhere in human culture rather than in biological nature, the more amenable
it must be to alteration and reform. I remember the buoyant enthusiasm with
which feminist scholars used to greet the finding that one or another brutal
form of oppression was not biological but 'only' cultural! I have often
wondered what the basis was for our optimism about the malleability of
culture by any one group or programme. At any rate, never so far as I
know has there been a sufficiently powerful place from which to argue that
such manipulations, however triumphal the ethical imperative behind them,
were not a right that belonged to anyone who might have the power to
perform them.

   The number of persons or institutions by whom the existence of gay
people – never mind the existence of *more gay people* – is treated as a
precious desideratum, a needed condition of life, is small, even compared to
those who may wish for the dignified treatment of any gay people who
happen already to exist. Advice on how to make sure your kids turn out gay,
not to mention your students, your parishioners, your therapy clients, or
your military subordinates, is less ubiquitous than you might think. By contrast, the scope of institutions whose programmatic undertaking is to
prevent the development of gay people is unimaginably large. No major
institutionalized discourse offers a firm resistance to that undertaking; in the
United States, at any rate, most sites of the state, the military, education,
law, penal institutions, the church, medicine, mass culture, and the mental
health industries enforce it all but unquestioningly, and with little hesitation
even at recourse to invasive violence. So for gay and gay-loving people, even
though the space of cultural malleability is the only conceivable theatre for
our effective politics, every step of this constructivist nature/culture
argument holds danger: it is so difficult to intervene in the seemingly
natural trajectory that begins by identifying a place of cultural malleability;
continues by inventing an ethical or therapeutic mandate for cultural

manipulation; and ends in the overarching, hygienic Western fantasy of a world without any more homosexuals in it.

That's one set of dangers, and it is against them, I think, that essentialist understandings of sexual identity accrue a certain gravity. The resistance that seems to be offered by conceptualizing an unalterably *homosexual body*, to the social engineering momentum apparently built into every one of the human sciences of the West, can reassure profoundly. Furthermore, it reaches deeply and, in a sense, protectively into a fraught space of life-or-death struggle that has been more or less abandoned by constructivist gay theory: that is, the experience and identity of gay or proto-gay children. The ability of anyone in the culture to support and honour gay kids may depend on an ability to name them as such, notwithstanding that many gay adults may never have been gay kids and some gay kids may not turn into gay adults. It seems plausible that a lot of the emotional energy behind essentialist historical work has to do not even in the first place with reclaiming the place and eros of Homeric heroes, Renaissance painters, and medieval gay monks, so much as with the far less permissible, vastly more necessary project of recognizing and validating the creativity and heroism of the effeminate boy or tommish girl of the fifties (or sixties or seventies or eighties) whose sense of constituting precisely a *gap* in the discursive fabric of the given has not been done justice, so far, by constructivist work.

At the same time, however, just as it comes to seem questionable to assume that cultural constructs are peculiarly malleable ones, it is also becoming increasingly problematical to assume that grounding an identity in biology or 'essential nature' is a stable way of insulating it from societal interference. If anything, the gestalt of assumptions that under-gird nature/nurture debates may be in the process of direct reversal. Increasingly it is the conjecture that a particular trait is genetically or biologically based, *not* that it is 'only cultural', that seems to trigger an oestrus of manipulative fantasy in the technological institutions of the culture. A relative depressiveness about the efficacy of social engineering techniques, a high mania about biological control: the Cartesian bipolar psychosis that always underlay the nature/nurture debates has switched its polar assignments without surrendering a bit of its hold over the collective life. And in this unstable context, the dependence on a specified *homosexual body* to offer resistance to any gay-eradicating momentum is tremblingly vulnerable. AIDS, though it is used to proffer every single day to the news-consuming public the crystallized vision of a world after the homosexual, could never by itself bring about such a world. What whets these fantasies more dangerously, because more blandly, is the presentation, often in ostensibly or authentically gay-affirmative contexts, of biologically based 'explanations' for deviant behaviour that are absolutely invariably couched in terms of 'excess', 'deficiency', or 'imbalance' – whether in the hormones, in the genetic material, or, as is currently fashionable, in the foetal endocrine environment. If I had ever, in any medium, seen any researcher or popularizer refer even once to any supposed gay-producing circumstance as the *proper* hormone balance, or the *conducive* endocrine environment, for gay generation, I would be less chilled by the breezes of all this technological confidence. As things are, a medicalized dream of the prevention of gay bodies seems to be the less visible, far more respectable underside of the AIDS-fuelled public dream of their extirpation. In this unstable balance of assumptions between nature and culture, at any rate, under the overarching, relatively unchallenged aegis of a culture's desire that gay people *not be*, there is no unthreatened, unthreatening conceptual home for a concept of gay origins. We have all the more reason, then, to keep our understanding of gay origin, of gay cultural and material reproduction, plural, multi-capillaried, argus-eyed, respectful, and endlessly cherished.

AXIOM 5: THE HISTORICAL SEARCH FOR A GREAT PARADIGM SHIFT MAY OBSCURE THE PRESENT CONDITIONS OF SEXUAL IDENTITY.

Since 1976, when Michel Foucault, in an act of polemical bravado, offered 1870 as the date of birth of modern homosexuality,[4] the most sophisticated historically oriented work in gay studies has been offering ever more precise datings, ever more nuanced narratives of the development of homosexuality 'as we know it today'.[5] The great value of this scholarly movement has been to subtract from that 'as we know it today' the twin positivist assumptions (1) that there must be some *transhistorical* essence of 'homosexuality' available to modern knowledge, and (2) that the history of understandings of same-sex relations has been a history of increasingly direct, true knowledge or comprehension of that essence. To the contrary, the recent historicizing work has assumed (1) that the differences between the homosexuality 'we know today' and previous arrangements of same-sex relations may be so profound and so integrally rooted in other cultural differences that there may be no continuous, defining essence of 'homosexuality' to *be* known; and (2) that modern 'sexuality' and hence modern homosexuality are so intimately entangled with the historically distinctive contexts and structures that now count as *knowledge* that such 'knowledge' can scarcely be a transparent window onto a separate realm of sexuality but, rather, itself constitutes that sexuality.

These developments have promised to be exciting and productive in the way that the most important work of history or, for that matter, of anthropology may be: in radically defamiliarizing and denaturalizing, not only the past and the distant, but the present. One way, however, in which such an analysis is still incomplete – in which, indeed, it seems to me that it has tended inadvertently to *re*familiarize, *re*naturalize, damagingly reify an entity that it could be doing much more to subject to analysis – is in counterposing against the alterity of the past a relatively unified homosexuality that 'we' *do* 'know today'. It seems that the topos of 'homosexuality as we know it today', or even, to incorporate more fully the antipositivist finding of the Foucauldian shift, 'homosexuality as we *conceive of it* today', has provided a rhetorically necessary fulcrum point for the denaturalizing work on the past done by many historians. But an unfortunate side effect of this move has been implicitly to underwrite the notion that 'homosexuality as we conceive of it today' itself comprises a coherent definitional field rather than a space of overlapping, contradictory, and conflictual definitional forces. . . .

As an example of this contradiction effect, let me juxtapose two programmatic statements of what seem to be intended as parallel and congruent projects. In the foundational Foucault passage to which I alluded above, the modern category of 'homosexuality' that dates from 1870 is said to be

> characterized . . . less by a type of sexual relations than by a certain quality of sexual sensibility, a certain way of inverting the masculine and the feminine in oneself. Homosexuality appeared as one of the forms of sexuality when it was transposed from the practice of sodomy onto a kind of interior androgyny, a hermaphrodism of the soul. The sodomite had been a temporary aberration; the homosexual was now a species.

In Foucault's account, the unidirectional emergence in the late nineteenth century of 'the homosexual' as 'a species', of homosexuality as a minoritizing identity, is seen as tied to an also unidirectional, and continuing, emergent understanding of homosexuality in terms of gender inversion and gender transitivity. This understanding appears, indeed, according to Foucault, to underlie and constitute the common sense of the homosexuality 'we know today'. A more recent account by David M. Halperin, on the other hand, explicitly in the spirit and under the influence of Foucault but building, as well, on some intervening research by George Chauncey and others, constructs a rather different narrative – but constructs it, in a sense, *as if it were the same one*:

> Homosexuality and heterosexuality, as we currently understand them, are modern, Western, bourgeois productions. Nothing resembling them can be found in classical antiquity. . . . In London and Paris, in the seventeenth and eighteenth centuries, there appear . . . social gathering-places for persons of the same sex with the same socially deviant attitudes to sex and gender who wish to socialize and to have sex with one another. . . . This

phenomenon contributes to the formation of the great nineteenth-century experience of 'sexual inversion', or sex-role reversal, in which some forms of sexual deviance are interpreted as, or conflated with, gender deviance. The emergence of homosexuality out of inversion, the formation of a sexual orientation independent of relative degrees of masculinity and femininity, takes place during the latter part of the nineteenth century and comes into its own only in the twentieth. Its highest expression is the 'straight-acting and -appearing gay male', a man distinct from other men in absolutely no other respect besides that of his 'sexuality'.[6]

Halperin offers some discussion of why and how he has been led to differ from Foucault in discussing 'inversion' as a stage that in effect preceded 'homosexuality'. What he does not discuss is that his reading of 'homosexuality' as 'we currently understand' it – his presumption of the reader's commonsense, present-tense conceptualization of homosexuality, the point from which all the thought experiments of differentiation must proceed – is virtually the opposite of Foucault's. For Halperin, what is presumed to define modern homosexuality 'as we understand' it, in the form of the straight-acting and -appearing gay male, is gender intransitivity; for Foucault, it is, in the form of the feminized man or virilized woman, gender transitivity.

What obscures this difference between two historians, I believe, is the underlying structural congruence of the two histories: each is a unidirectional narrative of supersession. Each one makes an overarching point about the complete conceptual alterity of earlier models of same-sex relations. In each history one model of same-sex relations is superseded by another, which may again be superseded by another. In each case the superseded model then drops out of the frame of analysis. For Halperin, the power and interest of a postinversion notion of 'sexual orientation independent of relative degrees of masculinity and femininity' seem to indicate that that notion must necessarily be seen as superseding the inversion model; he then seems to assume that any elements of the inversion model still to be found in contemporary understandings of homosexuality may be viewed as mere historical remnants whose process of withering away, however protracted, merits no analytic attention. The end point of Halperin's narrative differs from that of Foucault, but his proceeding does not: just as Halperin, having discovered an important *intervening* model, assumes that it must be a *supervening* one as well, so Foucault had already assumed that the nineteenth-century intervention of a minoritizing discourse of sexual identity in a previously extant, universalizing discourse of 'sodomitic' sexual acts must mean, for all intents and purposes, the eclipse of the latter.

This assumption is significant only if – as I will be arguing – the most potent effects of modern homo/heterosexual definition tend to spring precisely from the inexplicitness or denial of the gaps *between* long-coexisting minoritizing and universalizing, or gender-transitive and gender-intransitive, understandings of same-sex relations. If that argument is true, however, then the enactment performed by these historical narratives has some troubling entailments. For someone who lives, for instance, as I do, in a state where certain acts called 'sodomy' are criminal regardless of the gender, never mind the homo/heterosexual 'identity', of the persons who perform them, the threat of the juxtaposition *on* that prohibition against *acts* of an additional, unrationalized set of sanctions attaching to *identity* can only be exacerbated by the insistence of gay theory that the discourse of acts can represent nothing but an anachronistic vestige. The project of the present book will be to show how issues of modern homo/heterosexual definition are structured, not by the supersession of one model and the consequent withering away of another, but instead by the relations enabled by the unrationalized coexistence of different models during the times they do coexist. This project does not involve the construction of historical narratives alternative to those that have emerged from Foucault and his followers. Rather, it requires a reassignment of attention and emphasis within those valuable narratives – attempting, perhaps, to denarrativize them somewhat by focusing on a performative space of contradiction that they both delineate and, themselves performative, pass over in silence. I have tended, therefore, in these chapters not to stress the alterity of disappeared or now-supposed-alien understandings of same-sex relations but instead to invest attention in those unexpectedly plural, varied, and contradictory historical understandings whose residual – indeed, whose renewed – force seems most palpable today. My first aim is to denaturalize the present, rather than the past – in effect, to render less destructively presumable 'homosexuality as we know it today'.

9

A Brief, Slanted History of 'Homosexual' Activity

Donald E. Hall

Is a 'queer' history even possible? Without a doubt, queers of various sorts have existed throughout history: individuals who have challenged openly or simply lived abrasively toward notions of the sexual and social norm. And as the coming pages will explore, it is clear that there has always been some form of sexual activity between men and between women, though how that activity manifested itself and the ways in which it was socially castigated or tolerated have varied greatly.

Yet the concept of 'a' queer history is nevertheless a problematic one. One of the most useful insights of late twentieth-century critical theory and reconceptualizations of historiography is that 'history' is always an artificial construct, one that depends upon numerous acts of interpretation, exclusion, and information shaping that reflect inevitably and indelibly the beliefs and biases of the historian or critic. The construction of any simple historical 'timeline' is particularly problematic from such a theoretical perspective. Even a single life does not 'develop' in neatly linear fashion; there are contra-dictions, reversals, recurrences, and anomalous actions that make biography writing an act always of creative writing. And when you take the complexity of a single life and exponentially increase it by the complexity of all lives, the notion that human history is reducible to a nice, clean line of causes, effects, progressions, and developments is really a bit ridiculous (however popular and comforting those wall charts showing the advance of world 'civilization' may be).

But even more to the point here, linearity becomes particularly artificial for our purposes because queers have lived often in ignorance of each other and of queer-relevant historical information from the near, as well as distant, past. Sexuality itself has frequently been ignored as part of historical record keeping, and sexual nonconformity, in particular, has often (though not always) gone unrecorded. Indeed, it was commonly feared that simply discussing sexual nonconformity would give people ideas about forms of sexual expression and gratification that would never have occurred to them otherwise. And certainly there is something to that fear. It is not that we

96

have to have a name for our desires before they urge themselves upon us; desire may be there already for any number of reasons (though also hearing about different sexual pleasures and possibilities may, itself, generate new and different forms of desire). But certainly naming something and giving it a history (either within an individual life or over a great span of years) does make it available as a way of organizing one's identity and of seeing and proactively creating affiliations.

Indeed, history writing – as reductive, biased, and creative as it may inevitably be – is a singularly important political act. I would caution that it needs questioning – queering – aggressively so it is never naturalized or con-cretized, but it is vital as a component of identity-creation and communal validation. There would be no popular and effective lesbian and gay rights movement today without a process of historical data-recovery, which opens up the possibility of affirming contemporary lives by looking backwards over time to find that we are not alone in our experiences of oppression and struggles for acceptance. History *motivates* by offering examples of what can happen if one fails to organize and fight back, by stoking one's anger over the many horrors perpetrated by generations of oppressors, and by creating a 'telos' (an end-point or goal): the present moment where action simply must be taken or a future moment of 'liberation' that one must fight to realize.

I do not want to forget that Anglo-American history as it will be discussed here is not only an act of creative writing for what it includes within its own 'story', but also for the vast numbers of peoples and stories across the globe and through time that it must ignore. There are many, many histories still to be written, used, and learned from. As lesbian historian Leila Rupp has suggested, 'History, for most historians [today], is not the one "true story". Rather it is a story as best we can tell it, given the evidence, our own assumptions and values, and the perspective we take from our own place in a particular society, at a specific point in time' (*A Desired Past*, 13–14).

So let me begin to set some of the parameters for our own slanted little story with a question or two. When and why did something so small and (potentially) insignificant as a man touching another man's penis or a woman caressing another woman's genitalia become a source of profound horror and a seeming threat to the very foundations of human moral, religious, and political structures? Why have such expressions of desire and acts of tenderness motivated torture, murder, and vehement, frothing diatribes by politicians, clergy, and medical personnel? Why does an act of love (or simply piqued sexual interest) between two individuals of the same biological sex still today generate genocidal hatred? Even more concretely put, why, when I hold the hand of my boyfriend at a restaurant, do some people want to kill me?

To answer these questions we do have to move backwards through time, to look at changing ideas, references, and resonances, some of which are still used today to justify harshly different valuations of what we now term hetero- and homosexuality. And in moving across millennia, we immediately face the problem of terminology, for there is no term or phrase that accurately subsumes both my holding hands with my boyfriend in Los Angeles in the twenty-first century *and* anal intercourse between an adult man and an adolescent boy in ancient Greece. I could call that latter activity 'gay', as some have, but that is simply a backwards projection, a limited and imprecise usage that obscures far too many complexities for a book such as this one. 'Gay' represents a modern stance concerning a well-formulated, highly politicized sexual identity. Some have argued that it is most appropriate to see 'gay' as a late twentieth-century identity label; others have traced its usage back to the last decades of the nineteenth century. But certainly 'I am gay' is only possible as a statement in a world in which sexuality is perceived as having an identity-determining capacity, and even then only gains weight and meaning in a context in which 'I am straight' (or something to that effect) is the generally approved social norm. That is not how people thought of themselves (or their 'selves') for most of human history, as difficult as it may be for some of us to understand that fact, since we are looking backwards through the lens of our own language and reference systems.

Perhaps the easiest way to conceptualize such a dramatic epistemological shift for the student new to this discussion is to think of some physical or preferential characteristic today that does not carry any particular weight. Let us say a preference for hot cereal over cold cereal for breakfast. That is not a distinction that we generally think about or to which we attribute any social value. Of course, if I am eating cold cereal one morning in a restaurant and I see someone else eating hot oatmeal, I suppose I might think to myself, 'ick, how can she eat that?' but probably it would not even register with me. And I am quite sure that I would never place her in a category of 'hot-cereal-eater' that would colour my perception of her through the rest of the day and forever afterwards. If we work together in the same office and I happen to see her in the hallway, images of her eating oatmeal would not suddenly spring to mind, nauseating me, and making me wish her dead or incarcerated. That is simply not how we in the twenty-first century classify individuals. Perhaps in the future we may rearrange our worldviews in such a way that we will divide up the world into categories of people arranged by breakfast preferences. At that point, if the hot-cereal-eaters are in the majority or have particular political sway, cold-cereal-eating might be outlawed and cold-cereal-eaters violently oppressed. 'Coldies', existing covertly, might then form secret support networks; a few may risk arrest by campaigning publicly for a decriminalization of cold-cereal-eating, etc. Those individuals might not be able to look back on our day and imagine that it was possible that we did not see the profound identity difference between hot-cereal-eaters and cold-cereal-eaters. They would be looking at us through the lens of their own identity constructs.

Obviously the above analogy is a simplistic and problematic one. Sexuality and desire were never as wholly inconsequential as breakfast food preferences are today. But it is important to recognize that we cannot extrapolate from our own worldviews and think of them as 'natural' or 'normal' across vast expanses of time. Nor can we even use them accurately across cultures today. If I walk hand-in-hand with another man on the streets of Los Angeles, I am correctly interpreted as someone who has sexual contact with other men. If two men walk hand-in-hand down a road in rural Congo or India, it would be wholly erroneous to assume that they are sexually active with each other. Facile impositions of one individual's or group's conception of the 'normal' or 'natural' is precisely what the queer theories that we will explore later engage, critique, and ultimately reject as oppressive and grossly reductive.

In looking backwards over centuries, all we can do is attempt to tease out the identity constructs that were available and circulating in a culture and at a particular time. 'Gay' as a term signalling an assertion of self-aware and self-respecting sexual identity is one best left for referencing the twentieth century and today. And it is most accurately used for men alone. 'Lesbian' as an identifying term distinct from 'gay' identity is also centrally important here, even though lesbians and gay men have often interacted politically and socially and in ways also worth noting. 'Homosexual' and 'heterosexual' too are recent identifiers, dating from late nineteenth-century medical terminology. They are not at all accurate as terms for labelling identities from previous centuries, though they are useful for describing specific activities between members of the same sex or different sexes. In other words, two men from the medieval era, who had anal intercourse, could be said to have engaged in 'homosexual' activity (as a descriptor of sexual contact between members of the same sex), even if it would be wholly erroneous to describe them as self-aware 'homosexuals' of the nineteenth- or twentieth-century variety. In the coming pages I will use 'homosexual' only in that manner, to describe acts not individuals. And even then I acknowledge fully that it is an anachronistic and problematic usage (which is why I put 'homosexual' in quotation marks in this chapter's title). It is simply a convenient one that I will complicate as necessary.

So with these complications out of the way, let us return to the question posed earlier: when and why did one woman touching another's flesh or one man fondling another's body become invested with the power to elicit hyperbolic, even hysterical, social reactions? It was not always so. As historian David M. Halperin and philosopher Michel Foucault have explored, sexual paradigms during the Classical Greek era were far different. While we know much more about how men organized their sexual lives during that and most other eras than we do about how women interacted sexually, we do know that homosexual activity, within certain boundaries, was not regarded as a threat to society. Indeed, in some narrowly defined manifestations, it was idealized and celebrated. Greek mythology makes many references to same-sex erotic desire, especially between adult men and what we would now term 'adolescent' boys. And other philosophical and literary writings, as well as artistic representations, from the era suggest that such contact was countenanced by (perhaps was even common among) the privileged Greek citizenry. While this may seem shocking to us, and we may wish to project backwards our contemporary notions of 'child abuse' to condemn it, such an anachronistic imposition tells us much more about the power of our categories than anything particularly useful about the Greeks. That sexual contact between patrician men and boys was 'naturalized' at the time prompts us to see our own systems of organizing social/sexual relations as similarly time-bound. The 'natural' has little trans-historical grounding.

Indeed, as Halperin explores in *One Hundred Years of Homosexuality*, adult male sexuality during the Classical era had much more to do with power status and social positioning than it did with any expression of identity-determining desire for the same or other sex. Sexual contact between two adult men or two adult women, while it no doubt occurred, was not itself an activity that provided a basis for self-assertions of identity, as far as we know. Social standing – what we might loosely call social 'class' – was the means by which individuals conceived of themselves and their place in the world. Pederastic activity was one means by which privileged men manifested their dominance over others. Of course, how *dominance* specifically piqued sexual desire and what that may or may not tell us about sexual relationships during other eras or today is a topic still demanding considerable scrutiny, research, and theorizing.

And beyond those intergenerational manifestations, same-sex desire was referenced in several important ways during the Greek era that resonated through later time periods and that deserve special note here. During the sixth century BC, the poet Sappho wrote nine books of emotionally charged and erotic verses, many concerning young women (though only a few of them survive today as anything other than tiny fragments). Both the term 'Sapphic' and, of course, 'Lesbian' (which derives from the name of her home island, Lesbos) have come down to us through the ages as terms for women who desire other women. And Sappho's iconic status is no twentieth-century projection backwards; she and her homoerotic verses were very well known during her own day, and her poetry was highly celebrated by Plato and others.

And Plato is another major source of Classical articulation on same-sex desire that has implications still. His dialogues contain various references to pederastic desire as mentioned above, but also, in his *Symposium*, he foregrounds a major statement by Aristophanes that has relevance to our discussion of identity construction even in the twenty-first century. In his statement, Aristophanes theorizes that the world was once made up of conjoined beings, some of mixed sex, others of two men or two women. When Zeus divided these conjoined beings into separate individuals, sexuality was determined by the search for one's missing half, either of the same or different sex. This broad understanding of sexuality as metaphysically determined (even divinely ordained) is something that we will see queer theories question aggressively, as useful as it may be for the purposes of arguing that a particular identity is 'natural'. While the search for a 'soul mate' may be celebrated widely even today in popular discourse, queer theories will treat with scepticism the transcendental bases of such terminology.

But even if (we might say) some things thus stay the same, others certainly change dramatically. The Greek era's relative tolerance for select forms of homosexual activity (and expressions of homoerotic desire in literature) gave way to very harsh proscriptions against all sexual activity outside of heterosexual marriage during the Christian era. While John Boswell in *Christianity, Social Tolerance, and Homosexuality* (an immensely popular work from 1980) suggests that the early church sometimes countenanced same-sex relations, Carolyn Dinshaw and other recent medievalists have carefully pointed out the many horrors perpetrated against 'sodomites' during the entire era. Dinshaw summarizes, responds to, and substantially revises Boswell's readings as she explores the severe penalties for all erotic contact between members of the same sex. From church records, we know that sexual activity certainly occurred in the same-sex communities of convents and monasteries, but also that biblical injunctions against such contact (contained primarily in Leviticus and the story of divine wrath against Sodom and Gomorrah) fuelled a persecution of homosexually active individuals there and across society. Sodomites were punished with castration, incarceration, and by the thirteenth century (if not earlier) public execution. Fuelling this escalating persecution was the distinct fear that homosexual activity within religious communities would threaten the involved individuals' primary allegiance to the church hierarchy. Across society, one might also see the increased persecution of sodomites as a result of the ascendancy of a network of Christian theocratic states that was determined to repudiate pagan/Greek activities, enforce a gender order that kept women in a state of sexual and social servitude to men (and men channelling their sexual energies into creating new church members), and divide individuals into clear-cut domestic units that rendered political and social control much easier to achieve and maintain. Indeed, the persecution of such individuals was thus overdetermined, demonstrating for us how a 'norm' is often multiply reinforced. Thus

it is important to recognize that a medieval man engaging in anal intercourse with another man was committing a 'crime against nature' that was
really a crime against the church and the state. The category of 'nature' is
always influenced by – and in some instances wholly determined by – such
political interests.

Yet, as noted, these and other 'crimes' certainly still occurred among men
and also among women. Historian Judith Brown has carefully searched the
historical archive for medieval church articulations on and persecutions of
women who had sexual contact with other women, and has offered some
important insights. She first explores the context for St Augustine's fifth-
century warnings to his sister against homosexual carnality and carefully
accounts for new prohibitions against nuns sleeping together devised by
councils of Paris and Rouen in the early thirteenth century. Yet after
probing these few references, she stresses that given the clear 'knowledge
that Europeans had about the possibility of lesbian sexuality, their [relative]
neglect of the subject in law, theology, and literature suggests an almost
active willingness to *dis*believe' ('Lesbian Sexuality', 69). She concludes that
'Even more than male sodomy, sodomy between females was "the sin which
cannot be named"' and such '[s]ilence bred confusion and confusion bred
fear. On these foundations Western society built an impenetrable barrier
that has lasted for nearly two centuries' (75).

Indeed, 'naming' something – even in prohibitive fashion – does carry
with it the possibility of identification 'with' as well as 'against'. Explicit
proscriptions against male sodomy served to heighten the possibility that
some individuals who enjoyed, for whatever reason, sexual activity with
another man would seek out ways of organizing, arranging, and structuring
their time, energy, and movements in order to gratify secretively their
desires. Oppression often breeds very creative forms of resistance. Sodomy
between men was made a crime punishable by death in English civil law
starting in the sixteenth century. Early seventeenth-century laws in the
American colonies were similarly harsh. Yet we know that around the same
time in England houses of male prostitution began to appear in London and
that men developed networks of subcultural connection through which they
could meet other men who also desired sex. As Alan Bray and other
historians have explored, 'molly-houses' were meeting places for men who
wished to arrange sexual encounters with other men. Most of these
individuals were probably married and as always it would be erroneous to
call them 'gay' or 'homosexual' since those terms were unavailable to them.
But unlike previous eras, a social and cultural space started to open up
whereby a secretive identity, one clearly centring on homosexual contact,
began to develop – and in ways that we can broadly see as a precursor to a
modern notion of homosexual identity. Thus even though it would be
reductive to chart the linear 'rise' of a homosexual identity, it is vital to

recognize how traditions and cultural/subcultural systems do develop over time. Identity constructs are belief systems that spread by word of mouth, by movements of people, and through the printed word and other media (the stage, the web today, etc.), all over time. Without seeing the patterns of social organization that resulted from increased persecution of homosexual activity during the medieval era and the creative arrangements that we know existed in the Renaissance, it would be hard to appreciate how the specific parameters of homosexuality today developed.

And certainly the narrowness of notions of 'proper' sexual activity led to resistance of some very interesting sorts. The 'libertine' identity of the seventeenth and eighteenth centuries, as explored by Randolph Trumbach and other scholars, was a radical sexual identity theorized by upper-class men who wished to challenge the power of the church and state to control their right to use their own genitalia as they wished. Its limitation to a certain class and gender tells us much about how narrow some 'liberation' or liberationist movements can often be – representing only the interests of a few privileged individuals – but it also reveals to us something about what was happening during the seventeenth and eighteenth centuries regarding a proliferating discourse of individual rights (over and above the rights of the church, king, or civil government). This is a watershed era during which notions of 'natural' social roles and unquestionable obedience to the aristocracy and church hierarchy began to give way to a sense of changeable and challengeable social relationships. Such increased social flexibility and fluidity were abetted by challenges to biblical beliefs posed by science, and the new mobility in social class fuelled by urbanization, industrialization, and a growing mercantile economy. The 'libertine' identity portrayed in the writings of the Marquis de Sade and others, in which sexual gratification of practically any sort – with members of the same or other sex, in whatever combination or grouping desired – is an important manifestation of a counter-discourse that reflected a new mind-set of challenge to what had been deemed normal and natural. In this way, libertinage serves as something of a precursor to queer theories today, though with its own rich historical context and complex internal rules, which George Haggerty has explored in *Men in Love: Masculinity and Sexuality in the Eighteenth Century*. And certainly de Sade's incarceration and the continued persecution and execution of sexual nonconformists make very clear just how threatening sexual 'individualism' was, even when other manifestations and celebrations of individual rights proliferated. The right to the 'pursuit of happiness', as proclaimed in the US Declaration of Independence, did not include the right to pursue sexual contact with another man or woman, however happy that might make one.

As we draw closer to our own day, the forms and functionings of sexuality become ever more recognizable. In Michel Foucault's well-known assessment from *The History of Sexuality: An Introduction*, '[t]he nineteenth-century homosexual became a personage, a past, a case history, and a childhood, in addition to being a type of life, a life form, and a morphology, with an indiscreet anatomy and possibly a mysterious physiology' (43). While he is clearly over-simplifying when he asserts that '1870' stands as the precise date of the 'birth' of the 'medical category of homosexuality' (43), Foucault makes an important larger point that we continue to live today with certain powerful Victorian classifications and identity categorizations.

As the breakdown of 'natural', 'fixed' social identities continued through the nineteenth century – with the continuing erosion of birthright in the determination of class identity, the challenge posed by the women's move-ment to 'natural' spheres in gender identity, and the undermining of religious authority through scientific research and evolutionary theory – the disquiet-ing potential for the loss of all fixed social references and stable definitions abetted the rise of the so-called 'social sciences': sociology, psychology, and anthropology, among them. Claiming scientific objectivity, practitioners in these fields set about charting human behaviour and social organization in ways that served to define and maintain forms of social 'order' that often protected the interests of select privileged groups. Nineteenth-century theorists of race, such as W. B. Stevenson and Joseph Arthur Gobineau, devised elaborate charts that classified individuals by skin tone and physiol-ogy into 'higher' and 'lower' forms of life and social development. As I have discussed in *Fixing Patriarchy*, theorists of gender, responding to the women's movement of the era, attempted to reinforce skewed notions of men's and women's roles by marshalling quasi-scientific 'evidence' to 'prove' women's inferior capacities outside of the domestic sphere. And as Foucault has explored, the medical and scientific community set out to chart sexual normality and abnormality, working to define and justify proper expressions of sexual desire, and diagnose, account for, and perhaps 'cure' improper expressions of same-sex desires and other 'perversions', ones that threatened the interests of a still expanding, reproduction-dependent economy organized and regulated through monogamous, patriarchally controlled domestic units.

Indeed, nineteenth-century sexologists began to construct elaborate theories detailing 'normal' and 'abnormal' sexualities, their manifestations, genesis, and social consequences. As Jonathan Ned Katz points out in *The Invention of Heterosexuality*:

In August, 1869, a German medical journal published an article by Dr. K. F. O. Westphal that first named an emotion he called 'Die contrare Sexualempfindung' ('contrary sexual feeling'). That emotion was 'con-trary' to the proper, procreative 'sexual feeling' of men and women. Westphal's contrary sexual feeling was the first, and became one of the best known, contenders in the late-nineteenth-century name-that-perversion contest. (54)

Other sexologists of the era began to work diligently to further refine sexual categories. Richard von Krafft-Ebing's encyclopaedic *Psychopathia Sexualis* from 1886 thoroughly pathologizes homosexuality, seeing it and a wide array of other 'perversions' not only as manifestations of individual illness but as clear indicators of a degenerating society. What an individual did with her or his own genitals and other body parts was thus ever more highly politicized and overloaded with meaning. Anxieties over social dissolution, circulating because of a wide array of economic, religious and political uncertainties, fixated (not solely, but certainly powerfully) on the figure of the sexual nonconformist. Having always been carried on in private, sexuality was 'a' secret (perhaps 'the' secret) that once fully revealed and properly controlled would secure us all. Not surprisingly, Krafft-Ebing seems especially disturbed by the possibility that an individual might move from sexual conformity to nonconformity by 'choice', which he calls 'cultivated pederasty' and terms 'one of the saddest pages in the history of human delinquency' (601). Temporal changes in sexuality or sexual self-identification and eager explorations across identity boundaries are particularly disquieting for the fixers and categorizers of identity.

Yet, as always, those expressions of explicit condemnation continued to breed resistance. Another early sexologist, Karl Ulrichs, devised an elaborate schema in his writings from the 1860s and 1870s to explain homosexuality as 'natural', partially through references back to Plato, just as we have explored here. Ultimately, Ulrichs based his defence of homosexuality on the premise that same-sex desiring individuals had the soul of the other sex's body trapped within them. Ulrichs thereby meant to validate homosexuality as metaphysically determined, yet as Joseph Bristow has noted, 'this idea would have a lasting and damaging influence on twentieth-century prejudices against homosexuals. For it set the trend for imagining that lesbians and gay men were "inverts"' (*Sexuality*, 21–2). 'Inverted' individuals were (supposedly) recognizable because they always demonstrated the gender characteristics of the sex of the soul within them: gay men were theorized as always effeminate and lesbians as always masculine. This conflation and confusion of gender and sexuality gained further implicit support in Havelock Ellis's treatise *Sexual Inversion* from 1897, which decried social prejudices against homosexuals but still used a model of easily recognizable 'normal' and 'abnormal' behaviour that attempted only to replace vicious homophobia with something like pity for the invert. Such pathos resonated through literary characterizations even well into the twentieth century, with Radclyffe Hall's characterizations of miserable 'inverted' women in *The Well of Loneliness* (1928) standing as the starkest example.

How did these changing theories and scientific paradigms affect the activities and daily lives of men and women during the nineteenth century who actually engaged in homosexual activity? Here as always it is difficult to know precisely. Most people going about their day-to-day activities do not leave written records of their thoughts and actions; the few documents that are readily available include arrest and court records, autobiographies, and personal letters. We do know from the very frank autobiographical accounts of the Victorian writer John Addington Symonds that same-sex erotic activity was rampant in boys' boarding schools at mid-century. Furthermore, we have many legal documents to chart an increasing persecution of 'homosexuals' toward the end of the century, as that term began to circulate and as fears of social disintegration and changeable social identity became ever more fixated on the scapegoat of the sexual degenerate. The best documented case was the 1890s trials of Oscar Wilde, the popular and eccentric Victorian playwright. Wilde unwisely and unsuccessfully challenged in court the labeling of him as a 'somdomite' (a misspelling of sodomite) by the father of his lover, Alfred Douglas. In that libel case and the subsequent prosecution of him for 'crimes against nature', the Victorian press publicized in wildly inflammatory ways Wilde's eccentric dress, effeminate manner, and haughty demeanour, all held up as important signifiers of his unnatural sexuality and the threat he posed to 'normal', middle-class values. But even though Wilde's case was certainly a tragic one – he died in 1900 after having served two years in prison at hard labour – the figure of Wilde the aesthete, dandy, and campy witticist, also became a powerful one as a new public icon for homosexual men in Britain and America. As the first person widely and publicly identified as 'a' homosexual, Wilde influenced generations of men who came to model themselves after (or sometimes define themselves against) him.

But the dramatic figure of Wilde obscures the many ways that same-sex desiring men lived their lives in hidden and anonymous fashion during the nineteenth century, as in centuries before and decades afterwards. As Jeffrey Weeks, Angus McClaren and William Cohen have explored through court documents from the era, we know that male prostitution existed, that men were occasionally arrested for dressing as women, and that others were prosecuted for soliciting and engaging in 'indecent' acts in parks and elsewhere. And, of course, untold numbers of men carried on active sexual lives with other men in ways that were never noticed or known. Victorian pornography details sexual activity between men and women, men and men, and women and women, in pairs and groups, that can hardly be deemed sociologically reliable, but certainly tells us something about the possibilities that existed within the imagination (and perhaps lived experiences) of some Victorians. As I have explored in my overview of erotica from the period, 'Graphic Sexuality and the Erasure of a Polymorphous Perversity', sexually explicit writings from the century demonstrate some clear shifts in points of reference and internal delineations of acceptable and unacceptable same-sex activity over the course of the century. These, too, however, are clearly most relevant to the lives – in or outside of print texts – of literate-class men.

We know much less about working-class sex lives and, as always, relatively little about women's sex lives of the period. Historian Leila Rupp tells of her close personal relationship with her 'maiden' Aunt Leila (born just after the end of the 'Victorian era') but admits that even she does not know if her now-deceased aunt was 'a lesbian'. Even though Aunt Leila lived all of her adult life with another woman, and even shared a bed with her 'friend', Rupp writes,

> I don't know anything about Aunt Leila's desire, sexual behavior, or self-conception. But of course we don't know about such things for most people in the past. And that's the problem. The difficulty of locating sources that document same-sex love and sexuality is legendary. Reflecting the modern Western association of women with love and men with sex, the evidence in the case of women, as the story of Aunt Leila so aptly illustrates, tends to reveal [only] emotional attachments to other women. . . . It's not that women never had sex . . . just that our evidence is skewed. (*A Desired Past*, 5)

Thus historian Lillian Faderman, in *Surpassing the Love of Men*, has traced the 'romantic' friendships of women across many centuries in Britain and America, but acknowledges that it is impossible to know when and in what form sexual contact occurred between women who cohabited or publicly expressed their ardent feelings for each other. She, Rupp, and others remind us that it would be foolish to surmise that sexual activity between women was rare or nonexistent simply because it was not written about or was rarely mentioned in the annals of legal activity. Patriarchal belief systems, serving the interests of men and male-dominated institutions such as the church, expressly denied women the capacity or right to feel sexual desires except as channelled into the structure of marriage and reproduction. Of course, prostitution, adultery, and other forms of castigated and punished sexual expression were discussed in legal and other venues as a mechanism whereby 'good' women (chaste and cheerful wives, devoted mothers, etc.) were differentiated from fallen or 'bad' women (whores, etc.): the former were pure, loyal to men, and, in theory, always sexually naive.

That women's sexuality was little discussed except in such exemplary cases had complex implications. The fact that women's independently acted-upon sexuality was thought improbable, except among greedy and unnatural prostitutes and morally bankrupt adultresses, meant that laws often wholly ignored lesbianism, even when sexual contact between men was outlawed and severely punished. As we have seen, homosexual activity between men

was a crime punishable by death for many centuries in Britain. Homosexual
activity between women was never explicitly criminalized. And, as Rupp
suggests above, the common patriarchal association between women and
emotion and the greater scope allowed for women's emotional expression
meant that women could openly express affection toward each other in
public without anyone interpreting it as an indicator of sexual activity.
Though we would never want to ignore the many ways that women were
harshly oppressed by sexist ideologies, it is clear that such obtuse beliefs
provided a very useful cover for women who did live sexually nonconformist
lives. Only with the rise of the women's rights movement – and its dramatic
successes in the twentieth century – did popular perceptions widen to
recognize and explicitly castigate sexual activity between women.

    And this does bring us to the remarkable and well-documented activity of
the twentieth century. The rise of political rights movements – which worked
to redress social injustices of race, class, and gender – began in the eighteenth
century and proliferated during the nineteenth century. As we discussed
above, this was not because oppression itself necessarily increased during
that time (though sometimes it did) but more directly because individuals
newly thought of themselves as having inherent rights that the state and
privileged groups too often intruded upon or denied them. And thus we can
say that 'identity' became ever more 'political' as individuals banded together
in organizations – small and large, highly public, and sometimes very
secretive – to explore their commonalities, discuss their common experiences
of injustice, and strategize to change oppressive laws, policies, and social
perceptions. Twentieth-century 'lesbian and gay' rights movements were
greatly indebted to women's rights movements and African-American rights
movements from previous generations. The somewhat later manifestation of
sexual rights movements when compared to most others is attributable to
several factors. Sexuality is less directly tied to specific physical characteristics and clear outer markers of identity, thus social designation and
self-perception occurred at a later date. With the social category of 'homosexual' arising only in the nineteenth century, the overt politicization of that
identity base lagged behind the politicization of well-defined categories
such as 'woman' or 'Black'. Furthermore, sexuality itself was often held to
be unmentionable and the breaking of silence on 'unnatural' sexual activity
involved an especially deep shame and embarrassment that had to be
overcome. While the self-identifying statement 'I am a woman' or 'I am
working class' certainly carried with it an extraordinary range of cultural
valuations and expectations, it did not carry with it the embarrassment or the likelihood of immediate public scorn and violent reaction that
the revelation 'I am a homosexual' did.

    And certainly we cannot discuss the general social stigma (and sense of
shame) associated with homosexuality that lingered through much of the

twentieth century without mentioning its most influential early theoretician, Sigmund Freud, whose systemization of the field of psychology in the decades around the turn of the century gave the discipline a new legitimacy and social power. His complicated legacy endures to this day. While Freud's statements on homosexuality are inconsistent over the course of his career, in most of his writings he does portray it as a state of misdirected erotic energies resulting from childhood traumas and unfinished developmental processes. Lesbian historian Margaret Cruikshank has noted that Freud

> speculated that homosexuality involved a narcissistic search for a love that symbolizes the self, a castration fear for men and penis envy for women. He did not regard it as a sickness, however, or as a condition that could be changed, and thus he opposed criminal punishments for homosexuality. Freud believed that the natural sexual feelings of children are both homosexual and heterosexual and that social conditioning usefully represses both bisexuality and homosexuality. Thus a homosexual person is arrested in his or her development. Followers of Freud, especially in the United States, interpreted this to mean that homosexuals are perpetually adolescents, immature, blocked in some way, incapable of leading normal lives. Abandoning Freud's tolerant views, his disciples advocated treatment for homosexuality. (*The Gay and Lesbian Liberation Movement*, 7)

Yet I would reiterate that Freud was certainly no paragon of tolerance. In his *Three Essays on the Theory of Sexuality* (1905) he fans fear and bigotry in warning that 'The education of boys by male persons ... seems to encourage homosexuality' (96) and clearly links homosexuality with mental illness in numerous claims such as 'The unconscious mental life of all neurotics (without exception) shows inverted impulses, fixation of their libido upon persons of their own sex' (32). As Peter Gay notes in *The Tender Passion*, 'For Freud, heterosexual genital love-making was ... an achievement, the culmination of a long, never painless, and never quite complete evolution. [This] perception of sexual unfolding retained the normative hierarchy that had gone barely challenged through most of the Christian centuries' (251–2). Freud's heterocentric, normative system of value and reference heavily influenced generations of psychoanalysts and therapists, whose all-too-frequent condescension toward homosexuals reinforced a sense of self-hatred and shame. And Freud's theories and values were widely known even beyond the medical community. As Lillian Faderman notes in *Surpassing the Love of Men*, 'It would not have been necessary to read Freud's essays on "Sexual Aberrations" or "The Psychogenesis of a Case of Homosexuality in a Woman" in order to know that love between women was now an indication of childhood trauma and arrested development. Writers of popular literature, who may or may not have gone back to the original sources themselves, regurgitated the information for mass delectation' (315).

Yet in spite of this pathologizing of homosexuality, individuals began to risk popular scorn and embarrassment, as well as imprisonment, in increasing numbers during the twentieth century to assert that homosexuality was not a criminal, degenerate, or mentally disordered state. At the same time as Freud and other sexologists were devising elaborate theories proving the centrality of heterosexuality to a healthy society, Edward Carpenter in *The Intermediate Sex* (1908) and other works was arguing that the increasing incidence of 'uranism' (or homosexuality) was the harbinger of a new day of sexual freedom for all. And while an open political rights movement on lesbian and gay issues only developed toward the end of the twentieth century, private movements and scattered public actions date from the last decades of the nineteenth century and proliferated thereafter. In Germany, Magnus Hirschfeld founded the Institute for Sexology in 1919, which was specifically devoted to furthering rights for women and homosexuals; while his Institute was destroyed by the Nazis in 1933 (and the Third Reich went on to incarcerate and murder many thousands of homosexuals), Hirschfeld's work was internationally known and planted the seeds of other activist organizations in Europe and America. George Chauncey's *Gay New York*, Lillian Faderman's *To Believe in Women*, and Leila Rupp's *A Desired Past* all document the many and inventive ways that lesbians and gay men created supportive communities in the United States, especially after the turn of the twentieth century. What these historians reveal is just how creative and brave oppressed individuals can be as they create their own codes of behaviour in order to recognize each other without risking public discovery, and also begin to form neighbourhoods and social groups that allow them a space for self-expression and validation. Chauncey's remarkable book shows that in certain areas of New York City during the period of the 1890s to the 1930s men lived relatively open lives as self-proclaimed 'fairies' and 'queers', in ways recognized by the general public and even commented upon by the press, though they always thereby risked arrest, harassment, and other forms of persecution.

What Chauncey, Faderman and Rupp urge us to recognize today is that as much as we like to consider ourselves in the twenty-first century as uniquely self-aware and political, earlier generations were certainly capable of dramatic political statements and were hardly the self-hating and silent individuals that we may too often consider them to be. In simply existing 'queerly', people were living in ways that had a political impact, sometimes large, sometimes small and more diffusive. Of course, if we define the 'political' more narrowly as well-organized efforts to challenge laws, policies, and perceptions, then lesbian and gay political movements only developed in Britain and America during the middle and later decades of the twentieth century. The first political 'action groups' date from the 1950s, with the creation of the Mattachine Society and the Daughters of Bilitis on the west coast of the United States. The former began as a small movement of men, led by Harry Hay in Los Angeles, with ideological ties to the anti-Korean War movement and Communist Party (though it became considerably less radical later in the decade), and the latter as a small group of women, led by Del Martin and Phyllis Lyon in San Francisco, seeking to create an alternative to the covert bar scene of the day. Both groups generated publications, *One* and *The Ladder* (respectively), that began to circulate and that helped inaugurate a national gay and lesbian rights consciousness. Recent queer, as well as gay and lesbian, rights movements owe much to the path-breaking work of such groups.

Equally foundational to a deepening twentieth-century consciousness and politicization of sexuality (and with implications that still bear consideration) were the Kinsey Reports on sexuality, first published in the 1940s and 1950s. While Kinsey's methodology was problematic and his statistics generally unreliable, the 'facts' and 'figures' of the first Kinsey Report on male sexuality still linger in our system of reference today. As Chauncey notes,

> [M]ost recent commentary on the Kinsey Report has focused on (and criticized) its supposed estimate that 10 percent of the population were homosexuals, [but] Kinsey himself never made such an estimate and argued explicitly that such estimates could not be based on his findings. His research is much more helpful is if used, as Kinsey intended, to examine the extent of occasional homosexual behavior among men who may or may not have identified themselves as 'homosexual'. Only 4 percent of the men he interviewed reported having been exclusively homosexual in their behavior throughout their lives, but 37 percent acknowledged having engaged in at least one postadolescent homosexual encounter to the point of orgasm, and fully a quarter of them acknowledged having had 'more than incidental homosexual experience or reactions' for at least three years between the ages of sixteen and fifty-five.   (*Gay New York*, 70)

Somewhat lower but similar patterns of experience were charted among women surveyed for the report on women's sexuality published in 1953. As John D'Emilio has explored in *Sexual Politics, Sexual Communities*, these reports had wide-ranging significance both inside and outside of the lesbian and gay community. The startlingly high numbers of homosexual activity (though not 'identity') that Kinsey reported served at times 'not to ameliorate hostility toward gay men and lesbians, but to magnify the proportions of the danger they allegedly posed' (37). But D'Emilio also points out that

> [a]mong homosexuals and lesbians themselves, Kinsey had a more clearly beneficial impact. Scientific evidence appeared to confirm what many gay

people in the 1940s were experiencing – the sense of belonging to a group. Moreover, by revealing that millions of Americans exhibited a strong erotic interest in their own sex, the reports implicitly encouraged those still struggling in isolation against their sexual preference to accept their homosexual inclinations and search for sexual comrades.   (37)

And Chauncey makes an important additional point worth mentioning here, for as understandable as these usages of Kinsey were for the purposes of self-validation, the implications of Kinsey's research – that sexuality can change dramatically over time and in response to context, and that sexual activity does not necessarily have to lead to self-identification – have yet to be fully acknowledged and grappled with by most sexual rights movements even today. It is easy but finally reductive to read onto complex human behaviour and emotions the artificial binary 'heterosexual/homosexual' and categorize often diverse activities and multi-faceted identities as belonging to one 'side' alone. Indeed, self-validation along those lines by lesbians and gay men has often led to a facile diagnosis of 'not accepting' one's 'true' homosexual self if one has occasional or passing erotic contact with members of both sexes. Even one homosexual encounter can be taken by some as proof of 'really' being lesbian or gay, and of living in an unhealthy state of denial if one fails to self-identify as such.

Yet certainly a general discourse of validation was working to heighten the political awareness, commitment, and activity of groups of lesbians and gay men after the mid-century. And if there is a watershed moment demonstrating this – one that is now commonly hailed by lesbian and gay rights groups – it is the 'Stonewall Riots' beginning on 28 June 1969. In the middle of a routine raid by vice cops on a gay bar in New York, several hundred incensed patrons, tired of harassment, resisted by throwing bottles, rocks, and other objects at police. Skirmishes between the law and groups of angry lesbian, gay, and transgendered individuals continued for several days. While obviously it is reductive to call this the 'birth' of the gay civil rights movement, since individuals and groups had been doing important work for many years, the Stonewall Riots are certainly important as a marker and as a common point of reference (one that continues to be celebrated today in the form of annual 'gay and lesbian' pride festivals and marches throughout the month of June). The late 1960s saw an increasing radicalization of social movements working for the civil rights of women and minorities, and Stonewall was an important manifestation of a newly broadened concern with oppression and a new willingness to take to the streets to demand an end to discrimination. Dennis Altman, in *Homosexual: Oppression and Liberation* from 1971, offers some superb insights into and historical details concerning these early days of the specifically 'gay liberation' movement in New York. Guy Hocquenghem provides important information on French activities and organizations of the same era in *Homosexual Desire* (1972). Jeffrey Weeks is equally incisive in his analysis of British social history in *Coming Out* (1977). I recommend these books highly for readers pursuing research on that era.

And this willingness to challenge oppression also manifested itself *within* civil rights movements and organizations, as well as in the larger public sphere. The relationship between the women's movement and the lesbian rights movement was strained in the third quarter of the twentieth century. Liberal feminists, wishing to achieve parity with men in business, education, and the political arena, often sought to distance themselves from lesbians seeking civil rights. The epithet 'dyke' hurled against all feminists served to fracture women's rights organizations, with the most infamous example of divisiveness being Betty Friedan's characterization of a 'lavender menace' seeking to take over the National Organization for Women (NOW) during the late 1960s. This led to overt resistance by lesbians within the organization, who used that term in 1970 to begin a successful campaign of consciousness-raising among all organization members, resulting in an explicit commitment by NOW in 1971 to work for lesbian rights.

Similar strides were made during the 1970s and 1980s to bring to the foreground of consciousness the double-oppression (sometimes triple- or quadruple-oppression, when one considers gender and social class) of lesbians and gay men of colour. Audre Lorde was an eloquent spokesperson, in prose and poetry, for the necessary inclusion of sexuality in discussions of civil rights for African-Americans and women. Similarly, Essex Hemphill and Joseph Beam in *Brother to Brother* and other works worked to challenge the heterosexism and chauvinism inherent in masculinist discourse within some sectors of the African-American male community. In *The Greatest Taboo: Homosexuality in Black Communities*, edited by Delroy Constantine-Simms, we find investigations both of the richness of African-American gay and lesbian life, and of the long and continuing struggles to challenge the homophobia of national movements such as the Nation of Islam. Multiple identities involving race, class, gender, and sexuality have also been theorized and superbly complicated by Cherríe Moraga and Gloria Anzaldúa in *This Bridge Called My Back* and other works.

As all of this implies, a perception of anything like a homogeneous lesbian and gay rights movement would hardly be an accurate one. Lesbians and gays, white and of colour, have sometimes worked together and sometimes in highly divergent ways. It is important here to recognize that coalitions among individuals whose only commonality is an experience of oppression based on sexual activity are always fragile ones, especially when gender, race and class diversity is obscured temporarily by a political agenda that concentrates on sexual identity alone. The entrenched sexism of some gay men, the culturally encoded racism of some white lesbians and gays, the

powerful classism of middle-class individuals of both sexes, and the many
ways that religious and political beliefs beyond specific sexual identity issues
fracture any sense of simple social identity mean that current gay and
lesbian politics are certainly fractious and friction-filled. ...

I will return often to that need to continue to legitimate a sense of
collective, powerful, and empowering identity even as intellectual inquiry
calls into question the very notion of 'sexual' identity. It is not an 'either/or'
situation. As always, such binaries are intellectually sloppy and reductive.
In a recent attack on the entire field of 'queer theory', gay anthropologist
Max Kirsch (in *Queer Theory and Social Change*) quotes approvingly two
lesbian critics who charge,

> we cannot afford to allow privileged patriarchal discourse (of which Post-
> structuralism is but a new variant) to erase the collective identity lesbians
> have only recently begun to establish. ... For what has in fact resulted
> from the incorporation of a deconstructive discourse, in academic
> 'feminist' discourse at least, is that the word *lesbian* has been placed in
> quotation marks, whether used or mentioned, and the existence of real
> lesbians has been denied, once again.   (7)

Kirsch notes that 'identity, however short-lived, [is] essential' (7). But, I
would argue, that does not mean that it cannot be critiqued rigorously as an
essential 'construct'. Putting time-bound concepts and identifiers in quotation marks does not deny anyone's existence today or yesterday. Indeed,
intellectual complication (in the service of greater freedom of expression and
activity for sexual nonconformists) should never be equated simplistically
with a wholesale denial of nonconformist sexual expression by religious
fundamentalists and other homophobes. Historicizing and 'deconstructing'
are ways of differently imagining our future as well as understanding our
past. Identity is always a fiction, in the sense that it must suppress complexity
and isolate a defining characteristic (or a limited set of characteristics) from a
wide range of possibilities, but to say this is in no way to deny the fact that I
may be killed or imprisoned because of it. We can grapple intelligently with
both aspects of 'identity': its reality and its fictionality. Even revisionary,
newly empowering notions of 'identity' inevitably suppress certain complications and supposedly 'peripheral' activities. Of course, when it is *my*
complication or peripheral activity that is suppressed, that may feel to me
like as much an act of violence or oppression as that which may have spurred
identity creation and affirmation in the first place.

10

Gender Fucking or Fucking Gender?

Stephen Whittle

Queer means to fuck with gender. There are straight queers, bi queers, tranny queers, lez queers, fag queers, SM queers, fisting queers in every single street in this apathetic country of ours.

(street leaflet, quoted in McIntosh, 1993:31)

AN INTRODUCTORY NOTE

In the politics of gender, sex and the body, the existence of the body is for us all a statement of gender from the moment of birth. No matter how hard you try to talk about somebody else, you are always going to be talking about yourself. This work is, in the words of Stuart Hall, a 'moment of self-clarification' (Hall, 1992:293). As well as a chronicle of cultural change it is an intervention in it, and we would do well to remember that this has both overt and implicit political aims.

Each and every one of us goes through a process of self-identification which is located in a specific history, a specific structure, a specific culture and a specific interaction with these aims. I will not deny my position as a transgendered activist. I also consider myself a neo-Marxist, a transsexual man, an English liberal, a legal theorist, a father without legal recognition, and so on. The list is very long, but most importantly I am gendered, not just by myself but by everybody who

---

My thanks must go to Cath Little for all her help, thoughts and wisdom, which greatly influenced the form and content of this piece of work. I must also thank my partner, Sarah Rutherford, who has contributed (as well as tolerated) so much over the years to the formulation of my ideas.

knows me, by all those who write of me and 'my sort', by all those who work with transgendered people and, nearly always, by transgendered people themselves.

I, like you, cannot escape the hegemony of gendering but I also have a place in the power struggle that surrounds it, and I hope to use it responsibly, as I contribute, from my privileged position, to the culture of gender blending.

THEORIZING THE SEXUAL

In order to appreciate current cultural contributions to theories of gender blending, it is essential to understand the history of theory surrounding sex, sexuality and gender. The most recent manifestation of that history is queer theory, but that has its basis in the history of the pathologies and dualism that surround these areas.

Queer theory does not stand in isolation; its origins lie in the medico-legal discussions of sexual pathologies. It would be naive to interpret queer theory without reference to them.

Transvestism and transsexuality became recognized phenomena, separate from homosexuality, through the work of the early sexologists. Moreover, by the 1930s, an active role was being played by psychologists, psychiatrists, endocrinologists and surgeons in the 'treatment' of transgenderists. This continues to the present day. This history of homosexual subcategorization highlights an inconsistency in the approach of psychiatric professionals. This was exemplified by the *Diagnostic Statistical Manual (DSM) III* (1974), which removed homosexuality from the list of psychosexual disorders whilst at the same time it added transsexuality. For a long time, and certainly in their origins as social categories, the two were inextricably linked.

It could be argued that queer theory's first major contribution to academic theory arose from the work done in the late 1960s by homosexuals, and by homosexual psychiatrists and psychologists in particular, to gain that removal from the *DSM* ratings of homosexuality as a psychiatric disorder. However, at the time, this work would not have been recognized as the start of a major theoretical movement – rather, as part of the process of political activism.

This political process and corresponding theoretical development is today being mirrored in the contributions that transgendered individuals are making to current queer theory. In particular, they have contributed to the work that removed from *DSM IV* (1994) the category of transsexualism. However, this category has been replaced by what is, arguably, an indistinguishable category of 'gender dysphoria'. There is little or no change to the symptomatic requirements, and hence gender dysphoria is made a modern name for transsexuality.

To realize the power of the contributions that transgendered behaviour, lifestyle, politics and culture are making to theory, it is necessary to recognize the framework within which these are being employed and the changes to that framework which they are bringing about. Queer theory has, for transgendered people, seemed one of the obvious starting points, along with the specific disciplines of law and psychology. Those disciplines, unlike sociology, history and cultural studies, are only just beginning to feel the impact of queer theory as a school of thought, and that has probably been indirectly through the work of postmodern theorists. However, queer theory is an increasingly powerful force in many other disciplines, not just those mentioned. . . .

THEORETICAL DIFFERENCE(S)

Queer theory is a theoretical attempt to deconstruct the gendered and sexed praxis of academia. Through queer theory, the hegemonic centrism of heterosexism as practised and taught throughout academic life, thought and writing, is being challenged to justify itself or to 'get out of the kitchen'.

Queer theory is about the deconstruction and the refusal of labels of personal sexual activity, and it is also concerned with the removal of pathologies of sexuality and gendered behaviour. It concerns 'gender fuck', which is a full-frontal theoretical and practical attack on the dimorphism of gender- and sex-roles.

Yet can queer theory formulate sex desire, as opposed to same-sex or heterosex desire? Queer theory attempts to be non-gender-specific, but is this possible when the very fact that it foregrounds same-sex desire, according to Sue-Ellen Case (cit. in McIntosh, 1993: 30), is gender-specific?

It could be argued that because of the gay, lesbian and bisexual history of queer theory itself, it can currently do nothing more than expound and further delinate these boundaries. The crossing of them still belongs to the world of 'vogue-ing' and the destruction of them must belong to those for whom they have always been unreal because of their inherent personal incongruity within a gender-specific world. . . .

Bob Connell said that the state of the field of feminist theory and research by the mid-1980s was a paradox. The previous twenty years had produced a mass of factual research and a lively theoretical debate around work that was highly original and very penetrating. But he did not see current work on theories of gender as converging: 'the differences between the lines of thought have become more distinct, the conceptual and political differences greater' (Connell, 1987: 38).

Feminist theory is now faced with the need to address the dichotomy of biological imperativism and social structure, the differences of sex and gender, which are no longer recognized as synonymous.

Sexual difference was easily quantifiable in the modernist enlighten-ment view: the sex to which an individual was assigned depended upon whether the person possessed, at birth, a penis or a vagina. The knowledge of the genital was to predetermine a person's life story such that even if their genitals were to be reconstructed in another form they would not become a member of the other sex grouping. Gender was irrevocably connected to this biological construction of sex differences. An individual's gender was not mutable.

With the designation as male or female fixed through the knowledge of the genitals, any assertion by someone that they had been assigned to the wrong gender grouping was a form of madness. For sex-role theorists, transsexuals and other members of the transgendered community were to become, at best, a surgical construction, according to Janice Raymond (1980); at worst, 'the victims of error', according to Catherine Millot (1990). To both, trans-sexuals did not become members of the opposite sex but were always part of their original gender grouping; Raymond's researchees were 'male to con-structed female transsexuals' or 'female to constructed male transsexuals' and according to Millot sexual differences belong to: 'the register of the real. It constitutes an insuperable barrier, an irreducible wall against which one can bang one's head indefinitely' (Millot, 1990: 15). As such, she referred to them as male and female transsexuals, the gender designating that to which they were assigned at birth.

The transgendered community and its individual members has a large amount of personal experience of hitting the brick walls of the main founda-tions of this binary paradigm – the dualities of sex and gender. For many this led to a process of self-apologia and attempted explanation which caused self-identified transsexuals to adopt the stance of being a 'woman trapped inside a man's body' (or vice-versa). Cross-dressers and transves-tites upheld a view that there was a feminine side to their masculinity and maleness, rather than challenge the actual construction of their gender-role. It was as if, without genital reconstruction, personal gender-roles could not be changed, and even with it, that reconstruction provided the point of change. A transformation took place, and the idea that gender was signified through the genital was repeatedly upheld.

In this way, surgical gender-reassignment treatment and the self-organization of transsexual and transvestite groups in the 1970s and 1980s endorsed, according to Anne Bolin, 'a formula for gender constitution in which social woman is equated with genital woman' (Bolin, 1994: 460). However, the 1990s has seen a change for many in the transgendered community of their own personal praxis concerning sex and gender, and it is this change and its cultural expression which challenges and offers to expand queer theory's 'gender fuck'. Through the real-life postmodernist practice of hearing (and listening to) many voices and the acknowledgement of their individual truisms, gender, sex and sexuality are facing not just deconstruction but also reconstruction in the practices of many individuals and in the community's view of who can claim membership.

Recent contributions to cultural studies and other academic disciplines concerning transgendered behaviour have offered an oppositional standpoint to the assumed 'naturalism' of sexual dimorphism. Marjorie Garber (1992) refers to the 'category crises' of class, race and gender; that is, the failure of definitional distinctions that we face as we enter the twenty-first century. To her, transvestism 'is a space of possibility structuring and confounding culture: the disruptive element that intervenes, not just a category crisis of male and female, but a crisis of category itself' (Garber, 1992: 17). In other words, transgendered behaviour not only challenges sexual dimorphism in that boundaries are crossed, but it provides a challenge to the boundaries ever being there. These are the boundaries that queer theory attempts to deconstruct.

The transgendered community is now facing up to this 'category crisis' in a way which has not yet been addressed in issues of race and class. Again there are several reasons for this happening at this point and in order to understand why this is the case it is important to understand something of the recent history and creation of the community.

RECENT TRANS-HER/HIS/STORY

The *transgendered* community is a concept of the 1990s. Prior to the late twentieth century,

> only a few organised groups of cross-dressers appeared in historical accounts, including the Hijiras of India, the Kabuki actors in Japan, and the Mollies of 18th century England. Despite these occasional homosexual cross-dressing groups, there is no evidence in Western culture of what might be called a transvestite consciousness. (Bullough and Bullough, 1993: 280)

Early organization of the community started through the work of Virginia Prince, a cross-dresser and biological male who now defines herself as transgendered. She not only organized the Phi Pi Epsilon (FPE) sorority group for transvestites, but she extensively published transvestite ephemera under the 'Chevalier Publications' publishing house, and in the 1960s she became involved in a wide-reaching enterprise to educate the public about cross-dressing (Bullough and Bullough, 1993).

From these beginnings a huge network of self-help transvestite groups has come into existence throughout the world, such as the Seahorse Society of Australia, the Elizabeth Club in Japan, the Beaumont Society in the United Kingdom and the Phoenix Group in South Africa. They have not, however, always had the same points of view concerning transvestism and other aspects of cross-dressing, and the 1980s saw a burgeoning of other ephemeral publications, many of them coming from members of different factions of the network of self-help groups.

Initially generally aimed at the heterosexual cross-dressing male, these groups were often approached by self-identified transsexuals for member-ship, and similarly, after some time, some members would declare them-selves to be transsexual, and commence hormone treatment and seek surgical reassignment.

A close network of individuals was very involved in the organization and motivation of these groups. Ironically, certainly in the United Kingdom, they were often the self-identified transsexuals. For example, the Beaumont Society saw itself as a solely heterosexual cross-dressing male organization, but faced great pressure from the fact that many of its organizing committee and main activists were transsexual, and as transsexuals, identified as heterosexual or lesbian women.

Because of some problems of diversity and incompatibility, the first orga-nization for transsexuals, as such, in the United Kingdom, the Self Help Association For Transsexuals (Shaft), was founded in 1979. Of those involved, certain people stand out; Alice was one of these. A lesbian-identified transsexual woman, she is still involved with the Beaumont Trust and now organizes the Gender Trust, which specifically caters for transsexuals. However, whilst being involved in the running of both organizations, she campaigned actively to remain in the Beaumont Society, to allow other trans-sexuals to be admitted including female-to-male transsexuals and, in the late 1980s, to remove the bar on homosexual transvestites from the organiza-tion. Such campaigning was to greatly affect how the transvestite community viewed itself and to allow a huge level of diversity, increased gender acknowl-edgement, and many issues to be brought to the fore for discussion.

World-wide many associations now exist for transgendered people, from local cross-dressers' clubs to international groups such as the two Female-to-Male (FTM) Networks that now exist and boast over 800 members between them. Though primarily North American and European, these Female-to-Male Networks have members from as far afield as Alaska, New Zealand, Russia and China.

Important to the understanding of the transgendered community's current ideas and thoughts on theories of gender are the transitions that their 'organizing centres' have gone through. From the self-help organizing of a few transvestite networks in the 1960s and 1970s, there is now a plethora of groups catering for a significant level of diversity in cross-gendered behaviour.

However, many of the people involved in the running of these groups have been involved for over a quarter of a century. They have an immense level of respect within their own community because of their strong commitment to, and knowledge of, the community and its history. Many of them have also gone through great changes, personally and socially, both in their own self-identification and in their public lives. This has not just been to do with aspects of their cross-dressing or transgendered behaviour, though that could be seen as being pivotal, but with their ongoing fight to get public respect and academic recognition for the work they have done in this area. Their personal roads to understanding gender and what it means have informed the current theories they hold and expound.

It has been only very recently that transgendered people have felt able to participate in the theoretical discussions. In the fight to be included they have faced several serious problems. Firstly, any discussion of gender by the transgendered community has been hampered by the medical discourse surrounding transgendered behaviour, which makes them both self-interested and decidedly barmy. Secondly, they have been hampered by social and legal restrictions which have made it very difficult to come out publicly as transgendered, and this adds another aspect of self-interest to any work they might do on gender issues.

Thirdly, Janice Raymond's thesis in *The Transsexual Empire: The Making of the She-Male* (1980) discredited for a long time any academic voice that they might have, in particular, with feminist theorists. As a result of her work, feminists saw transsexuals as misguided and mistaken men seeking surgery to fulfil some imaginary notion of femininity, and furthermore, upholding the gendered sex-role structure inherent in the patriarchal hegemony which sought to discredit feminist work. Fourthly, transgendered people have not been allowed either objectivity or sexuality. Objectivity was lost because of the combination of the other three factors; also, if they questioned gender and sex-roles, they were put in the invidious position of having to justify any sex-role change they might undertake to accommodate their gender incongruity. Sexuality was lost, as it was constructed for them in the form of repressed homosexuality being appeased through reassignment surgery or, alternatively, heterosexuality (in their new sex-role) was imposed on them by the medical profession in order to justify what was seen as a 'medical collusion with an unattainable fantasy' (*Lancet*, 1991; cit. in Raymond, 1994: xiii).

These difficulties have not been avoided by the transgendered community, but rather they have been tackled head on. Firstly, the postmodernist acknowledgement of a multiplicity of voices has been adapted to theoretical stances and there is an ongoing discussion as to whether the medical profession should take a diagnostic or merely an enabling role for those people who actively seek reassignment treatment. Secondly, the transgendered community has consistently fought through the courts and the legislature for legal recognition of any new gender-role adopted, also for anti-discrimination clauses to include not only sexuality but gender-role.

Thirdly, transgenderists have tackled radical feminist separatism by continuously asking for answers to awkward questions: for example, along with male-to-female transsexuals, Leslie Feinberg, a 'female' transgenderist and author of *Stone Butch Blues* (Feinberg, 1993), along with James Green, a transsexual man, challenged the 'Womyn born Womyn' policy of the 1994 Michigan Womyn's Music Festival (Walworth, 1994: 27) by asking for their right to enter the festival. Transgenderists have also been active in addressing heterosexism and patriarchy both within and without their own community.

Fourthly, transgendered people have questioned the whole notion of objectivity; they do not try to claim it and instead they have built upon the tradition the community has of autobiographical writing to give a voice to their self-acknowledged subjectivity. As to sexuality, they have begun to reclaim it. Through the work begun by Lou Sullivan (a gay female-to-male who died of AIDS in 1991) and other gay, lesbian or bi activists (along with the help of Ira Pauly, a psychiatrist), they have come out. The argument is simple, if you can acknowledge in yourself that what makes a person is what takes place between the ears and not between the legs, then you are in a privileged position to know that sexuality is a movable and mutable force within us all.

Unfortunately, the reclamation project by lesbian and gay historians, which could have provided support for the challenge of this sex dimorphism, has placed stereotyped gendered behaviour on individuals of whom we know little beyond their sexual activity, choice of sexual partners or platonic lovers. Julie Wheelwright (1989) revealed the 'hidden history of women who choose to live, work and love as men', but it does not occur to her that these 'women' might have in fact been non-gender-specific, or even, for that matter, actually men. Jason Cromwell refers to this as a process of 'default assumptions' (Cromwell, 1994: 4).

Default assumptions are (as they always have been) one of the biggest problems facing the transgendered community's contribution to any academic work or, for that matter, any issue of acceptance at all. There is the first assumption that females do not become men or males become women, they become pastiches, surgical constructions of imaginary masculinities or femininities. As Jason Cromwell says, there are other related default assumptions that arise from this initial one. These take various forms depending upon the social setting, but he cites the director of the film *The Ballad of Little Jo*, Maggie Greenwald, in which she says, 'I stumbled upon some information about the real Little Jo Monihan (*sic*), about whom almost nothing is known except that she lived as a man and nobody had discovered the truth about her until she died' (in Cromwell, 1994: 4). Cromwell says:

> The default assumption here is that the truth is that Monaghan was female and thus really a woman. Greenwald vividly reveals her default assumptions when she concludes in the interview 'Women discover themselves – and this is so much part of feminism – that they don't have to be fake men; to be strong; to be powerful ... Jo becomes a woman not a man. She passes through a phase to survive, ultimately to be a woman'. Now let me get this right: Monaghan lived as a man, no one knew otherwise until death, but 'ultimately' was a woman. (Cromwell, 1994: 4)

The default assumption that underlies any notion of a transgendered existence is that gender is immutable, it is fixed through biological constraints, and social construction merely affects any representation that the biological may take. Gender blending thus becomes a social play, a performance of the realms of the imaginary.

Performativity is a notion well known in queer theory but it has yet to tackle whether gender is just performance or whether it just 'is'. Lynne Segal has said;

> Studying how we live our sexual and gender identities as highly regulated performances does tell us something which is useful about the instabilities of both categories beginning with the impossibility of insisting, without a brutalising blindness, on their definitive connection. But we are not free to choose our performances or masquerades at will – like a type of 'improvisational theatre'. ... Mostly we can only enact those behaviours which have long since become familiar and meaningful to us in expressing ourselves. This remains so however much we realise that our self-fashioning was formed through the policing norms and personal relations of a sexist heterosexual culture; indeed however fulfilling or frustrating our routine performances may prove. Challenge to our gendered 'identities' may be more than we can handle. (Segal, 1994: 208)

Queer theory sets up a stall which is apparently deconstructive of categories and subjectivities – it is about getting away from binary thinking – but according to Kobena Mercer, 'binary thinking ends up with a static concept of identity rather than the more volatile concept of identification' (cit. in McIntosh, 1993: 31). Transgendered activists and academics are attempting to deal with the volatile concept of identification, but it is against all odds: the rigidity of a set of default assumptions concerning sex-roles that pervades all discussion of gender; the two have an incorruptible sameness that makes them all-pervasive.

Yet gender and sex are fundamentally different to the transgendered community, who face the everyday reality of that difference in their lives, and attempts to reconcile it have led to it being challenged in unanticipated ways. Many have had to move on from seeking the biological basis for their state of being: any search for aetiology has been unsuccessful. Any aetiology that has been proposed, whether social or biological, has been torn down by the mass of exceptions. It has been accepted that seeking aetiology is a fruitless occupation as the multiplicity of possible factors increases; and, even if there were possible points of interception, would the 'cure' be wanted?

Expressing the move to a theory in which gender- and sex-roles are clearly separated (at least for a large number of people) and what that means to the modernist view of gender theory is a challenge the transgendered community is not ignoring, nor is it prepared to come up with trite self-serving answers. Challenging their own sense of self, looking inwards to find who they are, using the process of autobiography that they know so well, is producing some very interesting answers which challenge not only the structured world that queer theory inhabits but the very binary structure of the complacent world in which gender was invented, and by which it has become obsessed. The transgenderist did not, after all, invent gender. Gender, like God, is a concept of the imagination that belongs within and supports the foundations of a patriarchal heterosexist hegemony.

Illustrating this move towards teaching us the limits of one aspect of the imaginary, I wish to look at two 'texts' and what they re-present.

GENDER OUTLAWS ON THE RUN!

Kate Bornstein's *Gender Outlaw* (Bornstein, 1994) takes us through a life story of sex-roles and gender confusion. It uses the politics of respectability, which she has acquired through her position as a respected performance artist, to argue for a fluidity of gender politics. She uses her experience of gender boundaries and the crossing of them to question the basic assumptions: the assumptions that there are only two genders, which are invariant and bound by the genitals; that everyone must belong to one gender or another, and that this is 'natural' and independent of science or social construction; and that any transfers from one gender to another are either ceremonial or masquerades – and any exceptions to the two genders are not to be taken seriously. She argues that there are rules to gender – but rules can be broken, ambiguity does exist, it is how we provide for that ambiguity that matters. But even more than ambiguity there is fluidity.

Fluidity provides for any number of genders: 'the ability to freely and knowingly become one or many of a limitless number of genders for any length of time, at any rate of change. Gender fluidity recognises no borders or rules of gender' (Bornstein, 1994: 52). This has meaning in the real world and in the real politics of sex and gender. To be fluid in one's gender challenges the oppressive process of gender and the power processes which use gender to maintain power structures. It makes it hard for them to know who, where or what 'you' are and to set up rules and systems which control. As Bornstein points out, transgenderists are only at the very beginnings of having any sense of community, but gender outlaws exist, though there are still few groups that 'encompass the full rainbow' (Bornstein, 1994: 68). According to her, however, any community must be based on a principle of constant change to avoid the traps that the rules of gender dictate. But to her 'a fluid identity, incidentally, is one way to solve problems with boundaries. As a person's identity keeps shifting, so do individual borders and boundaries. It's hard to cross a boundary that keeps moving' (Bornstein, 1994: 52).

In her discussion of gender terrorism she points out that it is not the transgendered community who are the terrorists, rather it is gender defenders – those who defend the belief that gender is 'real' and 'natural' and use it to 'terrorize the rest of us'. She quotes Murray S. Davis, who wrote:

> Anything that undermines confidence in the scheme of classification on which people base their lives sickens them as though the very ground on which they stood precipitously dropped away. ... People will regard any phenomenon that produces this disorientation as 'disgusting' or 'dirty'. To be so regarded, however, the phenomenon must threaten to destroy not only one of their fundamental cognitive categories but their whole cognitive system.   (cit. in Bornstein, 1994: 72)

Bornstein argues that the transgendered person as a gender outlaw causes the destruction of the gendered system of reality on which most people base major aspects of their lives. The gender terrorists react with acts of violence which range from the physical – as in the rape and killing of Brandon Teena, a passing female-to-male in Nebraska, in early January 1994 (Jones, 1994: 3) – to the theoretical – as in the attacks on transsexuals by feminists such as Janice Raymond (1980; 1994) and Catherine Millot (1990).

Bornstein offers a view of real-life gender fluidity, a refusal to be categorized by the limited gender-roles that are imposed, a refusal to be some cute and humorous representation of the 'third sex' as court jester. Neither is she willing to be invisible, instead she proposes a play with gender partitioning to ultimately make the partitions meaningless. She is not a third sex, but she is creating a third space; a space outside of gender: 'Every transsexual I know went through a gender transformation for different reasons, and there are as many truthful experiences of gender as there are people who think they have a gender' (Bornstein, 1994: 8).

WANTED: GENDER OUTLAW

The second piece I wish to look at is Loren Cameron's self-portrait (see Figure 2). It could be argued that this is a complete education in the current position of gender blending in the world of queer theory. 'Gender blending' is a misnomer to the transgendered community. Gender exists as itself, that is, as an idea, an invention, a means of oppression and a means of expression. Many in the community would see themselves as existing outside of gender, of being oppressed by it but using its icons and signifiers to say who they are.

Cameron's self-portrait says who he is through a celebration of the body. He resists imposed gender representations and assumptions by his nakedness. He acknowledges that in the struggle for himself, dress as such is not the solution. It cannot direct us to a way out of gendered or sexed roles – it merely directs us further into them.

If he was dressed, in the nature of the 'true' disguise that directs us away from questioning, he would lead us further into the traps of gender; as the passing cross-dresser he would become hidden. The gender outlaw is nearly always hidden in passing and, as a result, the gender defenders are fucked, in that their rules become meaningless because they are constantly broken, and nobody knows when or where or how that is happening.

However, Cameron chooses not to pass. Normally the nature of 'not passing' means that heads aren't really fucked, because gender rules are not transgressed, they are only highlighted. Transgenderists, if they could be hidden outlaws, have to choose to tell the story themselves, to make the autobiographical statement in order to present the gender fuck. Realistically, many will not, because their outsiderness, their otherness, means they are seeking a form of sanctuary in the gender-roles they adopt. Anyhow, once we know – won't we always know, and always have known – so the gender fuck disappears.

However, if the gender outlaw who can pass, refuses to pass, then they, once again, present the gender fuck. A world in which gender is transgressed, in which representations are resisted, is a world in which the struggle

Figure 2 *Loren Cameron's self-portrait*

is presented by subjects rather than objects. Cameron (and Bornstein for that matter) has chosen to show that, 'gender is always posthuman, always a sewing job which stitches identity into a body bag' (Halberstam, 1992: 51).

The human is first, the gender is an addition. Cameron takes his human form and imposes gender signifiers upon it through the place of the observer. We see a bodybuilder's physique. As Marcia Ian explains:

> bodybuilders plan ... [to] display as much tumescent muscle as possible, the skin must be well tanned and oiled, the physique rock-hard, showing striations and bulging veins ... in other words to look as much like a giant erection as possible ... a human fucking penis. (Ian, 1994: 79)

Cameron becomes the human fucking penis. He is what he does not apparently possess, and which by default we would assume he desires. Yet does he desire the penis? The photograph shows a man who is proud to be without, because his masculinity does not come from a penis but from himself. We see in him the female signifier of 'lack', yet in his case the meaning of 'lack' is meaningless: he chooses not to wear a phallus because that would not be him, he is without 'lack'. He has gender through himself and because of himself. He shows his fluidity of gender through the fluidity of his tattooed body. The flames signify his flame, he just 'is' and he is proud of his being. Cameron does not 'gender blend', instead he escapes gender because it can no longer be imposed by the observer as the boundaries keep moving.

What has all this to do with queer theory? As stated earlier, queer theory arose from the mix of academic respectability and street activism. Bornstein and Cameron represent the two sides of that association but they are, even then, constantly crossing and re-crossing the boundaries. They are both activists and academics in the eyes of their own small community, and they represent the forefront of that community's current political theory around gender and what it is, what it means.

However, they choose not to gender blend, they do not claim the position of a third sex (meaning gender), rather they claim to be unique in their diversity and, most importantly, themselves. This is the lesson that they offer up to queer theory:

> The identity politics of queer theory permit us, even require us, both to take seriously and experiment with ways of thinking and being which more conventional radical theory is ready to consign to its epistemological closet. (Ian, 1994: 77)

Both are seriously experimenting with ways of 'thinking identity'. Both are bringing to queer theory the challenge of diversity, not just in terms of race and sex but in terms of gender in its most complete and fullest sense. They are challenging the imaginary assumptions through their own imaginations:

> Celebrating and affirming insurgent intellectual cultural practice ... [it is] an invitation to enter a space of changing thought, the open mind that is the heartbeat of cultural revolution.   (hooks, 1994: 7)

11

GenderFusion

Del LaGrace Volcano and Indra Windh

Figure 3 *My man Luigi*

MY MAN

Now I'm going to tell you about my man. My man, Luigi Cabron de la Concha, is the person I want to tell you about.

His mates in the Men's Club call him 'Luggan' and he's almost always dressed in the same old worn black jacket. The silk tie often slips askew, the gaudy gold chain deliberately, yet nonchalantly exposed. He is a pleasure seeker that rarely denies himself anything. A bizniz fixer in the party tent trade, doing his best to impress by pretending to be wise in the ways of the world. Others characterize him as loud, charming, disturbing, sexy, impossible, seductive and immature. Those of us who know him a bit better are aware that, beyond that superficial first impression, he has a depth that is considerably further-reaching than the mint-flavoured toothpick that he's generally seen frantically chewing on. I feel for him, and he infuriates me.

Sometimes he sneaks up on me. Other times it is a resolute decision: now I am Luigi. Because that's it, you see – he is me. Or I am him. I get into character. I allow him to access my body. I take possession of him. Or does he possess me?

I do male drag. I transform myself into a drag king. That means something more than putting on men's clothes and stuffing a sock down your trousers. I appropriate attributes, take liberties with signals, play with poses, exaggerate expressions, stage manners and take on attitudes that are usually associated with 'male' anatomy: generally the exclusive territory of the 50 per cent of humanity to which I'm not classified as belonging. The effect? Well, I don't pass as a man and I don't intend to. However, I do try to generate enough credibility to put a spin on our habitual ways of viewing things, and on conservative gender norms.

You are looking at Luigi. You are looking at me. At us. At something completely different? The double-exposure creates a dissonance. Contains a gender paradox. Offers an alternative interpretation of masculinity. Perhaps you lose yourself in the illusion, but something isn't quite right. A gap appears. A tiny rip in the dense gender fabric?

With the help of Luigi and his actions I stage a parody of gender. I make a mockery – not of any particular man, nor even necessarily of the male collective *per se*. I'm devoting myself to an active, tangible exploration of masculinity, an investigation of compulsive gender confines, in the hope of creating alternatives to expand our spheres of action.

Dragkinging is a conscious act of intentional confusion on my part. I put a theatrical slant on gender and display its characteristics in a funhouse mirror. Welcome myself and you, as a spectator and/or participant in the masquerade. Could you look beyond your ingrained opinions? Make a thought experiment? See if it is possible to break free from the binary cognitive trap that so pervasively structures our reality and dictates

Figure 4   *Blue Vulva and Luigi Cabron*

the conditions of how we perceive each other as gendered beings? There is something else. Much more.

I make myself/Luigi into an imitation without original. Question the demands of authenticity that enclose gender. Play a nosy, cheeky game with supposedly fixed categories with the purpose of trying to loosen them up, and erase their assumedly clear contours; defy gender-conformist demands. I provoke. Ridicule. Stir passions. Create a travesty. Break moulds. Enhance stereotypes. Play tag with our imagination and our ideas of what is what, who is what, and who desires what and who. Feeling the elasticity of the boundaries, trying to transgress them, embodying a statement of gender politics: the setting free of masculinity from 'the man'.

Does this serious play really have a subversive potential? Is dragkinging, as I have described it, queer? Feminist? What if instead I am contributing to a cementing of existing clichés, consolidating rather than disrupting our limiting gender roles? Despite having more questions than answers, I believe I am able to state that dragkinging provokes important discussions, generates fresh hypotheses, and provides an invitation to converse. It is an offer of a well-needed – even if possibly illusory – freedom; a temporary breather from a dichotomized reality. At its best it is a mocking crotch kick to a gender system that tyrannizes and reduces us all. Together with Luigi I

Figure 5 *Hermselfportrait: Indra*

give the finger to the limiting gendered structures, and picture the future overthrow of sexist and heterosexist constructions.

However, I don't have any illusions that dragkinging is the almighty method. Perhaps it's not even the most efficient instrument of liberation I can think of. But it is one of the most fun and pleasurable ones. The gender-political struggle has to be fought on several levels and with multiple means. Dragkinging is one.

EMBODIMENTS

How do we develop a sense of our bodies? What does it mean to say one feels embodied as any particular gender? I think it's safe to say that most people take their gender for granted – that is, they've never given themselves cause to think about which pronoun to use, about whether they should call themselves a woman or a man, a boy or a girl, male or female. Yet a significant number of us have been given or have given ourselves reason to doubt whether we are (or want to be) categorized and conceptualized as *either* female or male. Sometimes these doubts are manifested as physical anomalies, such as 'ambiguous' genitals, and at other times they have a much more amphibious grasp.

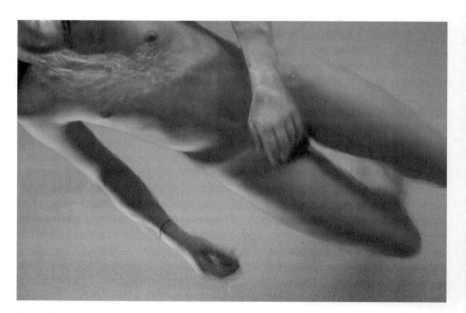

Figure 6 *Hermtorso*

From a young age I had a sense of myself as a force to be reckoned with. I had a sense of myself as a girl. I was proud to be female. Yet I seemed more adventurous, self-reliant and sexually active than any of the girls I was acquainted with. My mother became a 'feminist' and fortunately I was not expected to conform to sexist gender norms. My independence was seen as an asset, not a liability. There was nothing about my body or my behaviour that caused me to question my female gender assignation. Then I hit puberty. Or to be more accurate, puberty hit me.

Without warning the body that had previously been my best friend started to behave in strange ways and grow in places that I wasn't expecting. My left breast developed, excessively, as female while my right breast didn't grow much at all. Hairs began sprouting on my face and then on my chest. I was ashamed. I so desperately wanted to be female. Did having one breast and facial hair mean that I was really a man? Did it mean I would never grow up to be the lesbian I had hoped to be someday? I started searching for information. Quietly.

When I was seven years old my Mormon father taught me how to water-ski. Most of these joint-custody summers were spent at Keystone Lake, just outside of Tulsa, Oklahoma. As soon as the boat stopped I dived in the water. More often than not I suffered greatly afterwards due to my sun-sensitive skin becoming lobster red with bubbling blisters. But I didn't care because when I was in the water and on my skis I couldn't get enough. Much to my surprise and delight I was amazingly good at it, unlike most other sports. Once up I was flying; graceful and impressive. Zipping across the waves, high jumping the wakes, making razor-sharp turns. Showing off what my body could do and then daring it to do even more. It was in these moments I felt most like the self I wanted to be. A self I already was but couldn't see. Wouldn't see for many years.

Fast forward 43 years. At 50 I'm completely and utterly alone. It's so quiet up here, inside my body, as I look down at the crowd far below: hushed and expectant, waiting with bated breath to see me jump off the platform and fly through the air, tutus streaming behind. It's my half-century birthday. I spin over the top of the swinging bar and fling myself backwards, catching myself by my knees at the very last moment. I can feel my biceps burn as they swing and stretch. I smile at the crowd and I hope I look as devilishly handsome as I feel. My moustache is waxed and curled just like a Villain in an old burlesque show. Am I the Villain or the Hero in this story? Eyes Wide Open (think *Clockwork Orange*), the other Kewpie Doll Cute. Symmetry is not my style. Cherry red lips that are perfectly kissable, no matter your gender, no matter your sex. Nipples that are sensate sparkling Mounds of Venus. Muscles that ripple and bulge, shiny with stardust and sweat. I swing out one last time high above the crowd, do a double somersault and dismount, landing on my feet. The crowd roars!

Figure 7   *Hermselfportrait: Del*

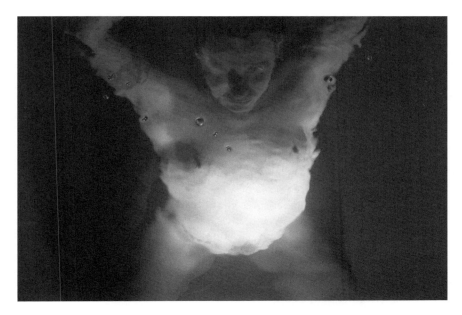

Figure 8 *Hermbirth*

GENDERFUSION

On the morning tube
They're all lookin' at me
None of them quite sure
What it is they see

DEL: In my day-to-day life I pass. Usually as male. Occasionally as female. Both passings are a compromise. I possess abundant facial hair and have a deep husky voice. I am read as male and often it is safer and more convenient just to blend into the woodwork like any ordinary bloke. *I'm* not being seen but sometimes that's okay. I need to protect myself.

INDRA: I sit next to herm. We are holding hands. My big hand holding herm's smaller. I pick up on their curious looks, their confused stolen glances, their defiant challenging glares, their insecure gazes. Smiles and whispers. Herm is attracting attention. Even when wanting to pass and blend. What part do I play in it? Does my presence make herm seem more familiar or more strange? Perhaps gender happens between bodies, not within them.

A pretty boy in make-up?
A faggot? A poof?
They be praying for
An UL TI MATE truth

DEL: There is something 'feminine' in the way I look, both in the way I look
at you and am looked at by you. This could be because my face is
relatively petite or because I have rather large hazel green eyes and small
features neatly balanced on a medium frame. I do have large well-
defined muscles, which I am obviously proud of, but they don't really go
that far in providing a masculine counterpoint. To the uninformed I
simply look like a gay man who goes to the gym. Occasionally.

INDRA: In my daily gender presentation I'm commonly perceived as
traditionally feminine. A tall, fit, able-bodied and rather normative
woman, according to certain prevailing values. I am aware that the way
I look gives me privileges in the world, if and when I am willing to 'play
my cards right' that is ... It all depends on any number of choices I
make. Or don't make. (Choices of clothing, amount of make-up, of the
company I keep, of whether and what I shave ...) And this range of
choices is in itself another privilege.

However, a lot seems to lie in the eye of the beholder. Some read me
as a femme or high femme; others ask themselves if I am a fag hag or a
drag queen. I have also had people considering if I might be MtF –
a transsexual woman. Seems like I'm no longer passing as normative.
What part does herm play in it? Does herm's presence make me seem
stranger, or more familiar?

They look me up and down
Searchin' for clues
They have no idea
Which pronoun to use

DEL: But I have a great deal of empirical evidence that the major signifier
of 'manliness' is facial hair, regardless of what other gender signals
might be in evidence. Wearing lipstick and a frock on a hirsute frame
creates a visceral dissonance in those I encounter. I must be queer, with
so many clues competing for a pronoun.

INDRA: 'What is a woman like her doing with a guy like him?! And
what is a guy like him doing with a woman like her?!' Their insulting
questions are both subtle and explicit, voiced and unspoken. I may be
perceived as a woman, and herm may pass as a man, but we cannot
even impersonate a traditional (heterosexual) couple. And nor do
we want to. The constellation that we create together seems oddly

threatening to those who you would think have nothing to fear. Even size and symmetry cause trouble for culturally constructed ideas and ideals. 'She is taller than he is ... he is wearing the skirt ... she insists on carrying the heavy bags ... and they *both* wear lipstick!'

But I do not
I DENT I FY
As FE-MALE OR MALE.
Those concepts don't apply
To my intersex tale

DEL: On the street I sometimes feel the need to pass (as male). But in my own queer community I don't want to pass as male or female. I want to be seen for what I am: a chimera, a hybrid, a herm. After seven years of living as a herm I have to question if it is even possible for others to see beyond the binary and validate those of us who choose to live outside its confines, as well as those who have never been given the chance to.

   With this task in mind I judiciously apply a bit of eyebrow pencil to my bottom lashes, and a little line just above my upper lip to accentuate my moustache. A little 'natural' red lip pencil blended with Vaseline will set off my lips nicely. I want the effect to be subtle rather than look like I'm on my way to a costume party. I want it to look like the most natural thing in the world to see a hunky 'guy' in a skirt and lippy on the rush hour tube. I call this 'criss-cross dressing'. I use my re-creation-al hermaphroditic body to full effect. If I turn up the volume, Blue Vulva emerges, or I let Tess Tickle take centre stage. But most often I'm just being Del. A herm, who has always loved glitz, glamour, shaving foam, a sharp razor, and as many tutus as I can afford.

INDRA: My strategy around gender subversion is inconsistency. Just when you think you know what to expect from me I transform. Vast sliding movements over different positions on the gendered spectrum. Slippery changes. We are talking big metamorphoses sometimes. People, even close friends and loved ones, don't always recognize me in my differing apparitions: Dragking, Dramaqueen, Cross-Dressed and Criss-Crossed. Or just Ordinary-Everyday. It's not simply that I disguise myself well; what they don't recognize is that I cannot be discovered *behind* these appearances. If anything, I am the differences *between* them.

So am I doing gender?
Or is gender doing me?
I wonder if you'll tell me
What it is that YOU see

Figure 9   *Tindra Windh and Blue Vulva*

INDRA: The lenses through which I perceive the world allow me to see more than double. In fact I take in a beautifully shifting, kaleidoscopic reality, an amazing mosaic of gender variance and norm deviance. Luckily, I have learnt to count past two and deliberately trained my eyes, and other senses, to detect a multiplicity of gendered possibilities all around and within me. I appreciate, value, respect, desire, admire and love what I see.

Herm Love
Criss-cross the line.
Herm Love
Cross it every time.
Herm Love
Times as it takes
Let's build a bridge that will not break!

12

Contagious Word: Paranoia and 'Homosexuality' in the Military

Judith Butler

In the recent military regulations on homosexual conduct, homosexual self-definition is explicitly construed as contagious and offensive conduct. The words, 'I am a homosexual', do not merely describe; they are figured as performing what they describe, not only in the sense that they constitute the speaker as a homosexual, but that they constitute the speech as homosexual conduct. In what follows, I hope to show that the regulation describes as performative the self-ascription of homosexuality, doing precisely that which it says. In describing the power of such acts of utterance, the regulations produce such utterances for us, exercising a performativity that remains the tacit and enabling condition for the delineation of 'I am a homosexual' as a performative utterance. Only within that regulatory discourse is the performative power of homosexual self-ascription performatively produced. In this sense, the regulations conjure the spectre of a performative homosexual utterance – an utterance that does the deed – that it seeks to censor, engaging in a circularity of fabrication and censorship that will be specified as paranoid.

If, however, the military can be said to produce a paranoid construal of homosexual utterance as contagious and offensive action, as performing or constituting that to which such utterances refer, how is this attributed performativity to be distinguished from the kind of performativity that is explicitly owned by the movement to authorize greater homosexual publicity, the clear aim of queer politics? According to this latter movement, coming out and acting out are part of the cultural and political meaning of what it is to be homosexual; speaking one's desire, the public display of desire, is essential to the desire itself, the desire cannot be sustained without such speaking and display, and the discursive practice of homosexuality is indissociable from homosexuality itself. ...

The question of whether citizenship requires the repression of homosexuality is not new, but the recent efforts to regulate the self-declaration of homosexuality within the military repose this question in a different light. After all, military personnel enjoy some of the rights and obligations of citizenship, but not all of them. The military is thus already a zone of partial citizenship, a domain in which selected features of citizenship are preserved, and others are suspended. Recent efforts of the US military to impose sanctions on homosexual speech have undergone a series of revisions[1] and at the time of this writing, continue to be contested in court. In the first version of these regulations proposed by the Department of Defense, the term 'homosexual' was disallowed as part of a self-ascription or self-definition on the part of military personnel. The term itself was not banished, but only its utterance within the context of self-definition. The very regulation in question must utter the term in order to perform the circumscription of its usage. The occasion for the formulation of this regulation was, of course, one in which the term 'homosexual' already proliferated in military, state, and media discourse. Thus, it is apparently not a problem, within the terms of the regulation, to utter the word: as a consequence of the regulation, in fact, it appears that public discourse on homosexuality has dramatically increased. Indeed, the regulations might be held accountable, paradoxically, for the apparent fact that the word has become more speakable rather than less. And yet the proliferation of public sites in which it has become speakable seems directly tied to the proposal to make it unspeakable in the military as a term that might be taken to describe oneself. The regulations propose the term as unspeakable within the context of self-definition, but they still can only do this by repeatedly proposing the term. Thus, the regulations bring the term into public discourse, rhetorically enunciating the term, performing the circumscription by which – and through which – the term becomes speakable. But the regulations insist as well that there are conditions under which the term is *not* to be insisted on at all, that is, in the service of self-definition. The regulation must conjure one who defines him or herself as a homosexual in order to make plain that no such self-definition is permissible within the military.

The regulation of the term is thus no simple act of censorship or silencing; on the contrary, the regulation redoubles the term it seeks to constrain, and can only effect this constraint through this paradoxical redoubling. The term not only appears in the regulation as that discourse to be regulated, but reappears in the public debate over its fairness and value, specifically as the conjured or imagined act of self-ascription that is explicitly prohibited by the regulation, a prohibition that cannot take place without a conjuring of the very act. We might conclude that the state and the military are merely concerned *to retain control* over what the term will mean, the conditions under which it may be uttered by a speaking subject, restricting that speaking to precisely and exclusively those subjects who are not described by the term they utter. The term is to remain a term used to describe others, but the term is not to be used by those who might use it for the purposes of self-description; to describe oneself by the term is to be prohibited from its use, except in order to deny or qualify the description. The term 'homosexual' thus comes to describe a class of persons who are to remain prohibited from defining themselves; the term is to be attributed always from elsewhere. And this is, in some ways, the very definition of the homosexual that the military and the Congress provide. A homosexual is one whose definition is to be left to others, one who is denied the act of self-definition with respect to his or her sexuality, one whose self-denial is a prerequisite for military service. . . .

In what sense are the military regulations symptomatic of a paranoia that forms the possibility of military citizenship? The specific performativity attributed to homosexual utterance is not simply that the utterance performs the sexuality of which it speaks, but that it transmits sexuality through speech: the utterance is figured as a site of contagion, a figure that precipitates a return to Freud's *Totem and Taboo*, in which the speaking of prohibited names becomes the occasion for an uncontrollable communication. Through recourse to Freud's view of conscience, in which the repression of male homosexuality becomes the prerequisite for constituting manhood, the analysis of the military regulations can be read as producing a notion of the 'man' as a self-denying homosexual. Against a psychological reductionism that might locate military acts as acts of individual psyches, I propose to turn to psychoanalysis as a way of reading the text of a highly symptomatic regulation of military citizenship.[2]

Psychoanalysis not only sheds theoretical light on the tensions between homosexuality and citizenship, but psychoanalytic discourse is itself a textual allegory for how the production of the citizen takes place through the rejection and transmutation of an always imagined homosexuality. Indeed, I hope to show that the peculiar form of imagining against oneself which is paranoia constitutes homosexuality not only as a form of inversion, but as the exemplary model for the action of conscience, the turning against oneself that involves the inversion and idealization of the sexual aim. In this sense, Freud's text proves to be as much diagnosis as symptom, and though I propose to read his text psychoanalytically (and, hence, not merely as the enunciation of psychoanalytic practice), I will also be proposing a way to read psychoanalysis allegorically.[3] What this means, more simply, is that Freud will appear to tell us a story about how citizenship and social feeling emerge from the sublimation of homosexuality, but his discourse will be, in the course of this narration, implicated in the very sublimation it describes.[4]

To understand the act of homosexual self-definition as an offence, it seems reasonable to ask, what set of relations or bonds are potentially offended or threatened by such an utterance? It makes sense to turn to Freud's text, 'On the Mechanism of Paranoia', in which he links the suppression of homosexual drives to the production of social feeling. At the end of that essay, he remarks that 'homosexual drives' help to constitute 'the social instincts, thus contributing an erotic factor to friendship and comradeship, to *esprit de corps* and to the love of mankind in general' (31). And at the close of the essay 'On Narcissism', he might be read as specifying the logic whereby this production of social feeling takes place. The 'ego-ideal', he writes, has a social side: 'it is also the common ideal of a family, a class or a nation. It not only binds the narcissistic libido, but also a considerable amount of the person's homosexual libido, which in this way becomes turned back into the ego. The dissatisfaction due to the non-fulfilment of the ideal liberates homosexual libido, which is transformed into sense of guilt (dread of the community)' (81). This transformation of homosexuality into guilt and, therefore, into the basis of social feeling, takes place when the fear of parental punishment becomes generalized as the dread of losing the love of fellow men. Paranoia is the way in which that love is consistently re-imagined as always almost withdrawn, and it is, paradoxically, the fear of losing that love that motivates the sublimation or introversion of homosexuality. Indeed, this sublimation is not quite as instrumental as it may sound, for it is not that one disavows homosexuality in order to gain the love of fellow men, but that it is precisely a certain homosexuality that can be achieved and contained only *through and as* this disavowal.

In Freud's discussion of the formation of conscience in *Civilization and its Discontents*, the very prohibition against homosexuality that conscience is said to enact or articulate is precisely what founds and constitutes conscience itself as a psychic phenomenon. The prohibition against the desire is the desire as it turns back upon itself, and this turning back upon itself becomes the very inception of what is later called 'conscience'. Hence, what the noun form of 'conscience' suggests as a psychic entity is nothing other than an habituated reflexive activity, the turning back upon oneself, a routing of desire against desire, such that the prohibition becomes the site and satisfaction of desire. That repeated practice of introversion constitutes the misnomer of 'conscience' as a mental faculty.

The restrictions on homosexual self-definition suggest that the very circuit of self-prohibition necessary for the production and maintenance of social feeling can no longer be guaranteed by conscience, that conscience is no longer in the service of social regulation. If the military represents a fairly explicit extreme of this regulatory production of homoerotic sociality, it seems that this circuit by which homosexuality is enjoined to turn back on itself again and again has failed to close. This paradox was articulated perhaps most obviously in the claim that social cohesion in the military requires the prohibition on homosexuality, where that cohesion was then described as a magical *je ne sais quoi* that kept military men glued together. The formulation might read: *we must not have our homosexuality in order to have our homosexuality: please take it / don't take it away from us.*

The prohibition that seeks to restrict the outbreak of homosexuality from within this circle of collective introversion figures the very word as a contagious substance, a dangerous fluid. Contagion will be important here, as I will try to show, for homosexuality will be figured implicitly on the model of AIDS, and will be said to 'communicate' along the lines of a disease.

The text is overtly one which seeks to regulate homosexual behaviour, but as regulatory, it is also incessantly productive. What is conjured in this text is a kind of homosexuality that acts through the magical efficacy of words: to declare that one is a homosexual becomes, within the terms of this law, not merely the representation of conduct, offensive conduct, but offensive conduct itself.

> Sexual orientation will not be a bar to service unless manifested by homosexual conduct. The military will discharge members who engage in homosexual conduct, which is defined as a homosexual act, a statement that the member is homosexual or bisexual, or a marriage or attempted marriage to someone of the same gender.[5]

The statement begins by making a distinction between orientation and conduct, restricting the military to discharging only those who engage in homosexual conduct. But then homosexual conduct is defined through a set of appositions which, rather than delimit the barriers of homosexual conduct, proliferate the possibilities of homosexuality. Homosexual conduct includes 'a homosexual act' – even in the singular, which is to say that it is not yet a practice, a repeated or ritual affair. And though subsequent clarifications have made clear that a one-time act, if disavowed as a mistake, will be pardoned, the language of the policy maintains the one-time requirement, insisting on a conflation of 'act' and 'conduct'. What is perhaps more properly an *inflation* of act *into* conduct is significant, for it tacitly and actively imagines the singularity of the event as a series of events, a regular practice, and so imagines a certain force of homosexuality to drive the one-time practitioner into a compulsive or regular repetition. If the act is already conduct, then it has repeated itself before it has any chance to repeat; it is, as it were, always already repeating, a figure for a repetition-compulsion with the force to undermine all sorts of social morale.

Let us return to the phrasing in order to read this passage as an articulation of a homophobic phantasmatic:

> The military will discharge members who engage in homosexual conduct, which is defined as a homosexual act, a statement that the member is

homosexual or bisexual, or a marriage or attempted marriage to some-one of the same gender.

If the statement is conduct, and it is homosexual conduct, then the statement that one is a homosexual is construed as acting homosexually on the person to whom or before whom it is uttered. The statement is in some sense not only an act, but a form of conduct, a ritualistic form of speech that wields the power to *be* what it *says*, not a re-presentation of a homosexuality, but a homosexual act and, hence, an offence. . . .

The utterance which claims or proclaims homosexual identity is construed as offensive conduct only if we concede that something about the very speaking of homosexuality in the context of self-definition is disruptive. But what gives such words the disruptive power they are presumed to wield? Does such a presumption not imply that the one who hears the utterance imagines him/herself to be solicited by the statement? In a sense, the reception traces the Foucaultian formulation in reverse: if Foucault thought that there were first homosexual 'acts' and that only later did homosexuality emerge as an 'identity', then the military takes every ascription of identity as equivalent to the doing of an act. It is important to distinguish, however, between two ways of rethinking identity as act: where one might say that what I mean by saying that 'I am a homosexual' is that 'I perform homo-sexual acts, or engage in homosexual practices or relationships', I would still be referring to those acts, but not, strictly speaking, performing them and certainly not performing them through the act of speaking. The military reading of the claim, however, appears to be of another order. That read-ing takes the claim, 'I am a homosexual' to be one of the very acts of homosexuality, not a reporting on the happening of acts, but the discursive happening of the act itself. . . .

The statement, then, 'I am a homosexual', is fabulously misconstrued as, 'I want you sexually.' A claim that is, in the first instance, reflexive, that attributes a status only to oneself, is taken to be solicitous, that is, a claim that announces availability or desire, the intention to act, the act itself: the verbal vehicle of seduction. In effect, a desirous intention is attributed to the statement *or* the statement is itself invested with the *contagious* power of the magical word, whereby to hear the utterance is to 'contract' the sexuality to which it refers. . . .

Presumed in the military construal of the self-defining statement as offensive action is that the speakability of the term breaks a taboo within public discourse, the floodgates open, and expressions of desire become un-controllable. Hence, the one before whom the desire under taboo is spoken becomes immediately afflicted by the desire borne by the word; to speak the word before such a person is to implicate that person in unspeakable desire. The word – and the desire – is caught in precisely the way in which a disease is said to be caught. Within contemporary military discourse, the taboo status of homosexuality is intensified by the phobic reduction of homosexual relations to the communication of AIDS, intensifying the sense of homosexual proclamations as contagious acts.

Indeed, consider the salience of the metaphor of contagion for Freud's discussion of taboo in *Totem and Taboo*:

> taboo is a ... prohibition imposed (by some authority) from outside, and directed against the most powerful longings to which human beings are subject. The desire to violate it persists in their unconscious; those who obey the taboo have an ambivalent attitude to what the taboo prohibits. The magical power that is attributed to taboo is based on the capacity for arousing temptation; and it acts like a contagion because examples are contagious and because the prohibited desire in the unconscious shifts from one thing to another.   (35)

In this last remark, Freud makes clear that the prohibited desire in the unconscious shifts from one thing to another, is itself an uncontrollably transferable desire, subject to a metonymic logic that is not yet constrained by the law. Indeed, it is the incessant transferability of this desire that is instituted by the taboo, and that informs the logic of contagion by which the desire under taboo enters into discourse as a highly communicable name. If I say, 'I am a homosexual', in front of you, then you become implicated in the 'homosexuality' that I utter; the utterance is presumed to establish a relationship between the speaker and the audience, and if the speaker is proclaiming homosexuality, then that discursive relationship becomes constituted by virtue of that utterance, and that very homosexuality is communicated in the transitive sense. The utterance appears both to communicate and to transfer that homosexuality (becomes itself the vehicle for a displacement onto the addressee) according to a metonymic rush which is, by definition, beyond conscious control. Indeed, the sign of its *unconscious* status is precisely that it 'communicates' or 'transfers' between speaker and audience in precisely that uncontrollable way.

Earlier in this same text, Freud refers to 'dangerous attributes' applied indifferently and simultaneously to persons, their states, their acts; the attribute not only shifts between these registers, but it becomes tempting and terrifying precisely by virtue of this shiftiness: 'Anyone who has violated a taboo becomes taboo himself because he possesses the dangerous quality of tempting others to follow his example: why should *he* be allowed to do what is forbidden to others? Thus he is truly contagious in that every example encourages imitation' (32). Freud distinguishes between those kinds of taboos invested with contagious power that 'produce temptation and encourage imitation' and another in which the transmissibility of a taboo is its displacement onto material objects (34). These two forms converge later, however, when he refers to taboo *names* as that material instance of language that carries both the desire and its prohibition, that is, that becomes the discursive site for the displacement of ambivalence. The 'transmissability of taboo' is a function of metonymic displacement, 'the tendency ... for the unconscious instinct ... to shift constantly along associative paths on to new objects' (34).

The question that emerges in trying to read the logic of contagion as it operates within the military ban on homosexual statements and acts is how a name and the act of self-naming in particular becomes precisely such a material/discursive carrier for this displacement and 'transmissability'. The sign uttered in the service of a prohibition carries that prohibition and becomes speakable only in the service of that prohibition. The breaking of the prohibition through the uttering of the sign becomes, then, a disjoining of that sign from its prohibitive function, and an unconscious transfer of the desire that the sign has, until this re-signification, kept in check. The name, 'homosexual', is not merely a sign of desire, but becomes the means by which desire is absorbed into and carried by the sign itself. The sign, in the service of prohibition, has substituted for the desire it represents, but also has acquired a 'carrier' function that links homosexuality with contagion. It is, of course, not difficult to imagine which one. How are we to account for this symbolic conflation of the fluidity of the sign and 'dangerous fluids'? Homosexuality, within this paranoid metonymy, has become a paradigm for contagion. The self-descriptive utterance of 'homosexuality' becomes the very act of dangerous communication which, participating in a contemporary revaluation of that sacred scene, infects its listener – immaculately – through the ear.

Freud concludes his remarks with the reminder that the taboo can be reinstalled only through the speech act that *renounces* desire: 'The fact that the violation of a taboo can be atoned for by a renunciation shows that renunciation lies at the basis of obedience to taboo' (35). In a corollary move, the military makes provisions for those who would recant their indiscretion; the only way to counter the public force and threat of a public act of self-definition as a homosexual is through an equally public self-renunciation. In remarks intended to clarify how the policy would be implemented, the military makes clear that to assert one is a homosexual presents a 'rebuttable presumption' that one will act in a homosexual way. In other words, one may now say, 'I am a homosexual and I intend not to act on my desire', and in such a case, the first clause, 'I am a homosexual', loses its performative force; its constative status is restored through the addition of the second clause. In Freud, the renunciation takes the form of regret and atonement, but it makes no claims to having annihilated the desire; indeed, within renunciation, the desire is kept intact, and there is a strange and important way in which prohibition might be said to *preserve* desire.

In *Civilization and its Discontents*, the repression of the libido is itself a libidinally-invested repression. The libido is not absolutely negated through repression, but rather becomes the instrument of its own subjection. The repressive law is not external to the libido that it represses, but the repressive law represses to the extent that repression becomes a libidinal activity.[6] Further, moral interdictions, especially those that are turned against the body, are themselves sustained by the very bodily activity that they seek to curb:

> An idea ... which belongs entirely to psychoanalysis and which is foreign to people's ordinary way of thinking ... it tells us that conscience (or more correctly, the anxiety which later becomes conscience) is indeed the cause of instinctual renunciation to begin with, but that later that relationship is reversed. Every renunciation of instinct now becomes a dynamic source of conscience and every fresh renunciation increases the latter's severity and intolerance. (*CD*, 84)

According to Freud the self-imposed imperatives that characterize the circular route of conscience are pursued and applied precisely because they become the site of the very satisfaction they seek to prohibit. In other words, prohibition becomes the displaced site of satisfaction for the 'instinct' or desire that is prohibited, an occasion for the reliving of the instinct under the rubric of the condemning law. This is of course the source of that form of comedy in which the bearer of the moral law turns out to be the most serious transgressor of its precepts. And precisely because this displaced satisfaction is experienced through the application of the law, that application is reinvigorated and intensified with the emergence of every prohibited desire. The prohibition does not seek the obliteration of prohibited desire; on the contrary, prohibition pursues the reproduction of prohibited desire and becomes itself intensified through the renunciations it effects. The afterlife of prohibited desire takes place through the prohibition itself, where the prohibition not only sustains, but is *sustained by*, the desire that it forces into renunciation. In this sense, then, renunciation takes place *through* the very desire that is renounced, which is to say that the desire is *never* renounced, but becomes preserved and reasserted in the very structure of renunciation. The renunciation by which the military citizen is purged of his sin and re-established in his or her place, then, becomes the act by which the prohibition at once denies and concedes homosexual desire; it is not, strictly speaking, *un*speakable, but is, more generally, retained in the speaking of the prohibition. In the case of the homosexual who claims to be one, but insists that he or she will not act on his or her desire, the homosexuality persists in and as the application of that prohibition to oneself.

But consider how it is that a term or the proclamation of an identity might be understood discursively to carry or cause an injury. What is the theory of causation in this instance, and is this a 'cause' established in paranoia? Freud offers the following account of how it is that paranoia is *caused*, but not in the analysis of how the causal account of paranoia slides into the paranoid account of causation. He writes, 'paranoia is a disorder in which a sexual aetiology is by no means obvious; on the contrary, the strikingly prominent features in the causation of paranoia, especially among males, are social humiliations and slights'. So far Freud appears to be substituting a true for a false cause of paranoia: it appears that what causes paranoia are slights and injuries, but what truly causes paranoia is a sexual wish subject to an introversion; the imagined punishment by others is the idealized and exteriorized effect of a prohibition against one's desire that is at the origin of that idealization and exteriorization. The agency of that prohibition is in some sense displaced, and the reasons for the beratement have already become illegible. Freud then continues, claiming that if we go into the matter 'more deeply', we shall see that 'the really operative factor in these social injuries lies in the part played in them by the homosexual components of affective life' (30).

It is this last phrase that introduces ambiguity into Freud's account. For how are we to understand how 'homosexual components of affective life play a part in these social injuries'? To feel slighted or injured, to imagine oneself slighted or injured, how precisely is this to be read as a permutation of homosexuality? Is the slight, the injury, the imagined external form that the prohibition against homosexuality takes, and is one being slighted and injured by virtue of one's homosexual desires? Or is this being slighted and injured an imagining of the social injury to which an exposed homosexual might very well be subject? The uncertainty appears to be this: is the prohibition a social one which might be said to become diffuse and generalized, or is it a psychic and internal one which becomes externalized and generalized in the course of paranoia?

In the first instance, it is the social vulnerability of the homosexual to injury which is projected onto a more generalized sense of others as berating and slighting in their behaviour; but in the latter case, it is the psychic sublimation of homosexuality which creates the very notion of the social, the notion of Others as regulating, watching, and judging, an imaginary scenario which becomes what is known as 'conscience' and prepares the subject for that social feeling that supports citizenship. The two possible sequences differ dramatically in their consequences. The second view postulates a homosexual desire which turns against itself, and then produces a notion of the social as a consequence of that turning back against itself: social feeling, understood here as co-extensive with social regulation, is a consequence of sublimated homosexuality, the projection and generalization of a set of judging and watching Others. This is a formulation that postulates homosexuality as the outside to the social, as the presocial, and derives the social, understood as a primarily regulatory domain, from the self-suppression of this sexuality.

But how are we to understand this self-suppression apart from the social regulations by which homosexuality is itself cast as the asocial, the pre-social, the impossibility of the social within the social? If the two versions of prohibition (psychic and social) cannot be dissociated from one another, how are they to be thought together? The slights and injuries experienced within what is called paranoia are the psychic traces of existing social regulations, even as those traces have become estranged from the regulations from which they are derived. The slights and injuries are not only the effects of a desire turned back on itself, and the subsequent projection of those turned-back desires onto the judgements of others (indeed a blending of super-egoic functions with social ones); rather, it is the coincidence of the judgement of Others and that turning back upon oneself that produces the imaginary scenario in which the condemned and unlived desire registers psychically as the imagined slights and injuries performed by Others.

Thus, the turn to Freud is not an effort to read Freud as the truth of homosexuality, but, rather, as a way to exemplify or allegorize the circularity in the account of paranoia, a circularity that comes to afflict Freud's own account. For instance, in 'On the Mechanism of Paranoia', he writes approvingly of the way in which homosexual feelings are necessary to the love of mankind, how they euphemistically 'combine' with the instincts for self-preservation to produce 'man' in the 'proper sense' of that term. If, to use his terms, homosexual tendencies 'combine with' ego-instincts, where ego-instincts are defined as self-preservative, then it becomes part of the project of 'man's' self-preservation – the preservation of 'man, properly speaking' – to deflect, and preserve in deflection, his homosexuality (69). Hence, the aetiology that Freud offers us is already within the normative and regulatory domain of the social for which he seeks to give an account. It is not that there are first homosexual feelings which then combine with self-preservative instincts, but that, according to the social norms that govern the conditions of self-preservation *as a man*, homosexuality must remain a permanently deflected possibility. Hence, it is not man's homo-sexuality that helps to constitute his social instincts, and his general mindfulness of others, but, rather, the repression or deflection of the ostensible narcissism of homosexuality that is construed as the condition for altruism, understood as one of the benefits of an accomplished heterosexuality. In this sense, the desexualization and externalization of homosexuality makes for a 'man' – properly speaking – who will always feel slights and injuries in the place where homosexual desire might have lived, and for whom this transposition of desire into imagined injury will become the basis of social feeling and citizenship. Note that this unacted homosexuality becomes the condition for sociality and the love of mankind in general.

It is not simply that homosexuality must remain unacted and deflected such that man in his self-preserving and proper sense may live, but that the very notion of the 'ego-ideal' – the imaginary measure by which citizenship is psychically regulated – is itself composed of this unacted and deflected homosexuality. The ego-ideal is formed through the withdrawal of large quantities of homosexual cathexis.[7] This homosexuality, however, is neither simply withdrawn nor simply deflected or repressed, but rather, turned back on itself, and this turning back on itself is not a simple self-cancellation; on the contrary, it is the condition for the fabrication of the ego-ideal in which homosexuality and its prohibition 'combine' in the figure of the heterosexual citizen, one whose guilt will be more or less permanent. Indeed Freud will say that homosexual libido is 'transformed into sense of guilt' and citizenship itself – the attachment to and embodiment of the law – will be derived from this guilt.

How, then, do we return to the problem that emerges within the military, where the military is at once a zone of suspended citizenship, and one which, by virtue of this suspended status, articulates in graphic terms the production of the masculinist citizen through the prohibition on homosexuality? Although the military regulations appear to figure homosexuality in masculinist terms, it is clear that lesbians are targeted as well, but that, paradoxically, the interrogations into their personal life often take the form of sexual harassment. In other words, women cannot speak their homosexuality because that would be to threaten the heterosexual axis along which gender subordination is secured. And if men speak their homosexuality, that speaking threatens to bring into explicitness and, hence, destroy, the homosociality by which the class of men coheres.

The line that demarcates the speakable from the unspeakable instates the current boundaries of the social. Could the uttering of the word constitute a slight, an injury, indeed, an offence, if the word did not carry the sedimented history of its own suppression? In this sense, the word becomes an 'act' precisely to the extent that its unspeakability circumscribes the social. The speaking of the word outside its prohibition calls into question the integrity. and the ground of the social as such. In this way, the word contests the boundaries of the social, the repressive ground of the citizen subject, by naming the relation that must be assumed for that sociality to emerge, but which can only produce that sociality by remaining unnamed. Unwittingly, it seems, the military introduces that word into its contagious circuit precisely through the prohibition which is supposed to secure its unspeakability. And it is in this way that the military speaks its desire again and again at the very moment, through the very terms, by which it seeks its suppression.

In fact, it is crucial to consider that the military does not merely confront the homosexual as a problem to be regulated and contained, but it actively produces this figure of the homosexual, insisting that this homosexual be deprived of the power of self-ascription, remaining named and animated by the state and its powers of interpellation. In its military dimension, the state insists on the codification of homosexuality. The homosexual subject is brought into being through a discourse that at once names that 'homosexuality' and produces and defines this identity as an infraction against the social. But where it names this subject compulsively, it denies to this subject the power to name itself, thus the state seeks to curb not merely homosexual actions, but the excessive power of the name when it becomes unshackled from the prohibitions by which it is spawned. What and who will the name describe on the occasion when it no longer serves the disciplinary aims of military nomination?

How, then, do we think about the situation in which the self-ascription, the reflexive statement, 'I am a homosexual', is misconstrued as a seduction or an assault, one in which a desire is not merely described but, in being described, is understood to be enacted and conveyed? In the first instance, I think we must read this construal of homosexuality and homosexual acts as assault and/or disease as an effort to circumscribe homosexuality within that pathologizing set of figurations. This is not simply an account of how the words of homosexuals performatively produce homosexuality, but, as state-sanctioned figure, a restrictive definition of homosexuality as an assaultive and contagious action. Hence, the performativity attributed to the homosexual utterance can only be established through the performativity of a state discourse that makes this very attribution. The figuring of homosexual utterance as contagion is a performative sort of figuring, a performativity that belongs to regulatory discourse. Does the statement reveal the performative power of homosexual utterance, or does it merely underscore the productive or performative power of those who exercise the power to define homosexuality in these terms?

This discursive power to enforce a definition of the homosexual is one that finally belongs neither to the military nor to those who oppose it. After all, I have just produced the military production for you and entered into the chain of performativity that I've been charting, implicating myself in the reproduction of the term, with far less power, admittedly, than those whose acts I describe. Is anything like homosexuality being described in this chain of performativity? Perhaps it is a mistake to claim that we might have the power to produce an authoritative or affirmative notion of homosexuality when we go about naming it, naming ourselves, defining its terms. The problem is not merely that homophobic witnesses to self-proclaiming homosexuals hallucinate the speaking of the word as the doing of the deed, but that even those who oppose the military are willing to accept the notion that naming is performative, that to some extent it brings into linguistic being that which it names. There does seem to be a sense in which speech acts and speech, more generally, might be said to constitute conduct, and that the discourse produced about homosexuality is part of the social constitution of homosexuality as we know it. Conventional distinctions between speech and conduct do collapse when, for instance, what we might loosely call representation *is* co-extensive with, say, being 'out' as a cultural practice of gayness and queerness, between cultural representations that express homosexuality and homosexuality 'itself'. It would, after all, be somewhat reductive to claim that homosexuality is only sexual behaviour in some very restricted sense, and that there is then, superadded to this behaviour, a set of representations of homosexuality that, strictly speaking, *are not* homosexuality proper. Or are they?

Many would want to argue that homosexuality and its cultural representation are *not* dissociable, that representation does not follow sexuality as its dim reflection, but that representation has a constitutive function, and that, if anything, sexuality follows representation as one of its effects: this appears to be the presumption in the claim that public conventions organize and make possible 'sexuality' and that the acts, and the cultural practices that orchestrate and sustain the acts, as it were, cannot be strictly distinguished. To construe sexuality as an 'act' is already to abstract from a cultural practice, a reiterative ritual, in which it takes place and of which it is an instance. Indeed, the very notion of a sexual practice is precisely that which overrides the distinction between 'act' and 'representation'.

To insist, however, that discourse on homosexuality, including the discursive act of 'coming out', is part of what is understood, culturally, as 'homosexuality' is not quite the same as claiming that saying one is homosexual is itself a homosexual act, much less a homosexual offence. Although I think we can imagine queer activists who would claim that the self-appellation is a sexual act in some broadly interpreted sense of that term, there is a certain comedy that emerges when 'queer' becomes so utterly disjoined from sexual practice that every well-meaning heterosexual takes on the term. But we surely need to take seriously the contention that 'coming out' is intended as a contagious example, that it is supposed to set a precedent and incite a series of similarly structured acts in public discourse. The military may be responding precisely to the felicitous perlocutionary consequences of coming out, the way in which the example has spawned a rash of coming outs throughout the public sphere, proliferating itself as if it were a certain kind of linguistic contagion – a contagion, we might conjecture, that is meant in part to counter the force of that other contagion, namely, AIDS. What, then, is the difference between the logic that governs the military policy and the one which governs queer activism?

One way of understanding this, I think, is to note the way in which paranoid military listening consistently closes the gap between the speaking of a desire and the desire that is being spoken. The one appears to communicate the other directly in moments of seduction (but even there we know through painful examples that the communication is not always interpreted in quite the right way); in paranoia, though, the desire that the speaking elicits is imagined as emerging wholly and without solicitation from the one who speaks it. It comes from the outside, as an assault, or as a disease, and becomes registered as injury and/or contamination. Hence, the desire is already figured as assault or disease, and can be received in one form or the other, or both. How is that figuration to be understood as different from the production of a discourse about homosexuality, which might work against this pathological reduction and constitute a socially affirmative meaning for homosexuality?

I want to argue for the notion that a discursive production of homosexuality, a talking about, a writing about, and institutional recognition of, homosexuality, is not exactly the same as the desire of which it speaks. Whereas the discursive apparatus of homosexuality constitutes its social reality, it does not constitute it fully. The declaration that is 'coming out' is certainly a kind of act, but it does not fully constitute the referent to which it refers; indeed, *it renders homosexuality discursive, but it does not render discourse referential.* This is not to say that desire is a referent that we might describe in some other or better way; on the contrary, it is a referent that sets a certain limit to referential description in general, one that nevertheless compels the chain of performativity by which it is never quite captured. In an effort to preserve this sense of desire as a limit to referentiality, it is important not to close the gap between the performative and the referential and to think that by proclaiming homosexuality, homosexuality itself becomes nothing other than the proclamation by which it is asserted. Although Foucault might claim that discourse becomes sexualized through such an act, it may be that discourse is precisely what desexualizes homosexuality in this instance.[8] My sense is that this kind of account of the discursive production of homosexuality makes the mistake of substituting the name for what it names, and though that referent cannot be finally named, it must be kept separate from what is nameable, if only to guarantee that no name claims finally to exhaust the meaning of what we are and what we do, an event that would foreclose the possibility of becoming more and different than what we have already become, in short, foreclose the future of our life within language, a future in which the signifier remains a site of contest, available to democratic rearticulation.

In this sense, I would argue that the discourse about homosexual desire is not, strictly speaking, the same as the desire that it speaks, and when we think that we are acting homosexually when we speak about homosexuality we are, I think, making a bit of a mistake. For one of the tasks of a critical production of alternative homosexualities will be to disjoin homosexuality from the figures by which it is conveyed in dominant discourse, especially when they take the form of either assault or disease. Indeed, as much as it is necessary to produce other figures, to continue the future of performativity and, hence, of homosexuality, it will be the distance between something called 'homosexuality' and that which cannot be fully interpellated through such a call that will undermine the power of any figure to be the last word on homosexuality. And it is that last word, I think, that is most important to forestall.

13

I'd Rather Be the Princess than the Queen! Mourning Diana as a Gay Icon

William J. Spurlin

Before Diana's death, I prided myself in being rather smug about anything particularly royal. I found the Windsors an incredibly dull lot striving to maintain a sense of substantive purpose in the world by hopelessly clinging to outdated trappings of monarchy – ritualized ceremonies, the Queen's Christmas broadcast, stuffy public appearances, ostentatious palaces, shallow pretensions of happy family life. Frivolous Charles trying desperately to be taken seriously, dowdy Elizabeth, cranky Philip, Fergie's careless flaunting of royal wealth, and Diana without a single O-Level – except for Prince Edward, long rumoured to be gay, the Windsors had little appeal for me.

Diana's death in 1997 forced me to look at her again, critically this time. A good deal of my earlier cynicism for the other royals had been heightened to contempt following their reaction to Diana's death; recall, for instance, the Queen's uptight, almost angry, scowl upon first returning from Balmoral after Diana's death as she inspected the floral bouquets scattered in front of Buckingham Palace, left in Diana's memory – an expression of displeasure that seemed to say, 'Who made this mess?' Though I didn't pay much attention to Diana's life when she was alive, I became rather morbidly addicted to news reports about her death, and later, to the television narratives about her life. Like many others, I, too, visited the British Consulate in New York in the days before Diana's funeral – waiting in a long queue that wrapped around the block as if a new box-office hit film had just opened, struggling to etch thoughtful words in the elegant black leather condolence book once my turn finally came, trying not to be noticed as I turned back the pages to glimpse at what others before me had written, chatting with tearful mourners, some British, some American, some from other parts of the world, and, with my partner, laying down our own small bouquet of orange daylilies, yellow daisies, and violet chrysanthemums whose colours, along with others on the already flower-enshrined sidewalk, captured the balmy September afternoon sunlight just outside the austere Third Avenue building. Why was

158

I suddenly 'hooked' on Diana when the system of which she was part and, for most of her life, valued, seems so repressive to gay people – patriarchal family life enmeshed in primogeniture, obligatory heterosexual marriage and procreative sexuality tied to the production of heirs, the suppression of one's desires for the good of the family, the monarchy, and the State, and rigidly prescribed gender roles that reinvent and help sustain oppressive binary oppositions?

Is it possible for Diana to be a gay icon? I had once hoped that it would be Edward who would provide the initial queer trajectory for (re-)reading the current royal family; ironically, I have come to believe, it was Diana who did that and much more.[1] Her own sexual identity is not at issue; rather, it is her monumentality that enables resistant and critical rereadings. For me, Diana's death captured and reshaped her image in my mind, so much so that she nearly became more mythic than real. During most of her adult life, except for that brief period following her separation from Charles, the queer aspects of Diana's image were difficult to ascertain as they were often socially obscured by official images of her connections to royalty. Diana's betrothal to Charles, her wedding, the birth of the heir and the spare, her official functions as Princess of Wales, her divorce, and even her attempts to find happiness outside the realm of Buckingham Palace positioned her in some relation to the royal family (and therefore in relation to its personification of heteronormativity, at least in the present age) even as she tried to escape it. These events served, initially at least, to camouflage who Diana was, or could be, to her many audiences, and the ways in which her life could be read through multiple, sometimes contradictory, trajectories.

This does not imply, of course, that icons, in this case gay icons, whatever their sexuality, need to be dead to fascinate; obviously such is not the case with contemporary living icons like Bette Midler, Liza Minnelli, Madonna, or Barbra Streisand, to name a few, who, in their own way, signify as 'gay', and/or as 'lesbian', and/or quite possibly as 'queer', whether through camp, through taking on the persona of the 'bad girl', or through their status as 'diva', all in ways that Diana clearly did not. If we consider a cultural icon as that legible grid onto which our fantasies, desires and aspirations are pro-jected as a means to their conscious expression, given her brief life, I believe that it is predominantly, though perhaps not exclusively, after her death that queer identification with Diana's life, as it has been (and continues to be) represented, could occur – not identification with her actual life, which was knowable only to a relatively small circle of family and close friends, but her life *as depicted*, as represented. Diana becomes fixed in our systems of reference, but, as Wayne Koestenbaum points out, an icon is more of an *idea* than a person; sometimes the icon and actual person converge, sometimes they do not (Koestenbaum, 1996: 4). We respond to Diana, then, as a signifier, which we try to fix as it circulates in culture, whereas its signified remains endlessly deferred. But in a way that is similar to other cultural icons, strategies of identification with the admired person are often so intense that the distinction between self and Other becomes blurred. How then might Diana be read queerly?

Wayne Koestenbaum's work on Jacqueline Kennedy Onassis has helped to set an important precedent for studying cultural icons, especially the ways in which they are created, represented and read, and sustained largely through the various apparatuses of the modern media. He writes:

> We called Jackie an icon because she glowed, because she seemed ceaseless, because she resided in a worshipped, aura-filled niche. We called Jackie an icon because *her image* was frequently and influentially reproduced. ... We called Jackie an icon because her story provided a foundation for our own stories, and because her face, and the sometimes glamorous, sometimes tragic turns her life took, were lodged in our systems of thought and reference, as if she were a concept, a numeral, a virtue, or a universal tendency, like rainfall or drought.   (Koestenbaum, 1996: 4; emphasis added)

What is interesting is not only the similar way Diana can be interpreted as a (gay) icon but the parallel ways in which both women functioned as icons. Though Jackie was often conferred token royal status in the United States as the 'Queen' of the new Camelot that characterized the Kennedy campaign and carried over into JFK's years in the White House, the actual lives of Jackie and Diana, being a generation apart, were lived quite differently. At the same time, it must be acknowledged that the time between John F. Kennedy's assassination and Jackie's own death in 1994 allowed a more significant period for Jackie's life to be represented while she was alive. But it is possible to think about the representations of Jackie's and Diana's lived lives in parallel ways. For example, after President Kennedy's assassination in 1963, Jackie no longer held a legislated public or political position (Koestenbaum, 1996: 137) except as a former First Lady; similarly, following her divorce from Prince Charles in 1996, Diana relinquished her status and rank within the inner circle of the royal family (though she maintained her other titles) – yet both women went on to possess legitimacy more fully *in their own right*. Though widowhood and divorce respectively brought both women closer to the status of private citizens, they remained in the public eye, still able to transcend the domain of the familiar and everyday. Once 'on their own', the need to represent them, to see their lives depicted, became more intense than when they held their 'official' positions. In other words, their status as icons, as cultural signifiers, is marked by an *overdetermination* that exceeds and is not reducible to the signified positions through which they became public figures in the first place. Never did the now infamous paparazzi follow Diana more than when she was separated and later divorced from Charles, and while Jackie deliberately sought privacy after the JFK assassination, and more so after the death of Aristotle Onassis, she became even more of an enigma to the American imagination and to audiences world-wide. Their connections to being First Lady of the United States and Her Royal Highness, the Princess of Wales, cannot be totally severed from Jackie's or Diana's status as cultural icons; indeed, we could even proffer that Jackie 'came out' at the JFK Inauguration in 1961, as did Diana at her wedding twenty years later, as these respective events made their titles official and forever secured their celebrity positions. But their capacity to signify culturally is not reducible to those originary social positions. For this reason, I must extend Koestenbaum's point about Jackie to include Diana when he suggests, quite insightfully, that Jackie (like Diana) is 'remembered not so much for what she *was* but for what she invoked and catalyzed' (Koestenbaum, 1996: 272).

Yet, in looking back from our present perspective, especially in the case of Diana, their monumentality is evident even in their official capacities, prior to the JFK assassination, prior to Diana's separation and divorce from the Prince of Wales. In looking at photographs of the two couples, it is Jackie and Diana who dominate the photographic space in spite of the fact that it was their husbands who held the higher, more powerful social position. It is almost as if the materiality of the bodies of these two women physically operate somehow to refute the subordinate, feminized role socially constructed for them as wives of 'important men' like the President of the United States and the heir to the British throne; Jackie's and Diana's bodies exude an energy that claims the camera's centre. Along these lines, Koestenbaum describes how Jackie was able effortlessly to upstage JFK in his dark suits, his rather sleepy look, his gaze away from the camera in contrast to Jackie's sleek outfits (in fuchsia suits, her signature pillbox hats, her sleek 1960s hairdos), her direct gaze at the lens, 'a body that wants to move and to act, rather than be photographed or emblematic' (Koestenbaum, 1996: 118).

In photographs of Diana and Charles together, one notices a more gradual claiming of the centre of photographic space by Diana, in that early photographs of the couple, as Sir Roy Strong has pointed out, were carefully controlled (i.e. constructed) images of what the Palace conceived a Princess of Wales should look like – for the most part, the romantic English rose look, downcast face and eyes and dressed in 'billowing tides of soft diaphanous fabrics' (Strong, 1997: 133). From the time of her marriage until the birth of her second son, we see Diana largely as the shy and demure wife trying *not* to be at the camera's centre, though its lens seems more obsessed with her than with her husband. Even in the photo of the newlywed couple honeymooning at Balmoral in August 1981, Charles stands, fully decked in Scottish kilt, while Diana is seated behind him, holding his hand. Though Charles is erect, towering above and occupying more physical space in the photograph than his wife, our gaze none the less reverts to Diana. Most of her biographies indicate how uncomfortable she was in front of the cameras, especially in those early years, yet, in spite of suffering from bulimia at the time, she, similar to Jackie, unself-consciously and effortlessly upstages her husband in his drab suits or full military garb (or kilts, as the case may be!).

Koestenbaum, in speaking of Jackie and JFK, interestingly notes that prior to the 1970s, when gay male standards of beauty began to enter the mainstream media, as in the Calvin Klein ads, male escorts of famous women need not have been attractive; a double standard existed which demanded that the woman be beautiful but forgave the man his physical flaws (Koestenbaum, 1996: 144–5). Though Koestenbaum is speaking of JFK, the same seems to be true for Diana and Charles in the 1980s and early 1990s; Charles's body appears as uptight, rigid, and aloof, probably according to royal protocol. It isn't that Charles simply isn't physically attractive; his body exudes desexualization, as well as a lack of charisma, in stark contrast to Diana's. During the couple's first official visit to Wales in 1981, when each would take a side of the street to greet the crowds, audible groans could be heard from the spectators on the side of the street chosen by Charles, thereby expressing their disappointment at not being able to see Diana up close, a trend which would continue as Diana's popularity grew, much to the consternation of Charles and his family. But in the early photographs of Diana and Charles, despite the attempts of the Palace to place Charles more in the limelight as the Prince of Wales and future King alongside his decorous wife, the photographic space, including that occupied by Charles, is organized around Diana. Like Jackie in photos with JFK, Diana is the Barthesian *punctum*. In contrast to the *studium* of a photograph, which Roland Barthes describes as the cultural, conscious participation 'in the figures, the faces, the gestures, the settings, the actions' (Barthes, 1981: 26), the *punctum* pricks, ruptures, pierces the *studium* (Barthes, 1981: 26–7); while the *studium* refers to the political and historical contexts surrounding the photograph, the photographic *punctum* is absolutely personal – it changes our reading, it overwhelms us and causes us to *linger*.

Photographs play an important role in constructing cultural icons in the contemporary world. As Susan Sontag reminds us: 'The camera makes reality atomic, manageable, and opaque . . . to see something in the form of a photograph is to encounter a potential object of fascination. . . . Photographs, which cannot themselves explain anything, are inexhaustible invitations to deduction, speculation, and fantasy' (Sontag, 1977: 23). Diana, photographed with Charles, pierces, ruptures, and perhaps wounds the fantasy of the picture-perfect heterosexual couple; the spectator's attention seems drawn invariably to her, not to Charles and what he, and his family, stand for, as if there is a gap between Diana's represented image in the photo and her more or less 'real' life, which, to most of us, is largely unknowable.

And on that grid, our own desires, fantasies, thoughts and feelings for her are projected, which, in turn, render Diana her status as cultural icon.

Around the mid-1980s, some time after the birth of Prince Harry, in resistance to the sanitized image the Palace wanted portrayed of the Princess of Wales, Diana wilfully discarded the romanticized English rose look with her soft pastel fabrics and high necklines and became not only more fashionable, but glamorous; Diana became a more contemporary, worldly woman in tailored, custom-made designer suits, sleek sleeveless evening gowns, and dazzling hairstyles that radically revised her image as she joined 'the ranks of the international glitterati' (Strong, 1997: 133), very similar to the ways in which Jackie's outfits and hairdos stood out in stark contrast to the First Ladies who preceded her. In photos of the period leading to her divorce, and in those in the period between her divorce and her death, whether in the breathtakingly beautiful formal poses captured by French photographer Patrick Demarchelier (many of which appear on covers of her biographies), in those of her hugging people in need, or in photos of her wearing simple cotton shirts and jeans while campaigning for the abolition of land mines in Angola and Bosnia, Diana, similar to Jackie, 'disorganizes the 2-D flatness of a photo' (Koestenbaum, 1996: 239); she emanates a sense of presence, especially in these later photos, that *pricks* the spectator, giving the snapshot its *snap!* quality.

Of course one cannot take the Diana/Jackie comparison too far; Jackie, largely through Koestenbaum's readings of her, provides a salient lens from which to begin to read Diana as icon, opening up several matrices, as I will discuss shortly, through which to read Diana's iconicity queerly. While both women epitomized the system of celebrity in contemporary culture, one crucial difference is that Jackie tried to avoid public attention as much as possible, which, ironically, made her image more sought, more enigmatic. Jackie, as Koestenbaum notes, seemed more detached from her celebrity (Koestenbaum, 1996: 284), while Diana clearly did not. Diana was part of the 'globalized, electronically connected culture' (Appleyard, 1997: 165), which, unlike Jackie, she often used to her own advantage, whether as a forum for confessional (as in her BBC *Panorama* interview with Martin Bashir in 1994), as a means to highlight her charity work and the causes she felt deserved wider attention, or to complain about unscrupulous media intervention in her personal life. So while Jackie played a more unintentional role in fashioning herself as a cultural icon by deliberately avoiding public attention and scrutiny, Diana, one might surmise, sometimes consciously, sometimes not, played a more proactive role in shaping her own iconicity. Certainly the recent deaths of both women, only three years apart, help point to important parallels in terms of how they are received and interpreted as cultural icons, as I have tried to show. And surely the images we have of both women will remain in circulation and remain more or less fixed as the various social and cultural contexts that surround and read their images move on and change. But, at the same time, we must remember that, as I have already mentioned, their lived lives are not necessarily reducible to their iconicity, just as Diana as icon and Jackie as icon are not reducible to each other.

But the question remains of the more specific status of Diana as a gay icon. And this is where I think her iconicity, while sharing similar qualities with that of Jackie's, differentiates itself and develops in ways that Jackie's did not. First, let me mention that we must resist the easy temptation to read Diana's iconicity queerly simply because she touched and spontaneously hugged AIDS sufferers, many of them gay men, without gloves and without restraint. Such a reading not only patronizes her and trivializes her commitment to candidly addressing the social issues, particularly homophobia, surrounding AIDS and HIV infection, it also further demeans the lives of those already devastated by the disease. Quite un-Diana-like, it is a reading that merely tokenizes the Other, holding people marked by difference at bay, at arm's length (as opposed to Diana's physical embracements), without any genuine understanding (or interest) in the ways in which they are positioned in the world, which is very often at the fringes of hegemonic social formations. Indeed, the question to ask is why Diana, or anyone else, would *need* gloves to touch or to hold someone with AIDS. The patronizing gesture which I criticize also carelessly misreads her struggle, as a mother of a future King, to shape a more relevant monarchy that does not simply stand on ceremony, bask in royal tradition, and remain aloof and distant from its subjects. When she took her son William to the hospital to visit her friend Adrian Ward-Jackson, who was suffering from complications from AIDS and eventually died, her purpose was not to present him with the spectacle of AIDS. Because the person who was HIV-infected and suffering was someone whom she knew and for whom she cared deeply, Diana effectively disrupted (for William, and perhaps for others) the simplistic correlation of the spectre of illness and decay with death related to AIDS, providing a formative opportunity for William not only to develop compassion and empathy for those who suffer, but to think deeply about the specific medical, social and political complexities that exist at the nexus of AIDS. Donald Spoto has acknowledged that her involvement with AIDS charities and her closeness to AIDS patients led to criticism that she was 'bowing to gay propaganda' (Spoto, 1997: 63), and Andrew Morton, in *Diana: Her True Story*, points out that her counselling of AIDS patients often met with hostility and anonymous hate mail (Morton, 1997: 171); yet, in defending Diana from such attacks, both Spoto and Morton sanitize her commitment to AIDS by reducing the specificity of the disease to a concern for illness in general. The lack of an antihomophobic position in most biographical work on Diana fails to explore how hostile responses to her involvement with AIDS reveal contempt for those (like Diana) who do not feel or act the way it is felt they should feel or act towards others whom society holds in contempt.

I mention this because I also think it provides a useful lens to begin framing the question as to how one might consider reading Diana's iconicity queerly. Her representativeness is significant to gay men and lesbians not because she hugged AIDS victims without wearing gloves, but because this was one of several ways in which she crossed social and political boundaries. On one level, Diana's glamour, her social status, her jet-set lifestyle, her indulgences in pleasure, and her naughty indiscretions align her closely with Jackie O. And we must acknowledge that, like Diana, Jackie also did some boundary crossing of her own by breaking away from oppressive family relations in refusing the role of the mourning widow her in-laws had constructed for her, and by marrying, much to the chagrin of the Kennedy family, Aristotle Onassis. Koestenbaum reads the signifier 'O' of 'Jackie O' as 'Oh my!', as if we are in shock at her conduct in that she provokes open-mouthed awe (Koestenbaum, 1996: 156). Jackie's independence of mind, her transgression of conventional cultural norms held as right for a former US First Lady that were mired in the memory of her husband, duty to her children, and remaining chaste ('in the closet', sexually speaking), at least in the public eye, all of which served to efface her own desires, certainly have resonance for lesbians and gay men. Though we may use Jackie as a point of reference for talking about Diana as a (gay) icon, Diana went much further. While Jackie remained aloof like most of the British royal family today, Diana *flaunted* it – not her wealth and her privileged position as did Fergie – but her beauty, her weaknesses and vulnerabilities, her compassion for others.

Unlike the other Windsors, Diana didn't merely gaze out at the world, but moved effectively through it. Yet one cannot go so far as Spoto, who claims that because Diana mixed freely with many different kinds of people, she stood for a new classless society, which the world sees as the fruit of democracy (Spoto, 1997: 105). This is no more than Utopian; Diana did show us her vulnerabilities, which seemed to make her more human, yet she remained none the less an aristocrat, leading a life that was by no means classless or 'common'. But she did help revise the way we see, and are told to see, the British royal family, and she effectively shattered the myth of the Windsors as emblematic of heteronormative family life. As Morton points out, Diana's struggles within the royal family made her realize that she did not want to hide behind the conventional mask of monarchy to the extent that conventional royal life anaesthetizes individuals from the world (Morton, 1997: 205) outside its very visible, and clearly demarcated, borders. As she resisted the self-serving ideology of royal protocol, scapegoating by the royal family for its own problems with public relations, psychological abuse and emotional neglect from her husband, and, ultimately, attempts of the royal family and Palace courtiers to silence her, gay men and women watched Diana grow assertive. Indeed her *queer* 'coming out' was not her wedding, but was in her creation of multiple subject positions to inhabit rather than merely accepting those already appropriated for her.

It would be similarly Utopian to assume that, at some point, Diana simply became a self-determining subject, transcending ideological influence from the monarchy in particular and from her privileged class position in Britain and elsewhere. An important turning point that enabled her to cross social and political boundaries effectively was her own more critical reading of the interaction of ideological pressures in her life and her own subjective existence. Her resistance, following Paul Smith's work on subjectivity, was possible through her readings both of the ways in which she was implicated in systems of power and ideology and of the disturbances and contradictions in and among the multiple subject positions she held (P. Smith, 1988: xxxi, xxxv) – as princess, as (single) mother, as woman, as philanthropist, as citizen, as celebrity, to name a few. She becomes emblematic for queers not through her sexual identity, but metaphorically, through what Catharine R. Stimpson, in speaking of 'lesbian' as a political position, has eloquently described as 'that invaluable way of being in, with, and against the world' (Stimpson, 1990: 377).

More specifically, Diana crossed the boundaries of gender. In the early years of her marriage, she performed, and was expected to take on, the role of obedient, docile wife and dutiful mother. Spoto writes that during her courtship with Charles, the Queen saw value in Diana's shyness, which seemed to indicate submissiveness (Spoto, 1997: 54). Yet when it became evident to her that the marriage was collapsing, and when the royal family and its spin machines closed ranks against her, characterizing her as irrational, hysterical and unreasonable, once again (de-)feminizing her as one who had lost 'proper' gender, Diana refused to go away quietly. Joan Smith and others have written how royal women have traditionally been expected to relinquish personal satisfaction for the greater good of the monarchy (as was the case with Princess Margaret, who had to give up a marriage proposal from Peter Townsend who was divorced) (J. Smith, 1997: 155). Refusing the gender(ed) expectations that she would be dutiful and sacrifice personal happiness for the greater good of an institution that demonized, abused, and nearly demoralized her, Diana spoke out publicly, with an unusual blend of eloquence and defiance, about Charles's infidelities and his indifference to her bulimia and depression during most of their marriage. The contestation of regulatory regimes of gender is often central to queer politics to the extent that the social abjection of homosexuality, read as damaged or failed gender, is reworked into political agency and defiance.

Such contentious practices, as Judith Butler's work has illustrated, open up critical spaces to re-theorize relations between gender and sexuality beyond the causal and reductive ones posited by heteronormativity. The proliferation and persistence of gender identities that do not adhere to the 'norm' through which bodies, genders and desires are naturalized expose the limits of the cultural intelligibility of gender and help open up subversive matrices of gender dis-order within that very (heterosexual) matrix of intelligibility (Butler, 1990: 17). Butler is clear in her later work that cross-gendered identification is not the only paradigm for thinking about homosexuality, but one among others (Butler, 1997: 146); while Diana did not go so far as to make a cross-gender identification, her refusal to cite the gender norm none the less, I would argue, links her to queerness though such a refusal may not appear to be obviously subversive. As Alexander Doty reminds us in *Making Things Perfectly Queer*, queerness, in interpreting mass culture, can be read as 'a quality related to any expression that can be marked as contra-, non-, or anti-straight' (Doty, 1993: xv).

In *Bodies that Matter*, Butler indicates that gender norms operate by requiring the embodiment of certain ideals of femininity and masculinity, almost always tied to the idealization of the heterosexual bond (Butler, 1993: 231–2). Diana's wedding and her production of two heirs certainly were gender(ed) performances, nearly theatrical in their cultural representation, which enhanced the social idealization of heterosexuality in the strongest sense of the word, given the almost impenetrable bonds between femininity, hegemonically conceived, and the subject position of princess. But at the same time, Diana's later refusal to limit herself only to royal ideals of femininity, and her disavowal of the concomitant relations of discipline and regulation that accompany them, enabled a reformulation of gender, a redeployment of the categories of the dominant culture, and operated oppositionally. Her decision, and her subsequent actions resulting from it, reveal another failure of heteronormativity, which insists on fixed notions of gender and sexuality, to legislate its ideals fully. Through becoming more assertive, by publicly accusing her husband of infidelity and insensitivity, and by eventually moving out and into the world instead of simply receiving it, Diana didn't transcend royalty, or the monarchy as a political institution, but she did socially transform the role of princess and the archaic gender and family norms that attend it. Similar to queer performativity, Diana's life, especially after her marriage, both contained *and* exceeded the heterosexual matrix. As Butler sums up:

> Performativity describes this relation of being implicated in that which one opposes, this turning of power against itself to produce alternative modalities of power, to establish a kind of political contestation that is not a 'pure' opposition, a 'transcendence' of contemporary relations of

power, but a difficult labor of forging a future from resources inevitably impure. (Butler, 1993:241)

Closely related, Diana's life and memory work as a potential site of identification for queers not only because both are a critique of the British establishment, as Clive Aslet has noted (Aslet, 1997:159), but because her life and her memory also work more specifically as critiques of normalizing regimes, including that of the nuclear family, which serve the interests of patriarchal power. While she remained a dedicated and loving mother until the end of her life, and while she was sexually straight, Diana was able to expose the dysfunctionality of the Windsors, shatter their pretence to serve as a healthy model for family and domestic life, and effectively collapse the myth of her so-called 'fairy-tale' marriage to Charles. Her relationship with Dodi Fayed, who was also part of her children's lives, enabled not only the redeployment of gender norms insofar as she unapologetically enjoyed sexuality outside the confines of marriage and procreation, both of which are legibly inscribed in her position as princess, but also showed the world the ways in which it is possible to realign one's affectional and familial bonds in meaningful ways beyond those dictated by convention, by biology, or by marriage – a narrative which is so familiar to contemporary gay and lesbian life.

There has been speculation that, had she lived, Diana might have married Dodi Fayed. Perhaps so. But could it be possible that the happiness many of her friends reported that she had found with Dodi, and on her own after her divorce, came out of the fact that she and Dodi were not bound by marriage? I cannot agree with Spoto's seemingly racist and misogynistic implications about the Diana/Dodi relationship, that is, that Diana 'had *so recently* selected a *Muslim* playboy for the object of her affections' and that 'her subsequent marriage to a *man of color* would have outraged class-conscious Buckingham Palace even more than her maverick charitable causes and her earlier love affairs' (Spoto, 1997:188–9; emphasis added). One wonders who else would have been outraged besides the Palace, and one cannot help but invoke, once again, Jackie and the admonishment directed towards her for marrying Aristotle Onassis 'so soon' (i.e., five years!) after the Kennedy assassination. But, in considering the normalizing forces that organize and regulate heterosexual marriage and family life, I am not so sure that Diana would have married again – and if she did, given her unhappy first marriage, she would certainly not have done so as an act of retaliation against the royal family. Perhaps she had 'selected' Dodi simply because she loved him, because he, too, had reciprocally 'selected' and loved her. But I think Diana was more subversive (and more queer) as single. Indeed, the period between her divorce and her death was the most interesting in her life as she became a public figure in her own right.

Remarriage would have most likely represented a regression for Diana, a return, perhaps, to the metaphorical closet, where her desires for pleasure, for achieving good in the world, for personal fulfilment outside of the marriage might have been subordinated through the demands of married life. Obviously the Palace was somewhat aware of this; hence, the orchestration and redeployment of the fantasy of heteronormative life as it arranged Diana's funeral, with her former husband and ex-father-in-law following the funeral cortège (together with Princes William and Harry and her brother, Earl Spencer) to Westminster Abbey. Fortunately, this did not obfuscate our memory of Diana as colourful, defiant, glamorous, and having a bite. From a queer perspective, at a time when the signifier 'family' seems stubbornly lodged to the heterosexual nuclear family and legitimated only by marriage, Diana's stature and her realignment of familial bonds have helped to create a tear in the social conflation of heterosexual marriage with family life. Eve Sedgwick has written about the need for more inclusive understandings of family

> in order to project into the future a vision of 'family' elastic enough to do justice to the depth and sometimes durability of nonmarital and/or nonprocreative bonds, same-sex bonds, nondyadic bonds, bonds not defined by genitality, 'step'-bonds, adult sibling bonds, nonbiological bonds across generations, etc. At the same time ... a different angle ... onto the family of the *present* can show this heterosexist structure always already awash with homosexual energies and potentials, even with lesbian and gay persons, whose making-visible might then require only an adjustment of the interrogatory optic, the bringing *to* the family structure of the pressure of our different claims, our different needs.   (Sedgwick, 1993: 71)

Diana's life, whether consciously or not, provided that angle and put pressure on the revered and often static definition of family, which helped to open it up and make it more susceptible to other configurations including same-sex bonds. And the extraordinary blend of energy, dignity and defiance with which she accomplished this is part of the pleasure we take in reading icon Diana queerly.

Many gay men and lesbians identified with Diana's struggles to break away from the narrow confines of 'appropriate' gender behaviour imposed on her by her birthright (royal women do not go to rock concerts in leather slacks!), by marriage, and by patriarchal family relations, all of which exerted keen pressure on her to become something she clearly did not want to be – in her case, an emblematic Windsor without voice or subjective agency. In the last part of her marriage and in her brief life afterwards, similar to Jackie's, yet played out very differently in her own lived experience, Diana resisted inhabiting subject positions that inhibited the expression of her desires, and, in so doing, found new ways to create alternative affectional and familial bonds while keeping the traditional family ones that meant most to her (her sons). Through working hard to overcome bulimia, depression, intense alienation, an unhappy marriage and family life, and other personal difficulties, Diana won the respect and admiration of most of the world. However, this last stage of respect, indeed of admiration from the world at large, for overcoming what often appear to be insurmountable odds, has yet to be realized by lesbians and gay men for the continual struggles we face – this, perhaps, is a fantasy, a hope, a desire, that I project onto the grid of Diana's life and memory in the hope that one day it will.

14

Identity Judgements, Queer Politics

Mark Norris Lance and Alessandra Tanesini

Political identities have received bad press for quite some time. Sexual identities constitute no exception to this trend. Nearly ten years ago Judith Butler expressed her ambivalent relation to identity categories by calling them 'necessary errors', whilst at the same time holding that 'there remains a political imperative to use [them]'.[1] In more recent times, Alan Sinfield has suggested that we might be entering a period which he labels 'post-gay'. This period is characterized by the realization that metropolitan post-Stonewall gay and, perhaps, lesbian identities 'are historical phenomena and may now be hindering us more than they help us'.[2] Sinfield gives voice, then, to the hope that in this new period 'it will not seem so necessary to define, and hence to limit, our sexualities'. For reasons not dissimilar to those advanced by Butler, however, Sinfield cannot bring himself to reject identities altogether. Instead, he enjoins us 'to entertain more diverse and permeable identities'.[3]

This uneasiness or discomfort with identities is widespread among queer theorists.[4] This common ambivalence has several sources. The reasons that motivate suspicion about sexual identities are well known. Among them, there is, of course, the tired, and by now tiresome, argument that identities presuppose essences. Perhaps more crucial is the assumption that sexual identities limit or constrain sexuality in ways that must be resisted. Sometimes this assumption is motivated by the desire to undermine the dichotomy between hetero- and homosexuality. At other times, it depends implicitly on a radical libertarian position that any constraint imposed on our sexual practices is oppressive, since it limits our freedom. Finally, a negative attitude toward identities is motivated by a discontentment with the shortcomings of identity politics as traditionally understood.

Nevertheless, theorists never advocate the end of all sexual identities as a proposal for the immediate future. There is little doubt that many individuals take their sexual orientation to be a feature which plays an important role in their perception of who they are. They feel that in some sense they would not

171

be the same person if their sexual orientation were to change. For this reason it seems deeply unrealistic to deny that sexuality is, in the current situation, one component of personal identity; hence the tendency to preserve, despite numerous reservations, talk of sexuality as an identity.

Awareness of the views shared by the vast majority of gay men and lesbians, activists included, must also be part of what motivates theorists to preserve the idea of sexual identities. Most gay people take their sexuality to be fairly fixed, something which is unlikely to change. They often also perceive it as something about which they had very little choice. More strikingly, in recent times many gay men and lesbians believe that they were born gay.[5] A widespread belief that sexual identities can be explained biologically stands in direct opposition to the social constructionist view which is now the orthodoxy among scholars working in queer theory, history and politics.[6]

This formulation of the division between academics and the majority of gay people leads to an impasse. This stalemate, however, cannot be ignored if we care about politics, since it has given rise to incomprehension as well as several degrees of separation between theory and political practice. Given this background we intend in this article to reconsider the notions of personal and collective identities.

We do not want to begin, however, by asking a direct question about what sexual identities might be. Instead, we hold that questions about the importance of identity *claims* offer a better starting point. Thus, our question is: what is one committed to when one claims that one has a particular sexual identity?[7] We do not assume that there is a reality – either biological or socially constructed – which identity claims purport to describe. Instead, we argue that identity claims are not descriptive. Their correctness is not a matter of descriptive truth; it is not a matter of the presence of biological or social truth-makers. Identity judgements, we hold, are normative.[8] They are political endorsements of particular sorts of psychological and sociological placings, whose appropriateness can be evaluated only within specific political contexts. We hope that the theoretical advantages of choosing this starting point will become clearer as our argument develops. Nevertheless, it might be useful to begin with a consideration which speaks in favour of this approach.

There is a common tendency, widespread among academics, to avoid the difficulties involved in genuinely political questions. Nowhere is this tendency more manifest than in recent discussions about identity politics among feminists and queer theorists. In these discussions political issues of commitment and strategy have been transformed into metaphysical questions about essences – or the lack thereof – and social constructs. Hence Cindy Patton's suspicion that 'deconstructionists may believe in the imputed essentialist identities much more than those in the political sphere who are purported to have them'.[9]

In this manner, theorists dream of an end to all disagreements. They hope to home in on the right theory about identity which will answer their problems once and for all. This theory will either explain what identities are or dissolve them. In either case, theoretical discoveries will be a substantial guide for political decisions. This approach, we argue, is misguided. Discussions about identities cannot ever be settled solely by looking at the biological, social or even cultural facts. They are genuine political discussions, and – as such – not based on any metaphysics, even a negative one. Disagreements which cannot be settled by means of non-normative considerations will, thus, always arise.

In this article we first explain and defend our account of identity judgements as normative claims, showing why it is a mistake to conceive of identities in biological terms. Some social constructionist accounts are, however, equally defective. Perhaps surprisingly, one consequence of our account is that the claim to be straight as a matter of identity is unlikely ever to be appropriate. Further, we argue that most current accounts of political identities are descriptive. Even performative accounts of identity categories, we contend, fall within this camp since they amount to descriptive interpretations of normative judgements.

AM I THAT NAME? THE PSYCHOLOGICAL SIGNIFICANCE OF IDENTITY ATTRIBUTIONS

We all take ourselves to have several identities. One might, for example, be a mother or a father, a woman, a socialist, or a philosopher. These identities carry with them desires and inclinations. Philosophers, for instance, like abstract thinking, and fathers are inclined to play with their children. These desires and inclinations, however, do not in themselves constitute identities. One might like ice-cream without taking being an ice-cream lover to be a matter of identity. Identities play a far more prominent role in our psychology than mere likes and dislikes. Further, identities are often associated with social roles and mere inclinations do not have this sort of social significance.

We claimed that identity judgements are endorsements of psychological and social placings and also that identity judgements are normative. In order to make good our positions, however, we need to turn first to questions concerning the psychological and social significances of taking oneself, and being taken by others, to be of a given identity. Our immediate concern is thus not with what identities themselves might *be*, but with the significance of identity attributions. Borrowing from Anthony Appiah's account of the psychological significance of identity claims,[10] we label the three aspects of this account 'felt demand', 'call to coherence', and 'normative projection'.

Appiah claims that identities provide scripts by which to live. These scripts are not fully determined, but they offer reasons for and against some ways of acting. It is hard to see, for example, how one could take oneself to be a socialist as a matter of identity without being thereby committed to working towards ending specific forms of injustice. If one never engages in this kind of work, sees no reason to do so, and does not even perceive this as a problem, then one is simply not a socialist. In this way identities pose demands on us to which we are sensitive, provided that we take that identity to be part of who we are.

Related to the fact that identities pose demands on us is the fact that we feel the need to try to reconcile the scripts that accompany each of our different identities. Thus, identities issue a call to coherence. It might never be possible to achieve full coherence between our identities since they might always make demands on us that take us in different and, perhaps, incompatible directions. In these cases one will perceive some sort of rational tension which one might try to alleviate in a variety of ways. For example, there might be tensions between those commitments to our parents which follow from our identities as their sons and daughters, and our commitments to our partners which stem from a different aspect of our identity. In this case, we will attempt to find strategies to make these two sets of commitments more compatible.

Sometimes, however, one might find two aspects of one's identity to be so irreconcilable that one will feel a demand to abandon one of them. One might, for example, come to the conclusion that being gay is incompatible with being a religious believer. In this case one holds that the commitments and demands that follow from being a religious believer conflict with those which follow from taking being gay as a matter of identity. If one believes that there is no justifying story which can bestow some discursive coherence on these two aspects of one's identity, one might stop taking oneself to be a religious believer.

These examples show that self-attributions of identities come with commitments. They also show that we expect – in the sense of call for – some discursive coherence between different aspects of our and others' identities. Hence, it is perfectly appropriate to be critical of somebody who does not even perceive a conflict between his gayness and his membership of, say, the Catholic Church.[11] As these examples show, then, identity attributions are subject to normative constraints.

Since identities carry commitments, they project normatively rather than merely causally into the future. Suppose being a mother is one of your identities. Of course you can predict that you will care for your children in the future. More importantly, however, your identity places future demands on you; it carries a commitment to care for your children in the future.

Caring for your children in the future is not simply something you know you will do. It is also something you feel you ought to do.

Of course, things can change: people get divorced, change sexual orientation, give up philosophy. However, if they do so on a whim, and feel no need to provide themselves and others with reasons for the change, we will doubt the extent to which being married, having that sexual orientation, or being a philosopher were ever significant parts of their identity.

Identities also have a significance for one's place in society besides being, as we have already explained, of psychological significance. Thus, whether one is taken to be a woman, or a man, single or not, makes a difference to how others treat you as well as to how it is generally assumed you ought to be treated. Identities are a matter of social significance. There is a world of difference in the significance of knowingly serving pork to someone who dislikes it and to a practising Muslim. Generally people could not carry out the commitments that are, for them, associated with their identities were they not facilitated by others. People need their identities to be recognized as a matter of psychological and social significance. When social facilitation is not forthcoming, as in the cases of working mothers or gay parents, we are dealing with *prima facie* cases of oppression.

TWO MISTAKES: BIOLOGICAL AND SOCIAL DESCRIPTIVISM

What we have said so far should already be sufficient to show that biology is not even a candidate for an explanation of sexual identities. Accordingly, the debate over gay genes is a red herring. We believe that there is very little evidence for the belief that there are biological causes of homosexual sexual inclination. But, even if sexual inclination was biologically determined, this fact would not make sexual identities a matter of biology.

An analogy should help to make this explicit. Consider the case of a person who is revolted by strawberry ice-cream. Suppose that this revulsion is genetically determined. This fact does not make hating strawberry ice-cream a matter of identity for the person in question. More specifically, mere likes and dislikes, whether or not they are genetically determined, do not project normatively into the future. The person who hates strawberry ice-cream might be in a position to predict that her dislike will not change. However, it makes no sense to say that she is committed to disliking this kind of ice-cream in the future. Further, were her dislike to change we might be surprised, but would not think that she needs a justifying story for her change. Similarly, mere likes and dislikes do not issue calls to coherence. We would be surprised if the person who disliked strawberry ice-cream so strongly loved fresh strawberries as well as ice-cream in other flavours. But, neither we nor the person in question would feel a need to alleviate any conceptual conflict.

This analogy shows that there can be behaviours which have a deep biological root and are, therefore, fairly fixed, but which are not a matter of identity. Further, there are identities, such as being a socialist, for which it seems absolutely ludicrous to suppose a biological aetiology. It is possible, however, that biological and social facts about the individual are a necessary condition for the correct attribution of some sorts of identities to that individual. Examples of such identities could be: being black, being American, or being a woman, as well as being queer. Even so, these facts do not *constitute* that identity. To suppose that they do is a category mistake.

In the case of biological facts this is quite clear. Suppose that the claim to be gay is the assertion that certain biological facts are true of oneself. We have seen that attributions of identities to oneself give reasons for and against some forms of behaviour, issue calls to coherence with other aspects of one's identity, and project normatively into the future. But, attributions to oneself of a certain biological nature have no such consequences. On the basis of biology we can expect – in the causal sense of 'predict' – a certain future behaviour to occur. On the basis of identity judgements we can expect – in the discursive sense of 'call for' – a certain future behaviour to occur. To think of identities in biological terms involves confusing normative for causal constraints.

The irrelevance of biology to identity judgements might, incidentally, explain why many activists who believe that they were born gay or lesbians do not necessarily engage in the kind of identity politics one might expect to be associated with so-called essentialist accounts of identity. These activists make a distinction between what they think has caused them to have homosexual inclinations, and what being gay or queer as a matter of identity means to them. The distinction may not always be clearly articulated, but it is sufficiently entrenched. No one looks to biology to find out how they ought to behave, whilst almost everybody holds that social and political commitments follow from attributing a given identity to oneself.

Even sophisticated accounts of identities as social constructions are not immune from the same category mistake of taking a descriptive claim for a normative one. More precisely, these accounts often employ a descriptive interpretation of normative judgements in their accounts of identity. They identify the normative nature of identity claims, which we have discussed in its psychological and social dimensions, with what is done in one's society. In other words, they reduce normativity to normality. It is, therefore, not surprising that identities have got such bad press. If we are right that current social constructionist accounts of identity ultimately take identities to be defined by what is normal in society, it becomes clearer why theorists have taken identities to be, as a matter of theoretical necessity, limiting in oppressive ways. But what, more precisely, is meant by a descriptive account of the normativity of identity, and what is the alternative proposal?

We have claimed that commitments and expectations follow from identity judgements. For example, being judged to be a woman makes a difference as to how one is treated. Thus, it is not uncommon to hear from some quarters that women ought to get married, look after children, stay at home, and so on. This is a particularly conservative view of the commitments associated with being a woman. Similarly, it is not unusual to hear that gay men and lesbians should not have children. This too is a conservative view of the sort of scripts associated with gay and lesbian identities. Social institutions and practices also define, sometimes implicitly, sometimes explicitly, the commitments and responsibilities which are taken to flow from given identities.

Some crude social constructionist accounts identify being of an identity with the occupation of such a social role. These accounts take identity claims to be purely descriptive of one's position in society. According to these accounts, whatever norms might be associated with identities, they are not constitutive of the identities in question. Rather, the identities, seen as social positions, logically precede the norms associated with them.

More recent social constructionist accounts are less crude. They acknowledge that identities are normative in the sense that being of a certain identity is constituted by, not just constitutive of, norms. However, they understand 'norm' in a weak sense that makes it a function of what is taken to be proper in society. In other words, they take the norms constitutive of identities to have merely a *de facto* normative force. Normative, here, refers to the kind of behaviour that is licensed or sanctioned within the society. According to this view, to be of a certain identity is to be the kind of person for whom certain forms of behaviour, but not others, are taken to be proper.

This new form of social constructionism is not committed to the belief that identities pre-exist the norms of identity. On the contrary, the view entails that identities are constituted by the current social-normative significance attributed to identities. Nevertheless, this view continues to be committed to a form of descriptivism. It assumes that claiming that one is of an identity is tantamount to asserting that one is the sort of person who is subject to the demands and commitments which society (or the majority, or some future idealized version of the majority) associates with that identity. It is rather obvious that identities so understood will always function as stumbling blocks. The grammar of identity claims, according to this view, entails that when making such a claim one implicitly accepts what the majority says is proper for an individual of one's own kind.

Given the current popularity of performative accounts of identities, our charge is bound to sound paradoxical, to say the least. It seems rather obvious that performatives are not descriptive (that is, constative). Yet, despite appearances to the contrary, we believe that these constructionist accounts ultimately rely on descriptive interpretations of normative judgements. In this regard, it is useful to consider Butler's accounts of gender identity, since she was the first to provide a sustained account of the performativity of identity.

In *Gender Trouble* Butler claims that the critical task of feminism is to identify and participate in 'those practices of repetition that constitute identity and, therefore, present the immanent possibility of contesting them'.[12] What are being repeated in the practices of repetition are norms.[13] But these norms are nothing other than what is taken to be proper, what has *de facto* normative force. Norms are tantamount to prescriptions of what is normal. They are merely the result of compulsory regulatory regimes. For this reason, Butler takes the repetitions that constitute identities to be imitations of the currently accepted norms of heterosexuality. However, since we are always bound to fall short, since we never fully embody what is proper in accordance with these norms, we are compelled to repeat our attempt to comply with them.

Butler argues that identity claims do not describe a pre-existing hidden nature. Thus, she abandons crude forms of descriptivism. She does, however, adopt a descriptivist account of identity judgements. This fact is obscured by her decision to call her view a performative account of identities.

There are at least three related problems with this view. First, it misreads what people do when they claim a currently despised identity for themselves. According to these sophisticated social constructionist accounts, self-attributions of identity amount to asserting that one occupies the psychological and social placings that are currently associated with that identity. For example, in the case of queer identity, to claim that one is queer would amount to asserting that one occupies a position about which it is appropriate to feel ashamed, and guilty. But, we contend, when people claim 'We're here, we're queer, get used to it!', they are not implicitly accepting what society takes to be proper for queers.

Second, the view makes it hard to explain why people take on despised identities. Usually, one will need to resort to accounts that show that individuals were forced into the mould of the despised identity. In this case, however, it becomes a mystery why people valorize their despised identities, since these identities would be purely the result of oppressive forces. Further, given the psychological centrality of identity attributions, these constructionist accounts will interpret individuals who take themselves to belong to an oppressed identity to be always clinging to, and valorizing, what is a direct result of their oppression.[14] Thus, these individuals will, of necessity, contribute to the continuation of their oppression. That we can achieve a political conclusion of such generality from a claim about the grammar of identity claims should make us extremely suspicious of these constructionist views.

Third, these accounts practically rule out the possibility of using identity attributions for progressive ends. If claiming that one is of an identity is a description of what society takes to be proper for individuals of that identity, then identity claims always function as implicit reassertions of the status quo.

In order to overcome these problems, we suggest that one take seriously the normative nature of identity judgements. Thus, we subscribe to a radical normativity thesis about identity claims. In our view, to claim an identity for oneself is to endorse a cluster of attitudes, behaviours and judgements on the part of oneself and of society, and to undertake a commitment to defend their appropriateness. In our opinion, therefore, identity judgements *are* moral and political evaluations. They do not describe the evaluations currently associated with the identity, as in the social constructionist interpretation; rather, they consist in an endorsement of a range of psychological and sociological placings, and of their consequences. The placings, attitudes and behaviours one endorses by claiming oneself to be of a given identity, however, could be somewhat at variance with those currently associated with that identity. (However, they cannot be totally at variance with current evaluations, because in such a case it would be nonsensical to hold that one is claiming that same identity, rather than a different one, for oneself.)

To summarize: in our view, to say that one is of a given identity is to say that one *ought* to take that identity to be part of one's script for one's life, that one ought to allow an associated script to demand coherence with one's other scripts, that one ought to take this identity to project normatively into the future, and that others ought to assign social priority to facilitating one's living according to the resulting narrative unity of the various scripts. To say who one is, then, is not to describe one's hidden nature, because it is not to describe at all. At the same time, it is therefore neither empty nor a mere description of how one is currently treated, for it is an endorsement.

'STRAIGHT' IS NOT AN IDENTITY

So far we have discussed the grammar of identity judgements, and suggested that they are political endorsements. But, we have not made fully clear what identities themselves might be. In our view, identities are a matter of the correctness of identity judgements. Thus, if one *claims* to be of an identity, and one's claim is correct, then one *is* of that identity. Since identity claims are normative – they are political endorsements – their correctness conditions are not a matter of corresponding to something in the world, some biological or even socio-cultural facts. Rather, identity judgements are correct whenever genuine political and moral goods are endorsed by making those claims.[15]

A consequence of our view is that it is impossible to have a totally bad political identity. One can, of course, make claims to such an identity. For example, one can make racist beliefs normative for oneself. One can hold that society should facilitate one's attempt to prevent miscegenation and so forth. However, these identity claims are never correct since what they endorse are not political and moral goods. By claiming such a racist identity for oneself one is claiming that society ought to give one a special status, accord one privileges and make it easier for one to act on one's racist beliefs. However, since the racist is not entitled to such status, and privileges, their claim to these entitlements is incorrect. In other words, the racist claim to identity is wrong, because by making it the racist claims entitlements, which would be constitutive of an identity, that he does not have. (This case shows why another sort of performative analysis – one which would equate having an identity with asserting that one has it – won't do. Since normative obligations on the part of others follow from an identity ascription, neither thinking nor saying that one has an identity makes it so.)

With reference to the specific case of sexual identities, we think that it is highly likely that, whilst it is sometimes appropriate to claim being gay or queer as a matter of identity, it is never appropriate to claim a heterosexual identity. Although it is foolish to make general claims at this level of abstraction, we are confident that, at least in the context of contemporary British and American cultures, being straight is not a genuine identity. Thus, we reach the surprising conclusion that there is an asymmetry in the case of sexual identities, since gay and queer identities exist, but heterosexual identities do not.

We shall deal with some of the obvious objections to this conclusion in what follows, after having provided some reasons in its favour. It must be stressed that these are exclusively political and moral reasons. We have entered at this juncture the fray of political discussions and disagreements. It is perfectly possible for somebody to agree with what we have said about the grammar of identity judgements, and about identities as a matter of normative status, and violently disagree with the purely political evaluations that follow. They are offered here because we recommend them, but also because these discussions allow us to clarify a few features of identity judgements as we understand them.

We have claimed that to accord to sexuality the status of an identity is to endorse the taking up of a particular script as normative for one's thought and behaviour, and to demand society's facilitation of one's living a life which coherently conjoins this script with one's other identities. But exactly which script is in question here? Three senses could be given to this normative issue, senses we label 'conservative', 'ideal' and 'tactical'.

A conservative identity endorsement is an endorsement of a range of psychological attitudes and social roles of the sort currently associated with that identity by currently dominant social practices. It is not thereby a mere description of these attitudes and roles, but rather a political act which attempts to preserve the status quo. All identity judgements are script-endorsements, and if the script in question is precisely the dominant one, then the act of so judging is a way of throwing one's social weight and epistemic authority behind current practice.

In the case of sexual identity, this would mean an endorsement of stereotypical psychological identities by either gay or straight people, and an endorsement of the oppressive social order of heterosexist practice. We have little to say about this potential endorsement as it is quite clearly inappropriate. No one who opposes homophobia could endorse taking up either social position definitive of that oppressive relationship.

When thinking of race, one would similarly not be likely to endorse the current scripts and social positionings of racist society. One might, however, be prepared to make what we call an 'ideal' identity judgement. To do this is to envision a future non-racist society, and to endorse an amended version of racial categories – presumably some sort of ethnic identity – which would be appropriate and defensible in that context. In the case of sexuality, however, we do not see any progressive role for ideal endorsements either. In other words, we do not believe that in a society free of heterosexist bias, it would make much sense to elevate one's sexual inclinations to the status of an identity. We see no reason why in such a society it would be morally and politically good to turn one's current *inclination* to find partners of a particular gender into a *commitment* not to change that inclination. In such a society people might still have fairly settled sexual inclinations towards people of one gender rather than another, and they might be able to predict that this will continue to be the case. But there seems to be no good reason to make this a matter of normative concern.

Contrast the elevation of one's inclinations to stay with a particular partner. Here there is a clear reason why, even in the absence of oppression, one would take this to be a matter of identity. The elevation of the inclinational to the normative that is constitutive of identity here serves a positive force in shaping the nature of the relationship. Families can only be what they are because they are taken on with normative significance. But we see no corresponding reason to take one's inclination, should one's current partner die, to be attracted to future partners of a given gender as a matter of normative concern in a non-homophobic world. And if no positive good is served, then there can be no grounds for demanding that society facilitates the identity.

The third and most interesting sort of identity judgement, and the one in which an asymmetry emerges, is what we refer to as a tactical identity endorsement. In this case, we claim that there are politically progressive gay identity claims and no progressive straight identity claims in the contexts of

British and American societies. We have said that to claim oneself to be gay is to make one's sexual inclination a matter of normative concern. To do so involves adopting a certain conception of oneself which gives reasons for and against attitudes and behaviours. One will feel the need to make the rest of one's life rationally cohere as much as possible with this aspect of one's psychology, and one will take this conception to project normatively in the future. In other words, one will endorse a commitment to preserve one's current set of desires and inclinations and, importantly, demand social facilitation of this stance toward one's life.

In the case of tactical identity endorsements, what is being endorsed is not the script which is currently associated with gay identity. Rather, this embracing of gay identity will involve substantial revisions of this script. There is no need to assume that everybody who makes a tactical endorsement of a gay identity will thereby endorse precisely the same revisions of the attitudes and self-conceptions which society takes to be proper for gay people. Just as in the case of an assertion of marital identity or of oneself as a socialist, there is scope for variance on this issue; and there is scope for ethical and political discussion.

Similar considerations apply on the social front. One can endorse society's taking oneself to be gay, and endorse that there are statuses, obligations, expectations and privileges carried by that attribution, without embracing the current set of such normative expectations as just, or good. Further, there is a politically progressive point to such endorsements. They are acts of solidarity whereby one affirms a commitment to being treated as others are being treated.

Such political acts belong to an old tradition of endorsing a social positioning for oneself with an eye to subverting the significance of that social position. For example, to be queer in the old usage was first to be excluded from what is 'proper', and then to be reviled for it. To call oneself queer in the new usage is to endorse that exclusion and to turn the evaluation on its head, to embrace difference as a challenge to what is regarded as proper.[16]

NOT ONE OF MY WORDS

There are no symmetrical political considerations that would indicate that genuine ethical and political goods are endorsed by means of straight tactical identity judgements. Let us begin with the psychological. It is hard to see anything of value in a tactical embracing of straight identity. One of us is not gay, and he is married to a member of the opposite gender. Suppose, for purposes of argument, that he were able to predict that he would only be attracted to women should he lose his current partner. What would be gained by taking this projection into the normative realm?

Why would one want to make this into a normative concern at all? In the case of gay identity, the point was to commit oneself to a project and to embrace one's place in the division of political labour. There is no corresponding point in the straight case.

The primary social markers of a positioning as straight are the trappings of privilege. One is considered by dominant society to be more trustworthy with children, more valuable as an employee, even more likely to be rational and unbiased when discussing gay politics. Obviously none of this privilege is deserved. Thus it would be wrong to endorse the social granting of it. This is not to say that one can avoid being granted it. One's inclinations, if known, will be enough for heterosexist society to grant one privilege, but to take one's heterosexuality on as a matter of identity is to endorse this granting of privilege and to make it central in one's life. Denying 'straightness', is a disavowal of such privilege. Such a refusal, though it won't prevent others from recognizing privilege, at least calls into question the universal assumption that such would be welcome.

One should not confuse this political act of refusal with a failure to acknowledge the unwarranted privilege that generally accrues to individuals who are taken to be heterosexuals. It is not uncommon to hear individuals complain that gay activists are too vocal about their sexuality. These individuals might even assert that they do not think of themselves as heterosexuals, but merely as fathers or professional men. These claims amount to denying that matters of sexuality currently have a social-normative significance. As such, these assertions are false. They are also politically pernicious because they make invisible the privileges granted to those who are taken to be straight. The explicit refusal to endorse heterosexuality as a matter of identity has the opposite political effect. It is an acknowledgement of these privileges as undeserved.

Yet, one might remain unconvinced, and argue that there are politically progressive tactical endorsements of heterosexual sexual identity. For example, one might cite the use of the slogan 'straight but not narrow' as an example of such an endorsement. We think this is a mistake. There is, of course, a political point in making the claim that one opposes heterosexist bias. One hopes that many non-gay people would perform such political acts of solidarity against homophobia. But it is hard to see why such acts should take the form of identity claims. One might suggest that what is at stake is the elaboration of new scripts which one might endorse as a heterosexual without endorsing homophobia. But, why, we ask, if one is attempting to refuse undeserved privilege, and the narrowness of current heterosexual scripts, try to do so by hanging on to the view that one's sexual inclinations should be elevated to a matter of normative status with accompanying entitlements and facilitations? We do not see any plausible answer to this question that does not rely, at least covertly, on the structures of authority and the privileges which are undeservedly bestowed upon people whom society takes to be straight, and who do nothing to disassociate themselves from that attribution. (Compare an eighteenth-century person claiming that it is a matter of identity that they are noble, but insisting that this doesn't really imply any sort of privilege. We find it hard to make sense of this act. Of course one could say, for example, 'These are my parents; this is my culture.' But one should simply go on to deny that one is noble, to deny the legitimacy of the very category as having to do with nothing but privilege.)

One must distinguish this point about tactical identity endorsements from questions of pure, brutal, short-term political effectiveness. It might be the case that straight but not narrow people could achieve results by claiming this identity for themselves. Virtually any act might, in some circumstance, be politically useful, but our contention is that their success will be partly predicated on the fact that straight people are often taken more seriously than queers by straight society even on matters of queer politics. In these cases strategic success is obtained by implicit reliance on homophobic expectations. Hence, we are sceptical about claims that such endorsements are politically progressive.

One might object, on another front, that these considerations ignore gender disparities in matters of sexuality. The psychological scripts and social roles currently associated with womanhood by dominant male society still prescribe sexual passivity as the appropriate behaviour for women. In the light of this, tactical revisionary endorsements of heterosexual identity might have a role to play in feminist politics. This conclusion is, however, premature, for it is politically important to call into question the current social norms governing women's sexual behaviour; it is hard to see what is gained by taking this project to be part of a revision of *heterosexual* identity. We see the point of embracing an active and independent sexuality for women as an important part of feminist politics, but such political acts of endorsement do not require that one makes the gender of one's sexual partners a matter of normative concern. Feminism does not require that we elevate the heterosexual dimension of some women's sexual inclination to the status of an identity.[17]

What about the more abstract objections to our position? First, it must appear odd to argue, as we have done, that heterosexual sexual identities do not exist. Such a conclusion seems intrinsically implausible. Second, our argument also seems to employ a notion of identity that does not correspond to the ordinary usage.

It is easier to address the first of these two objections by means of an analogy. Consider the case of claims to property, and more specifically to ownership of land. In several countries colonialists have appropriated for themselves, by means of genocide and pillage, the land which natives inhabited. It is not unusual nowadays for natives to reclaim entitlement to their land. These claims are, at least partly, based on the judgement that those individuals who now take themselves to own the land in question do not, and never did, own it. They do not own it because, due to the morally impermissible ways in which they have claimed it, they never really gained the sort of entitlement which is constitutive of genuine ownership.

Our claim about heterosexuality is the same. We do not deny that people have heterosexual inclinations and take themselves to have a heterosexual identity. Similarly, we do not deny that society attributes such an identity to many individuals. Politically bad identities can be attributed, undertaken and facilitated, but one cannot be entitled to them. So, given the meaning of identity judgements, one can't really be of that identity.

None of this implies that homophobia is not real. Since people take themselves to be straight, and society also takes them to have this sexual identity, privileges are granted to people with heterosexual inclinations. The claim that heterosexual identity does not exist does not prevent one from recognizing the very damaging ways in which incorrect identity claims operate.[18]

Our account of identity judgements as normative claims could also be accused of failing to fit ordinary usage. Thus, one might want to assert that there are descriptive uses of identity vocabulary. For example, one might point out that we have often used in this paper the expression 'straight people', although we have denied that being straight is ever a matter of identity. There is, however, no contradiction in our ways of writing. The expression 'straight people' stands as shorthand for 'people who take themselves and are taken by others to be straight', or for 'people with heterosexual inclinations'. We have never denied that there are such identity attributions. Also, one might point out that there are uses of the word 'heterosexual' in scientific contexts. We contend that in these cases, either the word is used merely to refer to a sexual inclination, or we have a normative use of the word which is mistakenly taken as descriptive. What we would have in this case is a politically conservative naturalization of identities.

Finally, we would like to consider briefly the charge that identity politics of the sort we have been defending always belongs to a kind of minoritarian politics. Related to this charge is the claim that identity politics in matters of sexuality reinforces, rather than undermines, the dichotomy between hetero- and homosexuality. We find these charges to be premature, and based on descriptivist readings of what identities might be. Whilst we agree that in an ideal society there would be no place for being gay as a matter of identity, there is no reason to conclude that in the current situation it is always counterproductive to claim being gay or being queer as a matter of identity. Similarly, there is no reason to assume that the political import of identity judgements is limited to making a demand for rights to be bestowed on a minority group. Rather, it is plausible that, by claiming to be gay as a matter of identity, and thereby endorsing for oneself a cluster of attitudes, behaviours, responsibilities and facilitations, one might be able to influence society's expectations about matters of sexuality in ways that are progressive for all members of the community.

In conclusion, one might ask what a non-queer person is to say to the question whether they are straight or gay, if they accept our position. We suggest that one follow the example of Oscar Wilde. When he was asked to state whether a certain passage in one of his books was blasphemous, Wilde, apparently, answered that 'blasphemy' was not one of his words. By extension, we recommend that those of us who are not gay, when asked whether we are straight, should insist that 'straight' is not one of our words.

15

Afterword

Mandy Merck

It is already customary, in Afterwords on queer theory, to note that its demise was pronounced very early in its existence and then somehow postponed. As early as the mid-1990s, some of its original exponents expressed doubts about the theory's continuing political edge in the face of its rapid canonization. Replying to these, Annamarie Jagose asks, 'Does queer become defunct the moment it is an intelligible and widely disseminated term?'[1] Not surprisingly, in her own *Introduction* to the theory, this proves a rhetorical question. For Jagose, queer is not what has gone before but what is yet to come, a perpetual dialogue between sexual identity and its critique, 'looking forward without anticipating the future'. If there can be no last word on this 'permanent becoming', it nevertheless seems useful to take the opportunity of yet another Afterword to look not forward but back – to the history of queer theory and its political development. Although its future may be, in Jagose's determined indeterminacy, 'unimaginable', queer's past is eminently available to investigation and analysis.

My first point – and it is not inconsiderable from the vantage of Britain – is that queer theory, like so much of twentieth-century sexual politics, was first articulated in the United States of America. Moreover, it was developed at a clearly identifiable period, the late 1980s. 1990 saw the publication of Judith Butler's *Gender Trouble*, with its extraordinarily influential combination of a Foucauldian theory of the productivity of prohibition with a psychoanalytic positing of sexual difference as signification to develop a performative theory of gender.[2] The year 1990 also saw the word *Gender Trouble* had not used – 'queer' – aggressively 'resignified' (a word it had used) in the parodic nationalism of a new political movement. The history of that movement, and the theory which shares its name, is inseparable from that of AIDS in the US, where the absence of universal healthcare and the prevalence of a phobic obsession with sex turned the epidemic into a crisis.

One notable response to this crisis was the formation in 1987 of the AIDS Coalition to Unleash Power, or ACT UP, a direct action movement for access to treatments. Eschewing the carnivalesque celebrations of Gay Pride, let alone politer pleas for tolerance, ACT UP was furious, harrying state

187

and medical authorities, as well as the general public, with the genocidal implications of their indifference. 'Silence = Death' their slogan proclaimed, on black posters with pink triangles, which spread across city streets and into the previously unpoliticized precincts of gay pornography. Meanwhile, new alliances were formed, not just between gay and lesbian activists, or homosexuals and sexual dissidents of other inclinations, but between these and others – intravenous drug users, ethnic minorities, sex workers and educators – with a range of sexual practices and identifications. All of this was accomplished with a huge output of cultural production – teaching, designing, filming, publishing. From its outset, ACT UP was also, in the words of one of its founders, the art theorist Douglas Crimp, 'an engaged, activist aesthetic practice' whose graphics, videos and 'actions' reconceived sexual politics in a state of emergency.[3] To mark this phenomenon the art theory journal *October* interrupted its normally mandarin modernism with 271 pages of cultural analysis of the epidemic, contributed by video producers, an attorney, a community activist, a medical editor, a former executive director of the New York Minority Task Force on AIDS and a performance artist campaigning for the rights of prostitutes, as well as critics and academics. (One notable author from the latter group was Paula Treichler, who offered an early application of the theory of performativity to AIDS discourse, quoting Bruno Latour and Steve Woolgar on how scientific 'interpretations ... do not so much *in*form as *per*form'.)[4]

Queer theory may have started with the AIDS issue of *October* in winter 1987, but the phrase didn't enter the language until some time later, after ACT UP's unapologetic chant 'We're here / We're queer / Get used to it' and the founding of its breakaway youth group, Queer Nation, in 1990. Although David Halperin has argued that the latter's emphasis on sexual rather than epidemiological issues was 'significantly less *queer*' than the 'broadly oppositional' coalition created by ACT UP, Queer Nation's eruption into All-American consumer space was another key moment in the development of the eponymous theory.[5] Rewriting the national signage of shopping malls, billboards, t-shirts and trademarks with alterations graphically disclosing the GAY in GAP, this collection of local affinity groups anticipated a decade's deconstruction of the unacknowledged perversity of the public sphere.

By 1993, and its celebration in an essay by Lauren Berlant and Elizabeth Freeman, Queer Nation had been appropriated by queer theory in an academic collection titled (after an album by the black rap group NWA) *Fear of a Queer Planet*.[6] But could queer theory go global? Some of the difficulties in doing so are illustrated in *Fear*'s list of contributors. Although subtitled 'Queer Politics and Social Theory', the collection's 15 authors include only two scholars of, respectively, sociology and law. And this was a representative sampling of what was becoming an established field. Where lesbian and gay studies had been pioneered in Anglo-American departments of history and social studies, its queer successor's poststructuralist turn was driven by critical theorists in literature, visual culture and rhetoric. This produced crucial new attention to a certain 'cultural' constitution of the sexual subject, but it also threatened the theory's analytical reach and capacities. As Steven Seidman complains in a lonely contribution to *Fear*, much is excluded in queer theory's opposition of a presumptively subversive sexuality to the norms of identity. 'In both defenders of identity politics and its poststructural critics there is a preoccupation with the self and the politics of representation. Institutional and historical analysis and an integrative political vision seem to have dropped out.'[7] A few years later Dennis Altman would count the cost of these omissions for any attempt to understand sexuality under globalization. All too often, he complained, the consequences of queer culturalism was the neglect of 'conventional sources of political and economic power' in favour of the particular symbolic phenomena which it had evolved to investigate.[8]

To be sure, this move from a concern with state and economic formations to those of high and popular culture was also followed by feminist studies from the 1980s. Both projects were undoubtedly influenced by the rejection of Marxism after the fall of Soviet communism, and the widespread adoption of a Foucauldian model of dispersed and pluralistic power. Although queer theorists retained the Marxist strategy of cultural critique (advanced in *Gender Trouble* to expose 'the contingent acts that create the appearance of a naturalistic necessity'), economic analyses of heterosexual dominance or of the distribution of resources among lesbian, gay and transgendered people were rarely undertaken.[9]

In 1997, this failing was addressed in a new critical collection which analyses phenomena ranging from the gentrification of gay neighbourhoods to campaigns for domestic partner benefits. But significantly, queer theory is hardly mentioned in *Homo Economics*, with the exception of Richard Cornwall's attempt to articulate interrelations between a property-owning individualism and both the proscription and the defence of homosexuality via readings of Wilde and Genet, as well as theories of market preferences. If Cornwall's speculations suggested that a 'Queer Political Economy' might be possible, Judith Butler's reply in the same year to Nancy Fraser's *Justice Interruptus* insisted on its salience.[10]

Fraser's analysis of the 'post-socialist condition' distinguishes claims for cultural or symbolic 'recognition' from those for socio-economic 'redistribution'. Although she acknowledges that most oppressed groups suffer from both maldistribution and misrecognition, she provocatively opposes the economic subordination of the working class to the cultural stigmatization of 'despised' sexualities. In response to her contention that queer politics stand outside those of political economy – since sexuality is neither a class-specific condition nor the basis for a division of labour – Butler revives an argument that informed socialist feminist analyses of the family in the 1970s and 1980s. Refusing any stable distinction between 'material' and 'cultural' life, she invokes structural anthropology to stress the economic functions of kinship bonds and regulations. Gayle Rubin's early 1970s claim that capitalism continues to require the pre-modern heritage of gender division, female subordination and heterosexism is redeployed – despite its subsequent abandonment by many gay and lesbian scholars, including Rubin herself. Where the latter, like Fraser, contend that capitalism has now commodified the functions that previously enforced familial dependency and heterosexual hegemony, Butler replies that the continuing exclusion of homosexuals from partnership rights in property, taxation and inheritance, as well as the economic disadvantages suffered by lesbians and people with AIDS, demonstrate its enduring heterosexism.

In 2000 the lesbian theorist Rosemary Hennessy made an ambitious intervention into this argument. *Profit and Pleasure* argues that while capitalism still makes uses of heteronormativity to enforce a gendered division of labour, neither those norms, nor gender subordination *per se*, are required for exploitation. What the market economy does require, Hennessy maintains, is the unequal division of labour now promoted by globalization, with its attendant transformation of the patterns of employment, family life, sexual practice, national identity, social migration and production itself – accelerated, decentralized, deregulated and made 'flexible'. This mode of production is said to find its subjective equivalent in the disciplined flexibility of the middle-class professional service worker: 'habitual mobility, adaptability in every undertaking, the ability to navigate among possible alternatives and spaces, and a cultivation of ambivalence as a structure of feeling'.[11] And who better to represent this cultivated ambivalence than that anti-identitarian identity, the queer subject – free floating, self-fashioning, apparently autonomous?

In proposing queer identity as both an expression and an instrument of globalization, Hennessy issues a severe challenge to its theorists, whose detachment of sexuality and signification from social contradictions she decries – and sometimes exaggerates. In any case, only two years after the publication of her study, a new anthology of essays on *Queer Globalizations* addressed many of the questions she raises. As its editors' introduction sets out, one concern of the collection is the 'sinister ... appropriation and deployment of queer subjectivities, cultures, and political agendas for the legitimation of hegemonic institutions presently in discursive crisis, institutions such as the nation-state or US imperial hegemony'.[12] Not only do the (US-based but internationally born) authors of these essays criticize queer theory for its unthinking Americancentrism, they search out relations between the cultural processes which naturalize social domination and the economics of exploitation. In particular, Janet Jakobsen and Cindy Patton offer rich accounts of the contradictory relations between global markets, the state, and sexual politics in the national imaginaries of the USA and Taiwan.

Is this the future of queer theory? Does it, for that matter, have a future in an era of increasingly short-lived academic fashions? Has it already queered the academy by opening (some of) its faculties and curricula to sexual dissidents? Or is this just one more example of educational entrepreneurism in the marketing of lifestyles? Will queer theory's increased engagement with global politics enable dialogue and coalition-building around the world? Or will that widening perspective reveal its strategies as peculiarly American responses to conservative hegemony in a nation where an unprecedented queer visibility has as yet yielded few improvements in legal or economic status? Writing as a lesbian who moved to Britain in the wake of the 1960s reforms which offered some limited rights to controversial sexual conduct, and who will soon be offered the dubious benefits of state-recognized couple-dom and divorce, I find myself increasingly distanced from the circumstances in which queer theory arose. But as this new reader and the theoretical developments I have briefly sketched indicate, queer has also moved on. Writing as a scholar with an immense debt to its boldness, originality and capacity for transformation, I cannot yet consign it to the past.

Summaries and Notes

1. IAIN MORLAND AND ANNABELLE WILLOX, 'INTRODUCTION'

Notes

1. Charles McDougall and Sarah Harding (dirs), *Queer as Folk* (Channel Four, 1999); Ron Cowen and Daniel Lipman produce the long-running American version (Showtime, 2000–present).
2. Russell T. Davies, *Queer as Folk: The Scripts* (London: Channel Four Books, 1999), p. 44.
3. On the moral backlash, as well as the series' glamorization of gay Manchester, see Sally R. Munt, 'Shame/Pride Dichotomies in *Queer as Folk*', *Textual Practice*, 14 (2000), 531–46.
4. BBC Online, 'Blair Appeals for Tolerance', 2 May 1999, <news.bbc.co.uk/hi/ english/special_report/1999/05/99/the_nail_bomb_terror/newsid_333000/333619. stm>.
5. BBC Online, 'Bomb Devastates Wedding Reunion', 2 May 1999, <news.bbc.co. uk/hi/english/special_report/1999/05/99/the_nail_bomb_terror/newsid_333000/ 333644.stm>.
6. Germaine Greer, *The Whole Woman* (London: Doubleday, 1999), pp. 64–74; for a critique, see Iain Morland and Annabelle Willox, 'Queer Feminism and the Politics of Difference' (paper presented at the Third Wave Feminism International Conference, Exeter University, UK, 2002).
7. Jay Prosser, *Second Skins: The Body Narratives of Transsexuality* (New York: Columbia University Press, 1998), p. 6.
8. Davies, *Queer as Folk*, p. 6.

2. SUZANNA DANUTA WALTERS, 'FROM HERE TO QUEER: RADICAL FEMINISM, POSTMODERNISM, AND THE LESBIAN MENACE'

(From 'From Here to Queer: Radical Feminism, Postmodernism, and the Lesbian Menace (Or, Why Can't a Woman Be More Like a Fag?)', *Signs*, 21:4 (1996), pp. 830–69.)

Summary

Suzanna Danuta Walters bracingly cross-examines the origins and purposes of
'queer'. She contextualizes the rise of queer in relation to AIDS, postmodernism and
poststructuralism, and academic politics. Queer, as a political strategy, developed
from the confrontational activism and radical refusal of sexual norms precipitated by
the 1980s AIDS crisis; postmodernism in Walters' account heralds a suspicious
rejection of totalizing narratives of human progress, while poststructuralism indicates a concomitant decentring of the post-Enlightenment subject. The emphases by
poststructuralism and postmodernism on the disruptive margins of culture and
identity lay the ground for Walters' later debate about the philosophy of coming out.
Prior to this, in a discussion of the academic politics of queer, she asks how far one
needs to have a particular sexuality to teach and research queer theory. Walters also
tackles the issue of whether queer is an improvement on feminism. Although feminists have been characterized in some queer discourse as the sex and gender police, she
argues that feminism productively complicates the notion of gender, contrary to
queer efforts to transcend it. Walters proposes that queer discourse makes exclusions
of its own by assuming a gay male subject – even a male lesbian.

Notes

I would like to thank David Bergman and Amy Robinson for their helpful comments
on earlier drafts of this article. Both have contributed meaningfully to the development of this piece. Erstwhile comrade Ara Wilson gave detailed and substantive
criticism, improving this essay in numerous ways. In addition, I would like to thank
the anonymous reviewers at *Signs*. Their thoughtful and thorough (if at times rather
contentious!) readings forced me to engage in this process of revision with equal
thoroughness.
 1. Briefly, the term *sex debates* is shorthand for a reinvigorated discussion of
    sexuality, power, pornography and fantasy that was, to a large extent, sparked
    by the events surrounding the 1982 Barnard Conference 'The Scholar and the
    Feminist'. At this conference, 'sex radical' feminists came into often angry con-
    frontation with antipornography activists who attempted to censor the speech of
    conference participants. Thus began a long and complicated series of debates
    about feminism and sexuality that has produced both acrimony and meaningful
    scholarship. See particularly Vance (1984).
 2. I do not mean to be facetious here; indeed, the very public debates over the 'place'
    of organizations like NAMBLA (North American Man–Boy Love Association)
    in the gay and lesbian movement illustrates the very pressing political concerns
    raised by a simple politics of nonnormativity. It is no accident that some of the
    strongest voices against NAMBLA's inclusion in marches, organizations, and so
    forth have been lesbian-feminist.
 3. See particularly Hartsock (1983); Bordo (1990); Nicholson (1990); and Modleski
    (1991).
 4. I say this only half-jokingly. Although clearly most queer theorists *are* gay, there
    does seem to be a proliferation of the 'Sedgwick' phenomenon in which married,
    heterosexual college professors throw off their married heterosexuality (but stay
    married and heterosexual) and claim 'queerness'. Although Sedgwick is certainly
    the most notorious, she is not the sole representative of this trend.

5. This is a very touchy issue and one, I must admit, I am very torn over. For, on the one hand, an essentialist position (one must be something to teach it, and that 'being' represents the truth of the experience) is unacceptable on any number of levels. On the other hand, if we believe that knowledge is always situated – that we always speak and think from somewhere – then to say it does not matter at all is equally unacceptable. Indeed, we do not argue for a more diverse faculty just to be more representative in our faculty statistics; we also do so because we feel diversity is not simply an intellectual acquisition but is embodied as well.

6. I would note, however, in disagreement with Harper, that the simple construction of a 'dichotomy' does not, in my mind, necessarily mean that those who use that dichotomy are negating other identities and meanings. For example, the fact that this article critiques queer theory primarily around its erasure of lesbian specificity and demonization of feminism does not mean that other critiques of queer are not important and valid (say, a critique of queer around its erasure of colour in the universalizing move of nationhood). Because I am primarily speaking of the queer occlusion of feminism and gender, this does not imply that I am myself 'privileging' gender as the most important marker of difference; it simply implies that this is the core subject of this particular (limited) article. In discussing other differences throughout this article, particularly around race and ethnicity, I try to make this point more forcefully.

7. David Bergman has written trenchant critiques of Sedgwick and her *oeuvre* (1991, 1993).

8. See particularly Creet (1991); Reich (1992); Hall (1993); and Roy (1993).

9. I recognize, of course, that oppositional cultures (including lesbian culture) do tyrannize their own members. Indeed, the brutal history of the Soviet Union and the sad and dogmatic hierarchies of the American Left provide vivid examples of this process. To some extent, I think it feels even more brutish when the 'clamping down' comes from within one's own ranks, e.g., from other lesbians. However, in recognizing this and arguing against it, we should not construct a monolithic new 'other' who can now serve as a historical reminder of the tedious past we have since transcended. And we need to make careful distinctions about this 'policing', based on questions of intentionality, power, structural location, etc. It seems to me that the 'policing' of lesbians by the homophobic state that, say, takes away our children is not of the same type or order as the 'policing' that comes from lesbians themselves around issues of sexuality, sexual practices, style, etc.

10. It is also interesting to note that these critics of identity shy away from the obvious analogies of racial and ethnic identity.

References

Anzaldúa, Gloria (1991). 'To(o) Queer the Writer – Loca, escritora y chicana', in *Inversions: Writing by Dykes, Queers, and Lesbians*, ed. Betsy Warland (Vancouver: Press Gang Publishers), pp. 249–63.

Bensinger, Terralee (1992). 'Lesbian Pornography: the Re/Making of (a) Community', *Discourse*, 15(1): 69–93.

Bergman, David (1991). 'Something about Eve: Eve Kosofsky Sedgwick's Closet Drama', review of *Epistemology of the Closet* by Eve Sedgwick, *Raritan*, 11(1): 115–31.

—— (1993). 'Disciplining Gay and Lesbian Studies', Andrew R. Hilen Lecture at the University of Washington, Seattle.

Bordo, Susan (1990). 'Feminism, Postmodernism, and Gender-Scepticism', in Nicholson (1990), pp. 133–56.

Butler, Judith (1991). 'Imitation and Gender Insubordination', in Fuss (1991), pp. 13–31.

Case, Sue-Ellen (1991). 'Tracking the Vampire', *differences*, 3(2): 1–20.

Creet, Julia (1991). 'Daughter of the Movement: the Psychodynamics of Lesbian S/M Fantasy', *differences*, 3(2): 135–59.

Däumer, Elisabeth D. (1992). 'Queer Ethics: Or, the Challenge of Bisexuality to Lesbian Ethics', *Hypatia*, 7(4): 91–105.

Dhairyam, Sagri (1994). 'Racing the Lesbian, Dodging White Critics', in *The Lesbian Postmodern*, ed. Laura Doan (New York: Columbia University Press), pp. 25–46.

Doty, Alexander (1993). *Making Things Perfectly Queer: Interpreting Mass Culture* (Minneapolis: Univeristy of Minnesota Press).

Duggan, Lisa (1992). 'Making It Perfectly Queer', *Socialist Review*, 22(1): 11–31.

Fuss, Diana (ed.) (1991). *Inside/Out: Lesbian Theories, Gay Theories* (New York: Routledge).

Hall, Lisa Kahaleole Chang (1993). 'Bitches in Solitude: Identity Politics and the Lesbian Community', in *Sisters, Sexperts, Queers*, ed. Arlene Stein (New York: Plume Book/Penguin), pp. 218–29.

Harper, Phillip Brian, E. Francis White, and Margaret Cerullo (1993). 'Multi/Queer/Culture', *Radical America*, 24(4): 27–37.

Hartsock, Nancy C. M. (1983). *Money, Sex, and Power: Toward a Feminist Historical Materialism* (Boston: Northeastern University Press).

Hennessy, Rosemary (1993). 'Queer Theory: a Review of the *differences* Special Issue and Wittig's *The Straight Mind*', *Signs: Journal of Women in Culture and Society*, 18(4): 964–79.

Herrnstein, Richard J., and Charles A. Murray (1994). *The Bell Curve: Intelligence and Class Structure in American Life* (New York: Free Press).

Maggenti, Maria (1993). 'Wandering through Herland', in *Sisters, Sexperts, Queers*, ed. Arlene Stein (New York: Plume Book/Penguin), pp. 245–55.

Martin, Biddy (1994). 'Sexualities without Genders and Other Queer Utopias', *diacritics*, 24(2–3): 104–21.

Minkowitz, Donna (1992). 'See What the Girls in the Backroom Will Have: a Dyke's Adventure', *Village Voice*, 30 June.

Modleski, Tania (1991). *Feminism without Women: Culture and Criticism in a 'Postfeminist' Age* (New York: Routledge).

Moraga, Cherríe, and Amber Hollibaugh (1983). 'What We're Rollin Around in Bed With: Sexual Silences in Feminism', in *Powers of Desire: The Politics of Sexuality*, ed. Ann Snitow, Christine Stansell, and Sharon Thompson (New York: Monthly Review Press), pp. 394–405.

Morgan, Tracy (1993). 'Butch-Femme and the Politics of Identity', in *Sisters, Sexperts, Queers*, ed. Arlene Stein (New York: Plume Book/Penguin), pp. 35–46.

Nicholson, Linda (ed.) (1990). *Feminism/Postmodernism* (New York: Routledge).

Phelan, Shane (1993). '(Be)Coming Out: Lesbian Identity and Politics', *Signs*, 18(4): 765–90.

Reich, June L. (1992). 'Genderfuck: the Law of the Dildo', *Discourse*, 15(1): 112–27.

Riggs, Marlon (1992). 'Unleash the Queen', in *Black Popular Culture*, ed. Michele Wallace (project manager) and Gina Dent (Seattle: Bay Press), pp. 99–105.

Roy, Camille (1993). 'Speaking in Tongues', in *Sisters, Sexperts, Queers*, ed. Arlene Stein (New York: Plume Book/Penguin), pp. 6–12.

Sedgwick, Eve Kosofsky (1993). *Tendencies* (Durham, NC: Duke University Press).
Seidman, Steven (1994). 'Queer Pedagogy/Queering Sociology', *Critical Sociology*, 20(3): 167–76.
Stein, Arlene (1992). 'Sisters and Queers: the Decentering of Lesbian Feminism', *Socialist Review*, 22(1): 33–55.
Vance, Carole (ed.) (1984). *Pleasure and Danger: Exploring Female Sexuality* (New York: Routledge).
Whisman, Vera (1993). 'Identity Crises: Who Is a Lesbian, Anyway?' in *Sisters, Sexperts, Queers*, ed. Arlene Stein (New York: Plume Book/Penguin), pp. 47–60.
Zita, Jacquelyn N. (1992). 'The Male Lesbian and the Postmodernist Body', *Hypatia*, 7(4): 106–27.

3. PATRICK CALIFIA, 'GAY MEN, LESBIANS, AND SEX: DOING IT TOGETHER'

(From Patrick Califia, *Public Sex: The Culture of Radical Sex* (Pittsburgh: Cleis, 1994), pp. 183–9.)

Summary

'When two gay people of opposite sexes make it, it's still gay sex', says Patrick Califia. Written during a period of tension within the lesbian and women's political movements – known affectionately as the lesbian sex wars – this testimonial essay disrupts notions of sexual identity not only within lesbian and gay subcultures, but also within mainstream culture. Califia had already challenged the political orthodoxy within the lesbian and women's movements with 'A Secret Side of Lesbian Sexuality' (1979; pp. 157–64 in *Public Sex*) at a time when sadomasochistic sexual activity was only just being acknowledged to exist within lesbian relationships. This later essay contests the idea that sexuality is fixed, ahistorical, and based on gender object-choice alone, and points towards a queerer focus on non-genital desires and specific sex acts. It also touches incisively on sexism, pornography, economics, rape, phallocentrism, and sexual health.

4. LARRY KRAMER, '1,112 AND COUNTING'

(From Mark Blasius and Shane Phelan (eds), *We are Everywhere: A Historical Sourcebook of Gay and Lesbian Politics* (London and New York: Routledge, 1997), pp. 578–86.)

Summary

In 2003, the United Nations' global estimate of HIV/AIDS sufferers was 38 million. Written at the same time that Califia was challenging the lesbian and women's political orthodoxy, Larry Kramer's article was composed as a wake-up call to the gay men whose lives and lifestyle were being decimated by the rise of HIV and AIDS. Kramer challenges the apathy of the New York City gay community, and importantly does so from a personal perspective. His explicit distancing of his words from any government or government-sponsored agency is historically significant because of the lack of funding for research into lesbian or gay communities and their sexual health issues. This in turn led to a lack of concrete information on HIV, AIDS, and disease transmission, and arguably escalated the speed and extent of the epidemic. Kramer's essay became widely disseminated at the time of writing, and helped to drive the work of queer political movements such as ACT UP (AIDS Coalition to Unleash Power).

5.   CAROL QUEEN, 'THE LEATHER DADDY AND THE FEMME'

(From Carol Queen, *The Leather Daddy and the Femme* (San Francisco: Down There Press, 2003), pp. 9–29.)

Summary

This story demonstrates the difficulty of defining sexuality within the parameters of gender. The protagonists experience their bodies differently in each scenario, but do not alter their biology to achieve this experiential volatility. Extending the premise of Califia's essay, Carol Queen shows how the acts in which a person engages may confuse or appear to contradict that person's identity. The erotic narrative exemplifies the queering of identity, both sexual and gendered, based on the lived experience and interaction of bodies. The story provides an illustration of the principles of phenomenology, which has become increasingly relevant within queer, and especially transsexual and transgender, theory. Phenomenology takes as its foundation *the world as it appears to us*, our subjective perceptual experiences. In this theory – a movement in continental philosophy which first stirred in 1765 – our embodied experiences are understood, and made meaningful, through perception. A queer understanding of phenomenology thus allows an appreciation of gender and sexuality as recursive interpersonal experiences, and so can account for those sexual embodiments which may jar with current culturally available categories, but none the less are perceived congruently by those individuals and communities who experience them.

6.   MARJORIE GARBER, 'THE RETURN TO BIOLOGY'

(From *Vice Versa: Bisexuality and the Eroticism of Everyday Life* (Harmondsworth: Penguin, 1997), pp. 268–83.)

Summary

In this chapter from her comprehensive study of the cultural politics of bisexuality, Marjorie Garber provides a succinct overview of the indeterminable relations between sexual orientation and biology. 'No calipers will fit the shape of desire', she claims, but nevertheless recourse to a biological ground for sexuality has frequently been made both by queer rights advocates and their homophobic opponents. Contextualizing such strategies in the light of nineteenth- and twentieth-century sexology, Garber demonstrates how bisexuality has tended to be filtered out of sex science as an omnipresent constant, an insignificant aberration, or a transitory illusion. (This is the key contention of her book about bisexuality's place in culture at large.) She dissects some of the claims made recently about gay genes and brains, as well as usefully demonstrating how measures of orientation such as the Kinsey scale can be at once liberating and constraining, not only for bisexuals and homosexuals, but for heterosexuals too – which suggests that *everyone* queers the science of sex.

Notes

1. Ann Landers, 'Teacher Needs to Learn Lesson – There Aren't Five Sexes', *Miami Herald*, 21 December 1992, p. 2C.
2. Anne Fausto-Sterling, 'The Five Sexes', *The Sciences*, March/April 1993, pp. 20–4. A briefer version of this article appeared on the *New York Times* op-ed page under the title 'How Many Sexes Are There?' (*New York Times*, 12 March 1993, p. A29).
3. Fausto-Sterling, 'The Five Sexes', p. 22.
4. Ibid., p. 24.
5. Steve Wolfe, letter to the *New York Times*, 26 March 1993, p. A12.
6. Gary Fairmount Filosa, letter to the *New York Times*, 26 March 1993, p. A12.
7. Ibid.
8. Simon LeVay, 'A Difference in Hypothalamic Structure between Heterosexual and Homosexual Men', *Science*, vol. 253 (30 August 1991), pp. 1034–7.
9. David J. Jefferson, 'Science Besieged: Studying the Biology of Sexual Orientation has Political Fallout', *Wall Street Journal*, 12 August 1993, p. 1.
10. Michael Bailey and Richard Pillard, 'Are Some People Born Gay?' *New York Times*, 17 October 1991, p. A21.
11. Mariana Valverde, *Sex, Power, and Pleasure* (Philadelphia: New Society Publishers, 1987), p. 112.
12. Richard von Krafft-Ebing, *Psychopathia Sexualis*, 7th edn, trans. Franklin Klaf (New York: Stein & Day, 1965) pp. 221–2.
13. Robert A. Wild, quoted in Natalie Angier, 'Male Hormone Molds Women, Too, in Mind and Body', *New York Times*, 3 May 1994, p. C13.
14. Roger S. Rittmaster, quoted in ibid.
15. Angier, 'Male Hormone Molds Women, Too', p. C13.
16. Sigmund Freud, 'Three Essays on the Theory of Sexuality' (1905), *Standard Edition*, 7: 140. The 'spokesman of the male inverts' is Karl Heinrich Ulrichs.
17. Robert J. Stoller, 'Facts and Fancies: An Examination of Freud's Concept of Bisexuality', in *Women and Analysis: Dialogues on Psychoanalytic Views of Femininity*, ed. Jean Strouse (New York: Grossman Publishers, 1974), p. 345.
18. Joe Dolce, 'And How Big Is Yours?' *The Advocate*, 1 June 1993, p. 40.
19. Ruth Hubbard and Elijah Wald, *Exploding the Gene Myth* (Boston: Beacon Press, 1993), p. 96.
20. LeVay, 'A Difference in Hypothalamic Structure', p. 1035.
21. Ibid., p. 1034.
22. LeVay mentions the possibility that his sample may be unrepresentative, since gay male AIDS patients might be thought of as belonging to a 'subset of gay men, characterized, for example, by a tendency to engage in sexual relations with large numbers of different partners or by a strong preference for the receptive role in anal intercourse', but he refutes this by noting that 'the majority of

homosexual men who acquired HIV infection during the Multicenter AIDS Cohort Study reported that they took both the insertive and the receptive role in intercourse and the same is likely to be true of the homosexual subjects in my study' ('A Difference in Hypothalamic Structure', p. 1036). This is the only mention of sexual roles or aims in the paper, and it is clearly intended to be discounted rather than counted as a differential factor.

23. Dolce, 'And How Big Is Yours?' p. 40.
24. Hubbard and Wald, *Exploding the Gene Myth*, p. 94.
25. Natalie Angier, 'Report Suggests Homosexuality is Linked to Genes', *New York Times*, 16 July 1993, p. A12.
26. Dean H. Hamer, Stella Hu, Victoria L. Magnuson, Nan Hu, Angela M. L. Patta-tucci, 'A Linkage between DNA Markers on the X Chromosome and Male Sexual Orientation', *Science*, vol. 261, no. 5119 (16 July 1993), p. 321; J. Michael Bailey and Richard C. Pillard, 'A Genetic Study of Male Sexual Orientation', *Archives of General Psychiatry*, vol. 48 (1991), pp. 1089–96.
27. Hamer et al. 'Linkage between DNA Markers', p. 326.
28. Ibid., pp. 321–2.
29. Amanda Udis-Kessler, 'Appendix: Notes on the Kinsey Scale and Other Measures of Sexuality', in *Closer to Home: Bisexuality and Feminism*, ed. Elizabeth Reba Weise (Seattle: The Seal Press, 1992), p. 316.
30. Ibid., p. 317.
31. In their article on 'The Multidimension Scale of Sexuality', authors Braden Robert Berkey, Terri Perelman-Hall, and Lawrence A. Kurdek cite J. P. Paul's use of 'sequential bisexual' and 'contemporaneous bisexual' in 1984, and G. Zinik's terms 'serial' and 'concurrent' in 1985. See *Journal of Homosexuality*, vol. 19, no. 4 (Winter 1990), p. 68; J. P. Paul, 'The Bisexual Identity: an Idea With-out Social Recognition', *Journal of Homosexuality*, vol. 9, nos. 2–3 (1983–4), pp. 45–63; G. Zinik, 'Identity Conflict or Adaptive Flexibility? Bisexuality Reconsidered', in Fritz Klein, MD, and Timothy J. Wolf, MD, *Two Lives to Lead: Bisexuality in Men and Women* (New York and London: Harrington Park Press, 1985), pp. 7–18.

7. PETER HEGARTY IN CONVERSATION WITH CHERYL CHASE, 'INTERSEX ACTIVISM, FEMINISM AND PSYCHOLOGY'

(From Peter Hegarty in conversation with Cheryl Chase, 'Intersex Activism, Feminism and Psychology: Opening a Dialogue on Theory, Research and Clinical Practice', *Feminism and Psychology*, 10: 1 (2000), pp. 117–32.)

Summary

Cheryl Chase's personal story highlights experiences familiar to many intersexed people: feelings of shame about one's body, medical secrecy and misinformation, and a scarcity of appropriate multidisciplinary healthcare, particularly psychological support. Then in a discussion of intersexuality's relevance to feminism, Chase details the sexism that has shaped medical decisions about intersexed patients. For example, female pain has been devalued, and names for surgeries ('clitorectomy' became 'clitoroplasty') have changed to serve political ends. The conversation turns to the ramifications of intersexuality for lesbian and gay issues. Chase shows how the traditional medical management of intersex has figured homosexuality as a failure of sexual development that needs to be surgically prevented. She also explains a key difference between intersex and gay essentialist discourse. Whereas the claim that homosexuality is biological has been made to shore up homosexual rights, the corresponding assumption has served only to stigmatize intersexuals. However, the Intersex Society of North America has learnt valuable lessons from the lesbian and gay rights movements about the power of activism to stimulate institutional change. Finally, Chase suggestively invokes 'queer' as a name for a transgressive difference that confounds precise definition.

Notes

1. See J. Money, J. G. Hampson and J. L. Hampson, 'Hermaphroditism: Recommendations Concerning Assignment of Sex, Change of Sex, and Psychologic Management', *Bulletin of the Johns Hopkins Hospital*, 97 (1955): 284–300; J. Money, J. G. Hampson and J. L. Hampson, 'An Examination of Some Basic Sexual Concepts: The Evidence of Human Hermaphroditism', *Bulletin of the Johns Hopkins Hospital*, 97 (1955): 301–19.
2. See S. Kessler, 'The Medical Construction of Gender: Case Management of Intersexual Infants', *Signs: Journal of Women in Culture and Society*, 16 (1990): 3–26.
3. A. Moreno, 'In Amerika They Call Us Hermaphrodites', in A. D. Dreger (ed.), *Intersex in the Age of Ethics* (Hagerstown, MD: University Publishing Group, 1999).
4. A. Fausto-Sterling, *Myths of Gender: Biological Theories about Women and Men* (New York: Basic Books, 1985).
5. A. Fausto-Sterling, 'The Five Sexes: Why Male and Female are not Enough', *The Sciences*, 33 (March/April 1993): 20–5.
6. More information about ISNA and other intersex organizations is available at the website www.isna.org.
7. See C. Chase, 'Hermaphrodites with Attitude: Mapping the Emergence of Intersex Political Activism', *GLQ: A Journal of Gay and Lesbian Studies*, 4 (1998): 189–211.
8. See R. E. Gross, J. Randolph and J. F. Crigler, 'Clitorectomy for Sexual Abnormalities: Indications and Technique', *Surgery*, 59 (1966): 300–8.
9. C. Chase, 'Affronting Reason', in D. Atkins (ed.), *Looking Queer: Body Image and Identity in Lesbian, Bisexual, Gay and Transgendered Communities* (Binghamton, NY: Haworth, 1998).
10. M. Hendricks, 'Is it a Boy or a Girl?', *Johns Hopkins Magazine*, November 1993: 10–16.
11. *New Yorker*, 'Dr Elders' Medical History', 26 September 1994: 45–6.
12. A. D. Dreger, 'The Limits of Individuality: Ritual and Sacrifice in the Lives and Medical Treatment of Conjoined Twins', *Studies in History and Philosophy of Biology and Biomedical Science*, 29 (1998): 1–29.
13. G. Greer, *The Whole Woman* (New York: Knopf, 1999).
14. AIS (Androgen Insensitivity Syndrome) is a condition in which XY foetuses have body cells that are insensitive to androgens. Consequently they develop, *in utero*, as females and have female-appearing external genitalia at birth. They are, as they always have been, raised female and develop female gender identities. See http://www.medhelp.org/www/ais for more information.

15. See R. Bayer, *Homosexuality and American Psychiatry: The Politics of Diagnosis* (New York: Basic Books, 1981). Contrary to many internalist narratives in modern lesbian and gay psychology, Bayer suggests that the declassification of homosexuality as a mental illness resulted less from the accumulation of scientific evidence than from the efforts of lesbian and gay activists within and without the profession, and from a shift away from psychoanalysis as the dominant paradigm in US psychiatry.
16. C. Dugger, 'New Law Bans Genital Cutting in the United States', *New York Times*, 12 October 1996: 1.

8.   EVE KOSOFSKY SEDGWICK, 'AXIOMATIC'

(From Eve Kosofsky Sedgwick, *Epistemology of the Closet* (Berkeley, CA: University of California Press, 1990), pp. 22–48.)

Summary

Eve Kosofsky Sedgwick dissects the illogical foundations of sexual ideology: the 'internal incoherence and mutual contradiction' of 'commonsense views' of human sexuality. She provides an axiomatic basis for her book's general contention that binary oppositions limit freedom and understanding, especially in relation to sexuality. First, Sedgwick says it is incorrect to assume that identity categories can define and contain the myriad individuals within culture: people are different from each other. She then challenges the assumption that feminism can provide the basis for antihomophobic analysis in axiom 2. Axiom 3 troubles the notion that lesbian and gay male sexualities can be studied as homogenous or co-extensive phenomena. In the fourth and possibly the most challenging axiom, Sedgwick maintains that the binary notion of 'nature versus nurture' is in itself a flawed concept. She suggests an alternative approach to the impasse of essentialism versus constructivism: a 'minoritizing' and a 'universalizing' view. The issue is not whether you are born or become homosexual, but whether the politics of your sexuality should bear upon only those who identify as you do (minoritizing), or upon all sexualities (universalizing). Put differently, the issue is: To whom is sexuality important – homosexuals or everyone? Finally axiom 5 sets up some of the issues addressed by Donald E. Hall. Whether past same-sex activities can be understood as analogous to, or even related to, same-sex activities today is a hotly contested point in queer historiography. Through analyses of work by Michel Foucault and David M. Halperin, Sedgwick proposes that any history of sexuality should aim primarily 'to denaturalize the present, rather than the past'.

Notes

1. Gayle Rubin, 'The Traffic in Women: Notes on the "Political Economy" of Sex', in Rayna R. Reiter (ed.), *Toward an Anthropology of Women* (New York: Monthly Review Press, 1975), pp. 157–210.
2. Gayle Rubin, 'Thinking Sex: Notes for a Radical Theory of the Politics of Sexuality', in Carole S. Vance (ed.), *Pleasure and Danger: Exploring Female Sexuality* (Boston: Routledge & Kegan Paul, 1984), pp. 307–8.

202   *Queer Theory*

3. This list owes something to Rubin, 'Thinking Sex', esp. pp. 281–2.
4. Michel Foucault, *The History of Sexuality*, vol. 1: *An Introduction* (Harmonds-worth: Penguin, 1978), p. 43.
5. See, for instance, Alan Bray, *Homosexuality in Renaissance England* (London: Gay Men's Press, 1982); David Halperin, *One Hundred Years of Homosexuality* (London and New York: Routledge, 1990); Jeffrey Weeks, *Sex, Politics, and Society: The Regulation of Sexuality since 1800* (London: Longman, 1981); George Chauncey, Jr, 'From Sexual Inversion to Homosexuality: Medicine and the Changing Conceptualization of Female Deviance', *Salmagundi*, no. 58–9 (Fall 1982–Winter 1983), 114–45; and Jonathan Katz, *Gay/Lesbian Almanac: A New Documentary* (New York: Harper and Row, 1983).
6. Halperin, *One Hundred Years of Homosexuality*, pp. 8–9.

9. DONALD E. HALL, 'A BRIEF, SLANTED HISTORY OF "HOMOSEXUAL" ACTIVITY'

(From Donald E. Hall, *Queer Theories* (Basingstoke: Palgrave Macmillan, 2003), pp. 21–47.)

Summary

Donald E. Hall begins by challenging the very possibility of reconstructing a queer history, given the difficulty of cross-cultural and ahistorical readings of identities and acts. He then explores the complexity of sexual paradigms in Classical Greece, and argues that these interactions may have had more in common with today's social class structures than with our sexual identity claims. The apparent sexual permissive-ness of Classical Greek society contrasts sharply with the following Christian era's idealization of heterosexual marriage, when sodomites were chastised and punished for their 'crimes against nature'. Molly-houses created a social space during the early seventeenth century which, Hall suggests, can be seen as 'a precursor to a modern notion of homosexual identity'. Building on Michel Foucault's key work on the history of sexuality, Hall explains how notions of 'natural' and 'fixed' character started to dissolve in the nineteenth century, even while notions of perversion began to be fashioned. The prevention and 'cure' of medicalized sexual 'abnormalities' gathered momentum, while always already being challenged. Hall suggests that the very public life, trial and death of Oscar Wilde provided a catalyst for the devel-opment of modern homosexual identity claims, but also acknowledges that this dramatic figure obscures many of the 'secret' sex lives of his era, especially those of working-class people. Turning to the twentieth century, Hall highlights Freudian psychoanalysis, the lesbian and gay rights movement, the women's movement and the African-American movement as important precursors to contemporary queer theory and sexual politics. The disparities and blind spots that inevitably surface when civil rights groups form alliances return Hall to his opening thesis that the history of queer is an interminable question, not an answer.

References

Altman, Dennis (1971). *Homosexual: Oppression and Liberation* (New York: Outerbridge & Dienstfrey).

Boswell, John (1980). *Christianity, Social Tolerance, and Homosexuality: Gay People in Western Europe from the Beginning of the Christian Era to the Fourteenth Century* (Chicago and London: University of Chicago Press).

Bray, Alan (1982). *Homosexuality in Renaissance England* (London: Gay Men's Press).

Bristow, Joseph (1997). *Sexuality* (London and New York: Routledge).

Brown, Judith, C. (1989). 'Lesbian Sexuality in Medieval and Early Modern Europe', in *Hidden from History: Reclaiming the Gay and Lesbian Past*, ed. Martin Duberman, et al. (New York: NAL Books), pp. 67–75.

Carpenter, Edward (1908). *The Intermediate Sex: A Study of Some Transitional Types of Men* (London: Mitchell Kennedy).

Chauncey, George (1994). *Gay New York: Gender, Urban Culture and the Making of the Gay Male World, 1890–1940* (New York: Basic Books).

Cohen, William (1996). *Sex Scandal: The Private Parts of Victorian Fiction* (Durham, NC, and London: Duke University Press).

Constantine-Simms, Delroy (ed.) (2000). *The Greatest Taboo: Homosexuality in Black Communities* (Boston: Alyson).

Cruikshank, Margaret (1992). *The Gay and Lesbian Liberation Movement* (London and New York: Routledge).

D'Emilio, John (1983). *Sexual Politics, Sexual Communities: The Making of a Homosexual Minority in the United States, 1940–1970* (Chicago, IL: University of Chicago Press).

Dinshaw, Carolyn (1999). *Getting Medieval: Sexualities and Communities, Pre- and Postmodern* (Durham, NC: Duke University Press).

Ellis, Havelock and John Addington Symonds (1897). *Sexual Inversion* (London: Wilson and Macmillan).

Faderman, Lillian (1981). *Surpassing the Love of Men: Romantic Friendship and Love Between Women from the Renaissance to the Present* (New York: William Morrow).

—— (1999). *To Believe in Women: What Lesbians Have Done for America – A History* (Boston and New York: Houghton Mifflin).

Foucault, Michel (1978). *The History of Sexuality*, vol. 1: *An Introduction* (Harmondsworth: Penguin).

Freud, Sigmund (2000). *Three Essays on the Theory of Sexuality* (1905; New York: Basic Books).

Gay, Peter (1986). *The Tender Passion: The Bourgeois Experience: Victoria to Freud*, vol. 2 (New York and Oxford: Oxford University Press).

Haggerty, George E. (1999). *Men in Love: Masculinity and Sexuality in the Eighteenth Century* (New York: Columbia University Press).

Hall, Donald E. (1996a). *Fixing Patriarchy: Feminism and Mid-Victorian Male Novelists* (New York: New York University Press).

—— (1996b). 'Graphic Sexuality and the Erasure of a Polymorphous Perversity', in *RePresenting Bisexualities: Subjects and Cultures of Fluid Desire*, ed. Donald E. Hall and Maria Pramaggiore (New York: New York University Press), 99–123.

Hall, Radclyffe (1990). *The Well of Loneliness* (1928; New York: Anchor Books).

Halperin, David (1990). *One Hundred Years of Homosexuality* (London and New York: Routledge).

Hemphill, Essex (ed.) (1991). *Brother to Brother: New Writings by Black Gay Men* (Boston, MA: Alyson).

Hocquenghem, Guy (1993). *Homosexual Desire*, trans. Daniella Dangoor (1972; Durham, NC, and London: Duke University Press).

Katz, Jonathan Ned (1996). *The Invention of Heterosexuality* (New York: Plume).
Kirsch, Max (2000). *Queer Theory and Social Change* (London and New York: Routledge).
Krafft-Ebing, Richard von (1965). *Psychopathia Sexualis* (1886; New York: Putnam's).
McClaren, Angus (1997). *The Trials of Masculinity: Policing Sexual Boundaries 1870–1930* (Chicago, IL: University of Chicago Press).
Moraga, Cherríe and Gloria Anzaldúa (ed.) (1981). *This Bridge Called My Back: Writings by Radical Women of Color* (Watertown, MA: Persephone Press).
Rupp, Leila (1999). *A Desired Past: A Short History of Same-Sex Love in America* (Chicago, IL, and London: University of Chicago Press).
Trumbach, Randolph (1985). 'Sodomitical Subcultures, Sodomitical Roles, and the Gender Revolution of the Eighteenth Century: the Recent Historiography', *Eighteenth-Century Life*, 9: 109–21.
Weeks, Jeffrey (1990). *Coming Out: Homosexual Politics in Britain from the Nineteenth Century to the Present* (1977; London: Quartet).

10.   STEPHEN WHITTLE, 'GENDER FUCKING OR FUCKING GENDER?'

(From Richard Ekins and Dave King (eds), *Blending Genders: Social Aspects of Cross Dressing and Sex-Changing* (London and New York: Routledge, 1996), pp. 196–214.)

Summary

In an introductory note to this essay on gender blending, Stephen Whittle states his personal position and explains why – despite queer theory's struggle against definitions – this declaration is politically important. The next two sections map the lines of force connecting transvestism, transgender and transsexuality first with sexology and then with queer theory. Whittle suggests that transgendered behaviour and queer theory share an interest not just in crossing sexual, bodily, and academic boundaries, but more radically in showing that these boundaries are already fallacious. In the centrepiece section, 'Recent Trans-Her/His/Story', Whittle outlines the development since the 1960s of trans communities, commentating on the institutional obstacles and personal prejudices they have fought. In particular, trans communities have contested medical authority by appealing to the postmodern notion of multiple narratives, fought for legal recognition and anti-discriminatory legislation, and challenged feminist assumptions about the biological purity of sexual difference. They have also insisted that objectivity is impossible – hence Whittle's declaration of his own standpoint. Accordingly, Kate Bornstein's *Gender Outlaw* (1994) and Loren Cameron's *Self-Portrait* (1993), two exemplary queer autobiographical texts, are deployed by Whittle to demonstrate that gender fluidity and gender fucking are first-person experiences before they become theory.

References

Bolin, A. (1994). 'Transcending and Transgendering: Male-to-Female Transsexuals, Dichotomy and Diversity', in G. Herdt (ed.), *Third Sex, Third Gender: Beyond Sexual Dimorphism in Culture and History* (New York: Zone Books).

Bornstein, Kate (1994). *Gender Outlaw: On Men, Women, and the Rest of Us* (London: Routledge).

Bullough, V. L. and B. Bullough (1993). *Cross Dressing, Sex, and Gender* (Philadelphia: University of Pennsylvania Press).

Connell, R. W. (1987). *Gender and Power* (Oxford: Blackwell).

Cromwell, J. (1994). 'Default Assumptions or the Billy Tipton Phenomenon', *FTM Newsletter*, Issue 28 (July): 4–5.

Feinberg, Leslie (1993). *Stone Butch Blues* (Ithaca, NY: Firebrand Books).

Garber, Marjorie (1992). *Vested Interests: Cross-dressing and Cultural Anxiety* (New York: Routledge).

Halberstam, Judith (1992). 'Skinflick: Posthuman Gender in Jonathan Demme's "The Silence of the Lambs"', *Camera Obscura*, 27 (9 September) 35–52.

Hall, S. (1992). 'Cultural Studies and its Theoretical Legacies', in L. Grossberg et al. (eds), *Cultural Studies* (New York: Routledge).

hooks, bell (1994). *Outlaw Culture: Resisting Representations* (New York: Routledge).

Ian, M. (1994). 'How do you wear your body', in M. Dorkenkamp and R. Henke (eds), *Negotiating Lesbian and Gay Subjects* (London: Routledge).

Jones, J. (1994). 'FTM Cross-dresser Murdered', *FTM Newsletter*, Issue 26 (February): 3.

McIntosh, M. (1993). 'Queer Theory and the War of the Sexes', in J. Bristow and A. R. Wilson (eds), *Activating Theory* (London: Lawrence & Wishart).

Millot, C. (1990). *Horsexe: Essay on Transsexuality* (New York: Autonomedia Inc.).

Raymond, J. G. (1980). *The Transsexual Empire* (London: The Women's Press).

—— (1994). 'Introduction to the 1994 Edition', in *The Transsexual Empire: The Making of the She-Male*, 2nd edn (New York: Teachers College Press).

Segal, L. (1994). *Straight Sex: The Politics of Pleasure* (London: Virago).

Walworth, J. (1994). 'Michigan Womyn's Music Festival 1994: Transsexual Protesters Allowed to Enter', *Cross-Talk*, Issue 61: 27–9.

Wheelwright, J. (1989). *Amazons and Military Maids: Women who Dressed as Men in the Pursuit of Life, Liberty and Happiness* (London: Pandora Press).

Useful addresses

The Gender Trust, PO Box 3192, Brighton BN1 3WR, England.
The Beaumont Society, 27 Old Gloucester Street, London WC1N 3XX, England.

11.   DEL LAGRACE VOLCANO AND INDRA WINDH, 'GENDERFUSION'

Summary

How queer can an easily comprehensible clothing switch be? Is a woman dressed as a man always necessarily understood to be a woman dressed as a man? This composition by Del LaGrace Volcano and Indra Windh introduces future possibilities for dragkinging, criss-cross dressing and gender performance in everyday life. Since the 1960s, scholars such as Susan Sontag, Esther Newton, Judith Butler, Marjorie Garber and Andy Medhurst have debated whether drag and camp are strategies of subversive caricature or performances that reinstate, even while transgressing, deterministic links between sex, gender and sexuality (see under 'Further Reading'). Critical discussion has centred upon the often humorous incongruities between the gender assumptions provoked by a drag queen's body, mannerisms, speech, and dress. Butler, for instance, has argued that drag plays with the distinction between clothing and anatomy (*Gender Trouble*, pp. 174–9), and thus reveals how gender more generally is disjointed from sex. But the signifiers of gender and sex can be more confusing than this. If we cannot decode the 'original' anatomy of the performer underneath their sartorial signifiers, the assumed incongruity between performance and performer itself becomes incongruous. When the biological ground that is presumed to contradict a parodic gender performance becomes unpredictable, so too does the drag performance *as performance* become uncertain. Through such complex and multi-layered criss-crossings, Volcano and Windh call for us to visibly transgress gender assumptions, play with the signifiers of gender, perform and expose desires, celebrate the perverse, and revel in 'what is already perverse in the normal' (Judith 'Jack' Halberstam in *The Drag King Book*, p. 152).

References

Butler, Judith (1999). *Gender Trouble: Feminism and the Subversion of Identity*, 2nd edn (London and New York: Routledge).
Halberstam, Judith 'Jack', and Del LaGrace Volcano (1999). *The Drag King Book* (London: Serpent's Tail).

12.   JUDITH BUTLER, 'CONTAGIOUS WORD: PARANOIA AND "HOMOSEXUALITY" IN THE MILITARY'

(From Judith Butler, *Excitable Speech: A Politics of the Performative* (New York and London: Routledge, 1997), pp. 103–26.)

Summary

Butler seeks to explain how the identity claim 'I am homosexual' can itself be interpreted as homosexual conduct. First she expounds her model of gender performativity, which has strongly influenced queer theory. A *performative* utterance – the term comes from linguist J. L. Austin – is an act rather than a description. So while 'the *Reader in Queer Theory* is on the desk' is descriptive or *constative* talk, 'I name this ship the *Queer Theorist*' is performative. Of course, in order to name the ship one must be in a position of appropriate authority, and it is this link between performativity and power that Butler explores with regards to the prohibition of 'homosexuality' in the US military. She uses Freudian psychoanalysis to elucidate – and also to provide an example of – this prohibitive mechanism. Freud sees homosexuality as a desire that is necessarily at once repudiated and turned back upon the individual to produce and maintain the conscience which organizes social bonds. In fact, this productive regulation is what *makes* the heterosexual citizen an individual. Homosexuality is hereby figured as necessarily unconscious, and so beyond a person's control. Butler then shows how this paranoid understanding of homosexuality has become infected by the discourse of AIDS: homosexuality is perceived as an uncontrollably contagious desire that may be performatively transmitted by the mere words 'I am homosexual'. Finally, Butler considers the broader relation between homosexuality and representation – whether the former can and should ever be wholly encapsulated by the latter. A queer stance, she indicates, would be to refuse such closure.

Editors' note: Some portions of this essay have been re-ordered for reasons of space. In the original text, Butler discusses in more detail how the US military regulations conflate homosexual speech, conduct and 'propensity', and situates her argument more precisely in relation to Austin's speech act theory.

Notes

1. The Pentagon announced its 'New Policy Guidelines on Homosexuals in the Military' on 19 July 1993, which included the following 'discharge' policy: 'Sexual orientation will not be a bar to service unless manifested by homosexual conduct. The military will discharge members who engage in homosexual conduct, which is defined as a homosexual act, a statement that the member is homosexual or bisexual, or a marriage or attempted marriage to someone of the same gender.' After discussions in Congress on the policy, the Department of Defense on 22 December 1993 issued a set of new regulations seeking to clarify problems concerning implementation of the policy. One of the key issues to be clarified was whether a 'statement' to the effect that one is a homosexual can be taken not only as 'conduct' but as sufficient grounds for dismissal from the military. The clarification offered by the Department of Defense made clear that 'statements that can be a basis for discharge are those which demonstrate a propensity or intent to engage in acts'. Over and against those who claim that statements of the desire or intentions of an individual are not the same as conduct, the Department of Defense insisted that what they now have is 'a conduct-based policy', one that is based on 'the likelihood that the person would act'. They explain, 'a statement creates a rebuttable presumption a person will engage in acts, but the service member then has an opportunity to rebut. . . .'

   Here, the 'statement' that one is a homosexual presents the occasion to rebut the presumption, but later in this same presentation, the spokesperson from the Department of Defense appears to suggest the opposite: 'Associational activities, like going to a gay parade or reading a magazine – in and of themselves – are not credible information [bearing on the conduct of the individual in question], and only rise to that level if they are such that a reasonable person would believe that *the conduct was intended to make a statement, intended to tell other people that the person is a homosexual*' (my emphasis). Here the question appears no longer to be whether the statement presents a rebuttable presumption that the person will engage in conduct, but whether conduct, of an associational kind, is sufficient to establish that a statement is being made. Whether the basis for dismissal is statement or conduct remains effectively open (*New York Times*, 20 July 1993, 22 December 1993).

   In addition to the former and current Department of Defense policy, Congress entered the fray by introducing legislation of its own: the National Defense Authorization Act for Fiscal Year 1994. This binding statute emphasizes the problem of homosexual 'propensity', and states that persons who demonstrate a propensity to act homosexually are deemed incompatible with military service. The statute also shows leniency for those who commit such acts on an occasion, but who repent or claim it was an accident. It also reintroduces the obligation of military officers 'to ask' servicemen about their orientation. Whereas it does not accept statements regarding one's own homosexuality as tantamount to homosexual acts, it does regard such statements as *evidence of a propensity* that poses a rebuttable presumption of homosexuality.

    Recent rulings on the new policy have split on the question of whether First Amendment rights are denied by the policy (suits concerning the 'old policy' continue to be litigated as well, with mixed results). For a thorough and incisive review of this litigation, one on which I heavily rely in this discussion, see Janet Halley, 'The Status/Conduct Distinction in the 1993 Revisions to Military Anti-Gay Policy', in *GLQ*, Winter 1996.

2. The following texts by Sigmund Freud are cited in this chapter: 'On the Mechanism of Paranoia' (1911), and 'On Narcissism: an Introduction' (1914), from *General Psychological Theory: Papers on Metapsychology* (New York: Macmillan, 1963), pp. 29–48 and pp. 56–82, respectively; *Civilization and its Discontents (CD)*, tr. James Strachey (New York: Norton, 1961); and *Totem and Taboo*, tr. James Strachey (New York: Norton, 1950).

3. By allegory, I mean a kind of narrative in which, most generally, one speaks otherwise than one appears to speak, where one offers a sequential narrative ordering for something which cannot be described sequentially, and where the apparent referent of the allegory becomes the very action of elaboration that allegorical narrative performs.

4. For an interesting and relevant account of allegory, see Craig Owens, *Beyond Recognition: Representation, Power, and Culture*, ed. Scott Bryson (Berkeley: University of California Press, 1992).

5. 'The Pentagon's New Policy Guidelines on Homosexuals in the Military', *New York Times*, 20 July 1993, p. A14.

6. Here one can see that Foucault's critique of Freud in *The History of Sexuality, volume I* is partially wrong.

7. Sigmund Freud, 'On Narcissism: an Introduction', *Standard Edition*, vol. XIV (London: Hogarth Press, 1957), p. 96.

8. This would be a way to both confirm and deny the recent suggestions by Leo Bersani in *Homos* (Cambridge, MA: Harvard University Press, 1995) that asserting a stable identity is a precondition of gay activism and that the intellectual scepticism directed at the success of that speech act is complicitous with a desexualization of gayness. To come out is still to perform a linguistic act and, hence, not necessarily to have sex or be sexual, except in that discursive way that may constitute a further instance of the linguistic sublimation of sex that Bersani laments.

13.   WILLIAM J. SPURLIN, 'I'D RATHER BE THE PRINCESS THAN THE QUEEN! MOURNING DIANA AS A GAY ICON'

(From Adrian Kear and Deborah Lynn Steinberg (eds), *Mourning Diana: Nation, Culture and the Performance of Grief* (London and New York: Routledge, 1999), pp. 155–68.)

Summary

William J. Spurlin sets out to explain how Diana – in many senses an extremely conventional, privileged heterosexual – might nevertheless be re-evaluated as queer.

Refusing to centre simply on either Diana's identity or her media representation, Spurlin focuses on how these axes can intersect in a productively queer way. The paper opens with a comparative discussion of the iconicity of Diana and Jacqueline Kennedy Onassis. Paying special attention to photography's tension between authoritative closure and personal disclosure (semiotician Roland Barthes's *studium* and *punctum*), Spurlin dissects the sometimes contradictory relations between the celebrity subject, the media, and the public. He counters the assumption that Diana's contact with AIDS sufferers gives her queer status. The media coverage that was crucial to Diana's iconicity framed her visits to AIDS patients in implicitly homophobic terms by blanching their sexuality out of the story. Spurlin proposes instead that Diana may be mourned queerly for her complex resistance to the very heteronormativity that brought her celebrity. She sought a sexual and familial identity that subversively reworked the expectations placed upon her. If Spurlin is right that Diana can be mourned as a queer icon, then not only sexuality can be queered; gender and sex can be too.

Editors' note: The endnotes have been abridged.

Note

1. I use the term 'queer' to denote an oppositional political praxis which operates against normalizing ideologies in general (e.g. race, gender, class, nationality) *in addition to sexuality*. This is an especially important distinction in the context of a discussion of Diana, who identified as sexually straight, but, as I shall argue, functioned as politically queer.

References

Appleyard, Bryan (1997). 'A New World, a Goddess, a New Kind of Heaven', in Brian MacArthur (ed.), *Requiem: Diana, Princess of Wales, 1961–1997: Memories and Tributes* (London and New York: Pavilion Books and Arcade Publishing).

Aslet, Clive (1997). 'The Legacy', in Brian MacArthur (ed.), *Requiem: Diana, Princess of Wales, 1961–1997: Memories and Tributes* (London and New York: Pavilion Books and Arcade Publishing).

Barthes, Roland (1981). *Camera Lucida: Reflections on Photography*, trans. Richard Howard (New York: Hill and Wang).

Butler, Judith (1990). *Gender Trouble: Feminism and the Subversion of Identity* (New York: Routledge).

—— (1993). *Bodies that Matter: On the Discursive Limits of 'Sex'* (New York: Routledge).

—— (1997). *The Psychic Life of Power: Theories in Subjection* (Stanford, CA: Stanford University Press).

Doty, Alexander (1993). *Making Things Perfectly Queer: Interpreting Mass Culture* (Minneapolis: University of Minnesota Press).

Koestenbaum, Wayne (1996). *Jackie Under My Skin: Interpreting an Icon* (New York: Penguin).

Morton, Andrew (1997). *Diana: Her True Story – In Her Own Words, 1961–1997* (London and New York: Michael O'Mara Books and Simon and Schuster).

Sedgwick, Eve Kosofsky (1993). 'Tales of the Avunculate: Queer Tutelage in *The Importance of Being Earnest*', in Eve Kosofsky Sedgwick, *Tendencies* (Durham, NC: Duke University Press).

Smith, Joan (1997). 'Unusual Normality, Jetset Glamour', in Brian MacArthur (ed.), *Requiem: Diana, Princess of Wales, 1961–1997: Memories and Tributes* (London and New York: Pavilion Books and Arcade Publishing).

Smith, Paul (1988). *Discerning the Subject* (Minneapolis: University of Minnesota Press).

Sontag, Susan (1977). *On Photography* (New York: Doubleday).

Spoto, Donald (1997). *Diana: The Last Year* (New York: Crown Publishers).

Stimpson, Catharine R. (1990). 'Lesbian Studies in the 1990s', in Karla Jay and Joanne Glasgow (eds), *Lesbian Texts and Contexts: Radical Revisions* (New York: New York University Press).

Strong, Roy (1997). 'An Icon for the Meritocratic Age', in Brian MacArthur (ed.), *Requiem: Diana, Princess of Wales, 1961–1997: Memories and Tributes* (London and New York: Pavilion Books and Arcade Publishing).

14. MARK NORRIS LANCE AND ALESSANDRA TANESINI, 'IDENTITY JUDGEMENTS, QUEER POLITICS'

(From Mark Norris Lance and Alessandra Tanesini, 'Identity Judgements, Queer Politics', *Radical Philosophy*, 100 (March/April 2000), pp. 42–51.)

Summary

Mark Norris Lance and Alessandra Tanesini's 'radical normativity thesis about identity claims' proposes that identities are politicized commitments to particular ways of living. Their argument turns on a critique of Judith Butler's theory of performativity, asserting that performativity cannot account for *why* and *how* people make identity claims, especially in the case of a historically derogatory identity such as 'queer'. So although identities are not grounded in biological or metaphysical essences, this is not simply because essentialism is a factual mistake. Rather it is because identities do not function descriptively. On the contrary, they are 'script-endorsements' – manifestos for specific ways of negotiating a person's cultural position. This leads to the issue of identity *judgements*. Understood normatively, the validity of an identity cannot be determined by its fittingness to describe a lifestyle. A moral judgement must be made about the kind of political future to which a given identity represents a commitment. By this measure, Lance and Tanesini protest that a straight identity serves to buttress the privileged position accorded to heterosexuals in contemporary Western culture. It follows, queerly, that a sexual *inclination* towards a particular gender should not be calcified into an identificatory *commitment* to have relationships with people of only that gender.

Notes

1. Judith Butler, 'Imitation and Gender Insubordination', in Linda Nicholson (ed.), *The Second Wave: A Reader in Feminist Theory* (New York and London: Routledge, 1997), p. 303.
2. Alan Sinfield, *Gay and After* (London: Serpent's Tail, 1998), p. 5.
3. Ibid., pp. 14, 199.

4. See, for example, Ed Cohen, 'Who are "We"? Gay Identity as Political (E)motion (A Theoretical Rumination)', in Diana Fuss (ed.), *Inside/Out: Lesbian Theories, Gay Theories* (New York and London: Routledge, 1991), pp. 71–92; and Lisa Duggan, 'Queering the State', *Social Text*, 39 (Summer 1994), 1–14.

5. See Vera Whisman, *Queer by Choice* (New York and London: Routledge, 1996). Alan Sinfield remarks on this fact in his 'Virtually Undetectable: the Andrew Sullivan Phenomenon', *Radical Philosophy*, 97 (Sept./Oct. 1999), 4.

6. Some of the most influential papers in the currently extinguished debate between biologism and social constructionism are collected in Edward Stein (ed.), *Forms of Desire: Sexual Orientation and the Social Constructionist Controversy* (New York and London: Routledge, 1992). Outside the context of queer theory, biological accounts of sexual orientation have been supported by Simon LeVay in his *Queer Science: The Use and Abuse of Research into Homosexuality* (Cambridge, MA: MIT Press, 1996).

7. Here we follow Robert Brandom in refusing to take the question of meaning to be a matter of identifying which bits of reality a linguistic expression refers to, together with an account of their relation. For a systematic account of this semantic view of language, see his *Making It Explicit: Reasoning, Representing, and Discursive Commitment* (Cambridge, MA: Harvard University Press, 1994).

8. For a sustained account of the nature of meaning claims as well as of normative commitments of the sort discussed in this article, see Mark Norris Lance and John O'Leary-Hawthorne, *The Grammar of Meaning: Normativity and Semantic Discourse* (Cambridge: Cambridge University Press, 1997).

9. Cindy Patton, 'Tremble, Hetero Swine!', in Michael Warner (ed.), *Fear of a Queer Planet: Queer Politics and Social Theory* (Minneapolis and London: University of Minnesota Press, 1993), p. 166.

10. See K. Anthony Appiah, 'Identity, Authenticity, Survival: Multicultural Societies and Social Reproduction', in Charles Taylor, *Multiculturalism: Examining the Politics of Recognition* (Princeton, NJ: Princeton University Press, 1994), pp. 149–63.

11. This is not to say that self-attributions of these two identities must be absolutely irreconcilable. But there is a rational tension between them, which individuals would need to do something about.

12. Judith Butler, *Gender Trouble: Feminism and the Subversion of Identity* (New York and London: Routledge, 1990), p. 147.

13. Ibid., p. 148.

14. In recent times, Butler, and others, have explicitly endorsed this consequence of their position. See, for example, Judith Butler, *The Psychic Life of Power: Theories in Subjection* (Stanford, CA: Stanford University Press, 1997). We find it astonishing that these writers do not think it a problem that they make *a priori* universal claims about matters which would seem to require case-by-case consideration.

15. Thus, the three criteria offered above – 'felt demand', 'call to coherence', and 'normative projection' – explain what it is to *take* oneself to be of an identity. One might fulfil them and yet not be of the given identity. This is no surprise since it is always possible to take oneself to be of an identity and be mistaken. On this matter, as on any other, we are not infallible.

16. Some readers might be troubled by our almost interchangeable usage of 'gay' and 'queer'. We do believe that these terms are employed in tactical identity endorsements which tend to differ from each other. It would, however, be a mistake to read queer as simply advocating an end for all identities.

17. There are deep and important connections between heterosexism and sexism.
    Further, there are also important differences in the socio-normative significances
    of identity claims made by men and women. These issues must be explored
    in detail in each particular political context. These considerations do not entail
    that women, unlike men, should make their heterosexual inclinations a matter
    of identity.
18. Similarly, Appiah's claim that there are no races does not prevent him from
    acknowledging the reality of racism. See K. Anthony Appiah, 'Race, Culture,
    Identity: Misunderstood Connections', in K. Anthony Appiah and Amy Gut-
    man, *Color Conscious: The Political Morality of Race* (Princeton, NJ: Princeton
    University Press, 1996), pp. 30–105.

15. MANDY MERCK, 'AFTERWORD'

Summary

If queer is a critique of fixed notions of identity, of norms and assumptions, then
might the project of 'queer' risk failure if it does not critique itself? Mandy Merck's
Afterword contemplates the contested genealogy of queer theory and activism, and
opens the debates of this volume onto the new critical terrain of globalization studies.

Notes

1. Annamarie Jagose, 'Afterword', *Queer Theory: An Introduction* (New York:
   New York University Press, 1997), pp. 127–32.
2. Judith Butler, *Gender Trouble: Feminism and the Subversion of Identity* (New
   York: Routledge, 1990).
3. Douglas Crimp, 'AIDS: Cultural Analysis/Cultural Activism', *October*, 43 (1987),
   p. 6.
4. Paula Treichler, 'AIDS, Homophobia and Biomedical Discourse: an Epidemic of
   Signification', *October*, 43 (1987), p. 52.
5. David M. Halperin, *Saint Foucault: Towards a Gay Hagiography* (New York:
   Oxford University Press, 1995), p. 63.
6. Lauren Berlant and Elizabeth Freeman, 'Queer Nationality', in Michael Warner
   (ed.), *Fear of a Queer Planet: Queer Politics and Social Theory* (Minneapolis:
   University of Minnesota Press, 1993), pp. 193–229.
7. Steven Seidman, 'Identity and Politics in a "Postmodern" Gay Culture', in
   Warner, *Fear of a Queer Planet*, p. 136.
8. Dennis Altman, *Global Sex* (Chicago: University of Chicago Press, 2001), p. 158.
9. Butler, *Gender Trouble*, p. 33.
10. Richard Cornwall, 'Queer Political Economy: the Social Articulation of Desire',
    in Amy Gluckman and Betsy Reed (eds), *Homo Economics* (New York: Rout-
    ledge, 1997), pp. 89–122; Nancy Fraser, *Justice Interruptus: Critical Reflections
    on the 'Post-Socialist' Condition* (New York: Routledge, 1997); Judith Butler,
    'Merely Cultural?', *New Left Review*, 227 (1998), pp. 33–44. See also Nancy
    Fraser's reply, 'Heterosexism, Misrecognition and Capitalism', *New Left Review*,
    228 (1998), pp. 140–9.

11. Rosemary Hennessy, *Profit and Pleasure: Sexual Identities in Late Capitalism* (New York: Routledge, 2000), p. 108.
12. Arnaldo Cruz-Malevé and Martin F. Manalansan IV, 'Introduction: Dissident Sexualities/Alternative Globalisms', in A. Cruz-Malevé and M. F. Manalansan (eds), *Queer Globalizations: Citizenship and the Afterlife of Colonialism* (New York: New York University Press, 2002), p. 5.

Further Reading

Atkins, Dawn (ed.), *Looking Queer: Body Image and Identity in Lesbian, Bisexual, Gay, and Transgender Communities* (New York: Harrington Park, 1998).

Bornstein, Kate, *Gender Outlaw: On Men, Women and the Rest of Us* (London and New York: Routledge, 1994).

Bristow, Joseph and Angelia Wilson (eds), *Activating Theory: Lesbian, Gay, Bisexual Politics* (London: Lawrence and Wishart, 1993).

Butler, Judith, *The Psychic Life of Power: Theories in Subjection* (Stanford, CA: Stanford University Press, 1997).

———, *Gender Trouble: Feminism and the Subversion of Identity*, 2nd edn (London and New York: Routledge, 1999).

Califia, Patrick, *Sex Changes: The Politics of Transgenderism* (San Francisco, CA: Cleis, 1997).

Cameron, Loren, *Body Alchemy: Transsexual Portraits* (San Francisco, CA: Cleis, 1996).

Carlin, Deborah and Jennifer DiGrazia (eds), *Queer Cultures* (Upper Saddle River, NJ: Prentice Hall, 2004).

Case, Sue-Ellen, Philip Brett and Susan Leigh Foster (eds), *Cruising the Performative: Interventions into the Representation of Ethnicity, Nationality, and Sexuality* (Bloomington and Indianapolis: Indiana University Press, 1995).

Church-Gibson, Pamela (ed.), *More Dirty Looks: Gender, Pornography and Power* (London: British Film Institute, 2003).

Corber, Robert J. and Stephen Valocci (eds), *Queer Studies: An Interdisciplinary Reader* (Oxford and Cambridge, MA: Blackwell, 2003).

Creekmur, Cory and Alexander Doty (eds), *Out in Culture: Gay, Lesbian and Queer Essays on Popular Culture* (London: Cassell, 1995).

Dollimore, Jonathan, *Sexual Dissidence: Augustine to Wilde, Freud to Foucault* (Oxford: Clarendon Press, 1991).

Dyer, Richard, *The Culture of Queers* (London and New York: Routledge, 2002).

Epstein, Julia and Kristina Straub (eds), *Body Guards: The Cultural Politics of Gender Ambiguity* (London and New York: Routledge, 1991).

Feinberg, Leslie, *Stone Butch Blues* (New York: Firebrand, 1993).

———, *Transgendered Warriors: Making History from Joan of Arc to Dennis Rodman* (Boston, MA: Beacon, 1996).

Foucault, Michel, *The History of Sexuality*, vol. 1: *The Will to Knowledge* (Harmondsworth: Penguin, 1998).

Fuss, Diana (ed.), *Inside/Out: Lesbian Theories, Gay Theories* (London and New York: Routledge, 1991).

Garber, Marjorie, *Vested Interests: Cross-Dressing and Cultural Anxiety* (Harmondsworth: Penguin, 1993).

Gluckman, Amy and Betsy Reed (eds), *Homo Economics* (London and New York: Routledge, 1997).

Halberstam, Judith, *Female Masculinity* (Durham, NC, and London: Duke University Press, 1998).

Halberstam, Judith 'Jack' and Del LaGrace Volcano, *The Drag King Book* (London: Serpent's Tail, 1999).

Harper, Phillip, Ann McClintock, José Muñoz and Trish Rosen (eds), *Queer Transexions of Race, Nation, and Gender*, special issue of *Social Text*, 52/53 (1997).

Herdt, Gilbert (ed.), *Third Sex, Third Gender: Beyond Sexual Dimorphism in Culture and History* (New York: Zone, 1996).

Jagose, Annamarie, *Queer Theory: An Introduction* (New York: New York University Press, 1997).

Jeffreys, Sheila, *Unpacking Queer Politics: A Lesbian Feminist Perspective* (Cambridge: Polity, 2003).

Kirsch, Max, *Queer Theory and Social Change* (London and New York: Routledge, 2000).

Lauretis, Teresa de (ed.), *Queer Theory: Lesbian and Gay Sexualities*, special issue of *differences: A Journal of Feminist Cultural Studies*, 3: 2 (1991).

Livia, Anna and Kira Hall (eds), *Queerly Phrased: Language, Gender and Sexual Politics* (Oxford: Oxford University Press, 1997).

Medhurst, Andy, 'Camp', in Andy Medhurst and Sally Munt (eds), *Lesbian and Gay Studies: A Critical Introduction* (London: Cassell, 1997), pp. 274–93.

Merck, Mandy, Naomi Segal and Elizabeth Wright (eds), *Coming Out of Feminism?* (Oxford and Cambridge, MA: Blackwell, 1998).

Nestle, Joan (ed.), *The Persistent Desire: A Femme-Butch Reader* (Boston, MA: Alyson, 1992).

Nestle, Joan, Riki Wilchins and Clare Howell (eds), *GenderQueer: Voices from Beyond the Sexual Binary* (Boston, MA: Alyson, 2002).

Newton, Esther, *Mother Camp: Female Impersonators in America* (Chicago and London: University of Chicago Press, 1979).

Patton, Cindy and Benigno Sánchez-Eppler (eds), *Queer Diasporas* (Durham, NC, and London: Duke University Press, 2000).

Phelan, Shane, *Sexual Strangers: Gays, Lesbians and Dilemmas of Citizenship* (Philadelphia: Temple University Press, 2001).

Pratt, Minnie Bruce, *S/He* (New York: Firebrand, 1995).

Prosser, Jay, *Second Skins: The Body Narratives of Transsexuality* (New York: Columbia University Press, 1998).

Queen, Carol and Lawrence Schimel (eds), *PoMoSexuals: Challenging Assumptions about Gender and Sexuality* (San Francisco, CA: Cleis, 1997).

Rimmerman, Craig A., *From Identity to Politics: The Lesbian and Gay Movements in the United States* (Philadelphia: Temple University Press, 2001).

Rosario, Vernon A. (ed.), *Science and Homosexualities* (London and New York: Routledge, 1997).

Schor, Naomi and Elizabeth Weed, *Feminism Meets Queer Theory* (Bloomington and Indianapolis: Indiana University Press, 1997).

Segal, Lynne, *Straight Sex: The Politics of Pleasure* (London: Virago, 1994).

Signorile, Michelangelo, *Queer in America: Sex, the Media, and the Closets of Power* (London: Abacus, 1994).

Simpson, Mark (ed.), *Anti-Gay* (London and New York: Freedom, 1996).

Sinfield, Alan, *Gay and After* (London: Serpent's Tail, 1998).

Sontag, Susan, 'Notes on "Camp"', in Fabio Cleto (ed.), *Camp: Queer Aesthetics and the Performing Subject: A Reader* (Ann Arbor, MI: University of Michigan Press, 1999), pp. 53–66.

Stryker, Susan (ed.), *The Transgender Issue*, special issue of *GLQ: A Journal of Lesbian and Gay Studies*, 4:2 (1998).

Stryker, Susan and Stephen Whittle (eds), *The Transgender Reader* (London and New York: Routledge, 2004).

Sullivan, Nikki, *A Critical Introduction to Queer Theory* (Edinburgh: Edinburgh University Press, 2003).

Thomas, Calvin (ed.), *Straight with a Twist: Queer Theory and the Subject of Heterosexuality* (Urbana and Chicago: University of Illinois Press, 2000).

Troka, Donna Jean, Kathleen Lebesco and Jean Bobby Noble (eds), *The Drag King Anthology* (New York: Haworth, 2003).

Turner, William B., *A Genealogy of Queer Theory* (Philadelphia: Temple University Press, 2000).

Warner, Michael (ed.), *Fear of a Queer Planet: Queer Politics and Social Theory* (Minneapolis: University of Minnesota Press, 1993).

Whittle, Stephen, *The Transgender Debate: The Crisis Surrounding Gender Identities* (Reading: South Street, 2000).

Wilchins, Riki Anne, *Read My Lips: Sexual Subversion and the End of Gender* (New York: Firebrand, 1997).

——, *Queer Theory, Gender Theory: An Instant Primer* (Boston, MA: Alyson, 2004).

Notes on the Contributors

Judith Butler is Maxine Elliot Professor in Rhetoric and Comparative Literature at the University of California at Berkeley, the author of *Gender Trouble* (1990), *Bodies that Matter* (1993), and several other works in philosophy, feminist and queer theory, and social and political criticism. Her forthcoming collection, *Undoing Gender*, will be published by Routledge in 2004.

Patrick Califia is one of the most outspoken and intelligent commentators on sexual politics writing today. Patrick Califia has authored sixteen books, including *Sex Changes* (1997), and *Speaking Sex to Power* (2002). He lives in San Francisco.

Cheryl Chase is the founder of the Intersex Society of North America, a patient advocacy organization dedicated to creating a world free of shame, secrecy, and unwanted genital surgeries for people born with intersex conditions. Ms Chase has produced *Hermaphrodites Speak!* (1997), the first documentary in which intersex people speak openly about their personal experience, and *The Child with an Intersex Condition: Total Patient Care* (2002), the video which introduced the model of patient-centred care to medical professionals and families.

Marjorie Garber is William R. Kenan, Jr, Professor of English at Harvard University and Director of the Humanities Center in the Faculty of Arts and Sciences. She is also Chair of the Department of Visual and Environmental Studies, and has written extensively on Shakespeare and on a wide range of literary and cultural topics. Among her books are *Dog Love* (1996), *Symptoms of Culture* (1998), *Sex and Real Estate* (2000), *Quotation Marks* (2002), and, with Nancy J. Vickers, *The Medusa Reader* (2003).

Donald E. Hall holds the Jackson Distinguished Chair in British Literature at West Virginia University. His most recent books include *The Academic Self: An Owner's Manual* (2002) and *Subjectivity* (2004).

Peter Hegarty is a social psychologist and a historian of psychology. His work centres on heteronormativity, particularly its instantiations in psychological and biological research. He has taught at Stanford University, California, City University of New York, Yale University, and currently teaches at the University of Surrey.

Larry Kramer is a novelist, playwright, and founder of both Gay Men's Health Crisis (GMHC) and AIDS Coalition to Unleash Power (ACT UP), and is one of the great polemicists of AIDS activism. In addition to *The Normal Heart* (1985) and a book of essays, *Reports from the Holocaust: The Making of an AIDS Activist* (1990), his publications include the poetry collection *Brilliant Windows* (1998).

Mark Norris Lance is an Associate Professor of Philosophy and Associate Professor of Justice and Peace at Georgetown University. He has published on philosophy of language, logic, epistemology, and political philosophy, and is co-author with John O'Leary-Hawthorne of *The Grammar of Meaning* (1997). He has also been an activist for 25 years on issues including Palestine, Latin America, South Africa, war, economic justice, and sexual minorities. He has been denounced by right-wing newspapers, radio talk shows, and at least one Catholic Bishop.

Mandy Merck is Professor of Media Arts at Royal Holloway, University of London, where she directs the MA in Gender and Sexuality on Screen. Her latest books are *The Art of Tracey Emin* (2002) and *In Your Face: Nine Sexual Studies* (2000).

Iain Morland has published scholarly articles on intersexuality and literary theory, and is a doctoral candidate in English Literature at Royal Holloway, University of London. He graduated with distinction from Sussex University's Sexual Dissidence master's programme.

Carol Queen got a PhD in sexology so she could impart more realistic detail to her smut. Queen is the author of *Exhibitionism for the Shy* (2002) and *Real Live Nude Girl: Chronicles of Sex-Positive Culture* (2003), and she has co-edited several anthologies, including the Lambda Literary Award winner *PoMoSexuals* (1997). She is Staff Sexologist at Good Vibrations in San Francisco and director of the Center for Sex and Culture.

Eve Kosofsky Sedgwick teaches in the PhD programme in English at the Graduate Center of the City University of New York. Her books include *Between Men: English Literature and Male Homosocial Desire* (1993), *Tendencies* (1994), *A Dialogue on Love* (1999) and *Touching Feeling: Affect, Pedagogy, Performativity* (2003).

William J. Spurlin is Senior Lecturer in English and Critical and Cultural Theory at Cardiff University. He has written numerous essays on queer studies, critical theory, and twentieth-century literature and culture. He co-edited *The New Criticism and Contemporary Literary Theory: Connections and Continuities* (1995) and *Reclaiming the Heartland: Lesbian and Gay Voices from the Midwest* (1996), and edited *The Teaching of Lesbian and Gay Studies: Positions, Pedagogies, and Cultural Politics* (2000). His next book is *Imperialism Within the Margins: Queer Representation and the Politics of Culture in Southern Africa* (forthcoming).

Alessandra Tanesini is Senior Lecturer in Philosophy at Cardiff University. She has been a Visiting Senior Lecturer in the Philosophy Department at the University of Sydney, and a Visiting Assistant Professor in the Philosophy Department at Georgetown University. She is the author of *An Introduction to Feminist Epistemologies* (1999) as well as of several articles on epistemology, feminist philosophy, and Nietzsche, and her latest book is *Wittgenstein: A Feminist Introduction* (2004).

Del LaGrace Volcano is a gender variant visual artist using life, love and the pursuit of happiness as source material. s/He has produced three monographs: *Sublime Mutations* (2000), *The Drag King Book* (1999) and *Lovebites* (1991) as well as several short films, the latest of which is *The Passionate Spectator* (2003).

Suzanna Danuta Walters is Professor of Sociology and Director of Women's Studies at Georgetown University. She is the author of three books: *Lives Together/ Worlds Apart: Mothers and Daughters in Popular Culture* (1992), *Material Girls: Making Sense of Feminist Cultural Theory* (1995), and *All the Rage: The Story of Gay Visibility in America* (2001).

Stephen Whittle is Reader in Law at Manchester Metropolitan University, as well as Vice-President of Press For Change, the UK's transgender lobby group. He also co-ordinates the FtM Network. In 2002 he received the Liberty/Justice Human Rights Award for 30 years of campaigning work for transgender rights. His publications include *Respect and Equality: Transsexual and Transgender Rights* (2002) and, with Susan Stryker, *The Transgender Reader* (2004).

Annabelle Willox is an independent trans queer scholar with a minor hockey obsession. She holds degrees in Philosophy, Sexual Politics, and Critical and Cultural Theory, has taught at Cardiff and Glamorgan Universities, and has presented papers at conferences throughout the UK and Ireland.

Indra Windh is a grown-up child of the 1970s from a small town in Sweden who has chosen psychology and drama as her main academic and applied disciplines. She has had an investment in the queer fraction of the bisexual movement, and is actively participating in the booming Swedish dragking scene. Feminist, Star Trek fan, self-help group supporter, hermlover and food enjoyer are some of the epithets to which she can relate.

Index

activism, 2, 5, 7, 36–8, 79, 111, 112–13,
116, 122, 124, 128, 155, 176, 187–8,
193, 200, 201 n.15, 212
ACT UP, 7, 187–8, 197
Admiral Duncan (pub), 3, 5
Advocate (gay newspaper), 35
AIDS/HIV, 2, 3, 7, 17, 23, 28–39, 59, 61,
63, 91, 92, 146, 148, 155, 187–8,
190, 193, 196–7, 198–9 n.22, 206,
209
phobia, 87, 164–5
AIDS Network, 37–8
Altman, Dennis, 112, 189
androgen insensitivity syndrome (AIS),
77–8
support group contact information,
200 n.14
androgyny, 93
Anzaldúa, Gloria, 12, 113
Appiah, K. Anthony, 173–4
Apuzzo, Virginia, 36, 38
Aristophanes, 101
Aslet, Clive, 168
Augustine, St, 102
Austin, J. L., 206, 207

Bailey, Michael *see* biological
determinism
Ballad of Little Jo, The (Greenwald), 123
Barthes, Roland, 162, 209
Bayer, Ronald, 79, 201 n.15
Beam, Joseph, 113
Bensinger, Terralee, 16
Berlant, Lauren, 188
Bersani, Leo, 208 n.8

binary oppositions, 8–9, 13, 17, 19,
55–6, 66, 68, 80, 83–4, 86–7, 112,
114, 118, 119, 123, 124, 139, 201
see also difference
biological determinism, 14, 54–5, 56, 77,
78–9, 85, 104, 118, 123, 124–5, 172,
173, 175–6, 197, 200, 201, 204, 210
Bailey and Pillard on the 'gay gene',
57, 58, 64, 65
Hamer on the 'gay gene', 58, 64–7
LeVay on the 'gay brain', 57, 58,
59–63, 64, 65, 66, 67, 69
bisexuality *see* sexual orientation
Blair, Tony, 3, 5
Blasius, Mark, 20
body, 4, 9, 54–6, 72, 77, 80, 83–4, 91–2,
115, 118, 126–8, 130–41, 197
see also biological determinism *and*
hormones
Bolin, Anne, 118
Bornstein, Kate, 124–6, 128, 204
Boswell, John, 101
Bray, Alan, 102
Bristow, Joseph, 105
Brown, Judith, 102
Butler, Judith, 4, 13, 19–20, 167–8,
171, 178, 187, 189–90, 205,
206–7, 210

Califia, Patrick, 1, 15, 196, 197
Cameron, Loren, 126–8, 204
Cameron, Paul, 57
camp, 159, 205
Carpenter, Edward, 110
Case, Sue-Ellen, 13, 15, 117